ALL ALONE

ALL ALONE

The Psychosocial Condition of
Nigerian Widows and Childless Women:
Implication for Survivor's Care

Adolphus Ezeakor

Library of Congress Control Number: 2012923631
ISBN: Hardcover   978-1-4797-6749-6
                Softcover   978-1-4797-6748-9
                Ebook   978-1-4797-6750-2

This book was printed in the United States of America.

Cover Illustration by Joel Ray Pellerin

To order additional copies of this book, contact:
Xlibris Corporation
0-800-644-6988
www.xlibrispublishing.co.uk
Orders@xlibrispublishing.co.uk
305205

Table of Contents

DEDICATION

This work is dedicated to the ethnic minority groups who are disinherited and suffer all forms of violence, abuse, and neglect, such as psychological threat, oppression, and stigmatisation in the society. It is also dedicated to my late father Chief Augustine Oforma Ezeakor.

FOREWORD

There has been considerable debate on how the experience of black and ethnic minorities in the UK psychiatric system can be improved. The dominant ideology in the UK Psychiatry has been characterised as being euro centric with understandings of illness and aetiology being transferred from the dominant European culture to other cultures e.g. black people from the African Diaspora without critically examining whether such understandings are valid when used across cultures. This includes the use of assessment tools in literature which purports to describe the incidence an prevalence of conditions affecting black and ethnic minorities. Anthropologically informed approaches to research, assessment and treatment are not popular and there is an ongoing battle between clinicians who are convinced of the efficacy and applicability of their models and service users or patients who describe the psychiatric system as coercive and unwilling to listen to them. The Americans have approached the understanding of psychiatric illness particularly as it affects minorities like African Americans differently and have readily embraced insights from anthropology and sociology. Cultural formulations have been devised and there is a growing body of literature on their use for different groups including ethnic minorities. Culturally competent services have been proposed as the way to address problems identified in the UK.

A Kleiman, P. Benson in 2006, criticised the concept of cultural competence which seemed to assume that culture could be reduced to a technical skill for which clinicians could be trained to develop expertise and attributed this to problems with how culture is defined in medicine. They point out that culture is inseparable from economic, political, religious, psychological and biological conditions and that culture is a process through which ordinary activities and conditions take on emotional tone and moral meaning for participants. They advocate training of clinicians in ethnography. This book is timely and it is a very good example of an ethno graphic study which looks at a form of stress in women in South East Nigeria, elicits the emic concepts and gives a detailed account of the context in which distress occurs. In the process of the study the aetiology of the distress is described in a way which makes the solution to the social, economic and political problems encountered by women apparent.

The book gives a detailed review of kinship, ritual, patriarchy and social theories on property relations. It leaves the reader feeling well informed about these concepts as well as being up to date and knowing how the concepts would relate to the area and subject under study. There is also a critical review of methlogical issues in trying to understand the psycho-social condition of the women in the study. The limitations of this study are clearly described but these should not deter the reader from celebrating the knowledge emanating from this study of a neglected subject using a qualitative research methodology.

At one level you can see why African countries continue to lag behind in the improvement of the health and well being of their people, as in this case more than 50 years after Nigeria became an independent country. The country seems to have a legal, political and governance structure that does not seem to work for all its citizens. Customary laws continue to affect the design and implementation of moderns laws to the detriment of the welfare of women. International laws on economic, civic and human rights are subscribed to at the national level including legal instruments agreed in international African bodies but they have limited or no impact on the ordinary people studied here. The problems of women do not feature in the manifestos of local or national political elites or their discourse and one fears that positive change, if it ever happens, will be very slow. What is described in this study is the chronic isolation, exclusion, humiliation, intimidation and stigmatization of women who are widowed (where husbands died intestate) and women who do not have children. Their fellow women, their families, the leadership of their communities, custom and politics seem to conspire to keep women in a poor chronically disadvantaged unhealthy existence.

In the study, the women describe their current level of functioning, their status, their feelings and emotions using their own language which is powerful in the trauma it describes. The women also describe things like spirituality, involvement in church activities, economic independence, literacy which reduce vulnerability to the negative effects of the emotional, physical and sexual abuse that they experience. What they describe points the way to what can be done to help them at the micro level, whilst at the same time, at the macro level, addressing and creating an economic legal and political framework that improves their condition in the short and long term. The importance of activities like education which empower women, comes across powerfully as it is the younger, poor unemployed, the illiterate or unskilled who seem to be most vulnerable and in the most hopeless situation.

The psycho social problems described, and in particular, 'Ariri' are accounts which come from people within their culture. This emic approach in my view, is the missing ingredient when those providing services e.g. statutory services in western developed countries like the UK and African countries which have copied psychiatric practices and systems from their former colonial powers are attempting to make psychiatry and psychology relevant to people in Africa and black and ethnic minorities in the diaspora. This book illustrates how one can go about understanding an issue in a way that allows the necessary culturally valid interventions to address a situation to emerge.

Dr. David Ndegwa
Consultant Forensic Psychiatrist
King's College University London

FOREWORD

It is a pleasure to be asked to write a foreword for this remarkable book by my friend and colleague Revd. Dr. Adolphus Ezeakor. This seminal work by author is ground breaking, not just timely—it is long overdue. He has cast a light on the stigma of widow-hood and childlessness in the lives of Igbo women, a neglected area of research. In doing so he does not only characterise the vulnerabilities within this particular culture but highlights the plight of women in many societies.

This scholarly work documents for the first time the customs and mores of Igbo women who have been widowed or who are childless. Some of the specific accounts are surprising, even startling, to Western ears and maybe to many Nigerians as well. They document a tale of degradation of the status of these women and the undervaluing of their contribution to society. This is a story of loss of dignity, leading to loss of respect, coupled with economic disadvantage, a pitiful waste of talent and loss of potential for society.

Some of the specifics may relate to Igbo women but the general themes of female societal disadvantages and its consequences are common to many cultures and, while receding in the West, were certainly a feature of Western culture in the recent past and many echoes remain.

Degrading or undervaluing the dignity and socio-economic status of women has widespread and long-lasting effects. As a medical practitioner I am especially aware of the risk of abusive behaviour and severe economic disadvantage when women are undervalued. This is true worldwide and is still a prominent feature of the lives of many women attending my own hospital in South Central London. Less specific but equally important is the impact of reduced status for women on their long-term health. Undervalued women are less likely to seek medical care, less likely to comply with treatment, less likely to adopt good preventative health measures, and have shorter life expectancy. It should not be a surprise that anyone who feels undervalued or suffers discrimination has low self-esteem and is more susceptible to self-destructive behaviours with the obvious consequences for their own health and well-being and those around them, particularly their children.

General observations on the status of women in Nigeria are even more stark in the case of widows. Their low socio-economic status leads to venerability and places them in peril on occasion. When one adds psycho-social constructs to the status of widows and childless women, leading to them being viewed almost as witches, then their social isolation becomes more profound and even more disabling.

The author of this book has shown himself not only to be an expert in psycho-social studies but also in pioneering a concept of pathology—'Ariri' as a culture-specific mental health problems in a more therapeutic manner, reflecting his own compassionate and caring nature. This book deserves, nay demands, to be read by all those with a leadership role in Nigerian society and its wider diaspora. It makes uncomfortable reading but addresses a vitally important issue which has been neglected and unaddressed until now. At the very least I would expect that caring professionals would recognise the trauma suffered by this group of women and would lead the response to their needs.

I consider this excellent study by the author will have a significant impact on women's health and well-being. I hope and expect that it will be an impetus for improvement, a voice of reason, and a call for action for this disadvantaged and denigrated group who deserve much more—who deserve our love and support.

Dr. Michael Marrinan FRCS Ed
Executive Chief Medical Director
King's College Hospital London

PREFACE

This book examines the patriarchal practice and how it adversely impacts the psychosocial, behavioural, and cognitive predictors of 'Ariri' (mental distress) amongst the female population in South-Eastern Nigeria. It is argued that patriarchal practice of inheritance of property (intestate) demonstrates that women, especially widows and childless wives are discriminated against. This not only affects their socio-economic status, but also stigmatises them.

In regard to the complex psychosocial condition of women, this book identifies the traumatic experience of women associated with disinheritance and with other forms of violence, abuse, and neglect in a patrilineal and kinship system. Broad in its scope and detailed in its research, this book analyses the plight of women on property relations and draws on a highly theoretical framework across anthropology, sociology, psychology, and law.

Initially, my experience as a parish priest working in a local community of different Christian denominations in Nigeria sparked my reflection on cultural ideology associated with women's rights and other forms of superstitious beliefs attributed to witchcraft, childless condition, and widowhood. I have pondered as I sat with key eminent people, men and women, who represent a generation of strong women who survived the Second World War as well as the Nigerian Civil War. I have taken the case of women's disinheritance to various non-governmental bodies (NGOs) in the south-eastern region of Nigeria, through their narrative experience (storytelling) process in rural and urban cities. In the midst of it all, I have taken time with population studies, as I have listened to the growing patterns of their prolonged grief. However, with my consultation from the participants, people believed that some widows and childless wives in families were successful in overcoming their trauma through family support or their socio-economic status (career/employment) to live above the experiences of trauma and abuse. However, through networking with the Roman Catholic Diocese of Awka Justice and Peace Development

Commission (JDPC) in Nigeria, I have reconnected with the narrative of human rights abuse which is still problematic on both regional and rural levels. In this context, I have also begun to discern a process through which women's rights and health care can be empowered, and individuals and communities can find the resilience to live.

Investigation on the impact of the psychosocial conditions of widows and childless wives in the south-eastern region makes this book most significant in analysing the long-term abuse and stigmatisation that underpin patriarchal practices. This correlated with the findings from the National Collaborating Centre for Mental Health in Great Britain, which recently completed a rigorous meta-analytic review of the clinical research literature on post-traumatic stress disorder (PTSD). Commissioned by the National Institute for Clinical Excellence (NICE), this meta-analysis served as the basis for the National Clinical Practice Guideline on PTSD (Royal College of Psychiatrists and the British Psychological Society, 2005). These studies reviewed trauma-based cognitive behavioural therapy (CBT), covering a range of vulnerable populations, including survivors of violence, abuse, and neglect (domestic violence and mixed trauma groups with multiple traumatic events). Being aware of the women's situation, I have made sincere efforts to represent the violence and domestic abuse suffered by them throughout my further studies and hope to present the psychological effects of abuse and its risk factors as a significant contribution to psychosocial conditions of women in gender studies and public health, as I seek to apply these in counselling and psychotherapy treatment.

It is out of women's stigmatisation that this book is authenticated. Also it is their abuse and trauma that motivated me to attempt this task of academic research. However, I believe that through modern counselling, the hopelessness and helplessness of many depressed women can be counteracted. Many supporting therapies and techniques are now available. Education is the starting point. My counselling experience working with children and families overseas for many years now, has enabled me to share, in this book, valuable insights.

The 'Why' of the Book

Women's abuse in a patrilineal and kinship system has become significant to this book, while looking at the pattern in the colonial and post-colonial periods. We need to perceive and interpret gender power and inequalities in Nigeria. This relates not only to the gender divisions of labour and the servicing activities of wives for their husbands but also to customary laws of inheritance, ownership of land, and other property relations.

This book allows readers to comprehend the cultural links in the patriarchal Nigerian environment, which relates to customary laws and functions of African cosmos and belief systems. It also addresses the internal problems of contemporary Nigeria and helps to create awareness on how kinship system reinforces the oppression of women which influence their long-term abuse and traumatic experience in the marital family. It also attempts to improve the understanding of the cultural factors influencing the mental health of Nigerian widows and childless women by bringing the traditional practices and beliefs of local communities into comparison with similar practices that continue to thrive across cultures in the world.

The south-eastern region, especially the Igbo society, is influenced by historical and external factors. These include slave trade, colonisation, and amalgamation of the present northern and southern regions of Nigeria which took place in 1914 by the British administration. Other factors include external economic social relations (trade, missionaries, and Western education), First and Second World Wars, independence, and the Nigerian-Biafra Civil War from 1967 to 1970 (Afigbo, 2006:155-178).

In addition, the Igbo society is influenced by a variety of customs, cultures, religions, and languages. Traditions among 250 ethnic groups give the country, Nigeria, a rich geopolitical diversity (Anyabolu, 2003:47).

The Igbo people take their name from the Kwa Family, meaning people from the same language. According to Ogbaa (1995:91) and Eberegbulam

(1990:34), the Kwa Family is an amalgamation of groups of people that formed a tribe known as Ndi Igbo. Both forms, Igbo' and Ibo, depict the same meaning. However, Igbo is more widespread among the people themselves; Ibo seems to have been first adopted largely by foreigners because of the difficulty in pronouncing the 'gb'. Igbo will be used throughout in this book, except when quoting authors who use the alternative form.

Historically, the Igbo are mainly located in the south-eastern part of Nigeria on both sides of the river Niger, but sizeable groups are found in different parts of the country, although less so after the Nigerian Civil War. One of the most powerful groups of Igbos is the Umu-Nri, guardian of the famous Nri Oracle, which wielded political influence over most of the peoples of the Niger Delta and its hinterland before colonisation. The correlation of symbolic power and political power is a characteristic of the society. The worship of traditional deity and ritual form the background of the environment, while Christian denomination and Islamic institutions are well established in rural as well as urban centres.

The ethnographic studies of Igbo by Afigbo (2005) and Nwagbara (2007) show a comprehensive and relatively accurate representation of the people. The Igbo language is spoken by 17 per cent of the people in Nigeria. English is referred to as the official language and is commonly used in education, commerce, and religion. For example, the local people in the urban and rural south-eastern region use pidgin English as a form of communication as a result of different dialects. Pidgin English is an amalgam of vernacular and English language and has variations throughout West Africa. According to Afigbo (2005), it is used as a form of lingua franca among the urban working class and is widely spoken in rural areas as well, particularly between the illiterate and semi-illiterate. Pidgin English is also used as a means of communication when conducting public education programmes, that is, family planning. Some writers have also written in pidgin to make their work accessible to a wider audience (Afigbo 2005:549-58).

The Igbos had a decentralised type of society, but the British created a native court area with a chief to whom they gave the warrant to rule. Not only was this system of white cap or warrant chiefs completely alien to the traditional system, but many of them proved to be corrupt as well as incompetent so that, in the period after pacification, village affairs were largely conducted by the council of elders.

Igboland is the most urbanised and possibly the most industrialised in Sub-Saharan Africa. There are eight major cities in Igboland—Enugu, Onitsha, Awka, Nsukka, Abakiliki, Umuahia, Owerri, and Aba, and it has an estimated population of 30-35 million. The population census in Nigeria puts the estimated figure of the south-eastern region of Nigeria at an approximate number. According to Nnadozie (2007:227-46), there is a precedence of tampering with census figures to show a larger population growth in the north than in the south in order to ensure a more generous revenue allocation from the government. Isichei (1997:246) argues that this has slowed down their socio-economic and political development in the south region, including Igboland. These factors contributed to the use of 'conflict situation' to relate my primary research within the south-eastern region in Nigeria.

The economic system in Igboland is based on agricultural subsistence. In this respect, Afigbo (2005:297) argues that Igbo people are enterprising and business oriented. In agriculture, men gain their status through yam cultivation, which is the most important root crop. Cassava and cocoyam are deemed to be secondary and generally cultivated and marketed by women, which may provide an explanation about their status in both the domestic and labour force. Thus, agriculture is located within kinship and family structures, which constrict men's and women's ability to act independently. Men control the more valuable yams and palm products and carry out more long-distance trading based on a subsistence economy. Labour consists of the members of the family, neighbours, friends, in-laws, and relations (Hafkin, 2000:56-70), and there is a clear gender division of labour. Women are rarely landowners or traders in yams and palm products. A man shows his strength and valour as the owner of productive resources, including family and kin, and by the size of land under cultivation, which is the case today.

Agricultural output, such as palm produce, contributed substantially to the gross domestic product (GDP) of Nigeria as a whole till today. Agricultural exports have been important and more pronounced in Igboland following the Second World War when earnings from it were buoyant and constituted the economic foundation of migration to the towns (Afigbo, 2005:80-84). Even from the 1960s, strong influence was exerted on the composition of the GDP. Palm produce, for a long time, also constituted a major source of income. However, it has over the years declined as a major source of income for rural dwellers. After independence, agricultural exports ceased to be a major earner. Petroleum emerged as the major export earner for Nigeria, which expanded industrialisation, commerce, and migration to the cities and is a major source of conflict with the government and the multinationals in the delta region, although this does not directly affect Igboland.

Apart from yam and other produce, which serve as the basis of livelihood in Igboland, the south-eastern region has, according to Afigbo (2005:83), the country's highest concentration of trade and commerce. Recent studies, such as the one by Ekechi (2002:75-82), demonstrate that commerce and colonialism have both significantly affected the structures of village life. The traditional relationship between men and women in subsistence agriculture was men's assumption of political and economic power over women. In recent times, however, some of the women in urban and rural areas have been able to buy plots of land for subsistence agriculture through the support of their natal family, relatives, and children overseas.

It has been argued that the changes in village life are related to urbanisation, which is sustained by the modernisation of agricultural production, transport, and industrial developments. These factors impact upon women and their participation in the labour force in the villages and the towns. Moore (1995:94-96) argues that in contexts of urbanisation, women are experiencing a profound reorientation of their social and economic lives towards the cities and urbanism, with a decline in economic opportunities in the countryside, which has meant that many more women are migrating to the cities than before. On the other hand, Korieh (2001:117-62) claims that the expansion of rural market and agricultural produce gave women increased independence in the household economy even in rural contexts. According to him, this applies to wives and mothers in their patrilineal household in the village structure. In the villages studied for this investigation, women earn cash through trading, farming, and jobs in both the public and private sectors, but their financial security and social status depend to a great extent on their kinship position and traditional gender ideologies.

In Nigeria, as elsewhere in Africa, colonial officials discriminated against women (Korieh, 2001:160). In other words, the issue of colonial taxation adversely affected Nigerian women. The irony behind the Aba Women's Riot in 1929, according to Chief Esiaba, is that the women's demonstration was a result of protest against British imperialism or indirect rule over the Ibo administration. Women used revolution to express their common interest. They displayed a degree of militancy associated traditionally with male rather than female behaviour. Information collected from the informants of the Aba crisis who actually took part in the riots clearly showed that the riots were instigated and stage-managed by the men, who hoped to achieve certain reforms in colonial administration. The women were prompted to act in the belief that the colonial authorities would not harm them, since in accordance with the tradition of the Igbo, women were never killed in warfare, and on many occasions, they acted as peacemakers in tribal wars. During the riots, more than 40 persons died amongst over 120 women, 51 were wounded, and 29 of the wounded were admitted in the hospital (see Reports of the Women's Aid Collective, 2005:12). This indicates a significant point in gender relations where traditional status of women as 'outside' warfare was ignored. Similarly, Adichie (2006:71) noted the 'aggressive' rape and murder of women in the civil war, which represent a 'normalisation' of physical violence against women, which was strengthened by the civil war in Biafra in particular.

The 1970s oil boom was one key factor that gave rise to migration with all the opportunities for making one's fortune in cities like Lagos, Port Harcourt, and Warri, the delta state as well as other areas that were indirectly stimulated by the oil economy. As a longer-term phenomenon, however, migration from the rural areas, especially amongst young men, is an accelerating and largely irreversible social process (Chukwuezi, 2001:50-57). This has affected the rural economy in the areas of migration by creating marked changes in the gender division of labour. For instance, as migration of men left gaps in the rural areas, the resulting labour gap was met by others, especially wives, children, or hired labourers (Afigbo, 2005:237). The tasks were modified or not performed and less land was made available for cultivation. For instance, the absence of men led to the neglect of such agricultural tasks as land clearing and heavy soil conservation work, which men generally performed. Thus, in forest areas from which there was much male migration, thickly overgrown land that had been left fallow for extended periods would not be cleared for cultivation; instead, the same parcels of land were used repeatedly, leading to rapid decline in soil fertility. There are also claims that the departure of men helped to generate a lively market for rural wage labour. The situation resulted in the confirmation of domination in cash crop production and confined women to the growing of subsistence or less valuable cash crops. Government efforts to increase agricultural output in fact led to a more clearly marked gender division of labour than previously the case (Chukwuezi, 2001:55-66).

Changing socio-economic circumstances related to limited female migration to urban areas are therefore contributing to changing gender relations especially through women's non-agricultural employment in the towns and their mixing with female counterparts in the city. In the villages studied, women earned cash through trading, farming, and public and private sectors. Moore (1995) argues that in some areas of postcolonial Africa, women's social movement is restricted by migratory behaviour. Migration raises fears and doubts about women's changing roles and, in particular, their increased participation in economic and political life in Igboland. Part of the dominant male ideology is that female migration to cities is not something to be encouraged. One of the male anxieties over this issue is a desire to control women's morality and sexual behaviour, but there is evidence that women identify their reasons for migration as solely based on social and economic grounds (Francis, 2002:531-50). The basic understanding here is that gender relations, and in particular conflict between men and women, are central to understanding rural and urban migration and why women experience changing social and economic pressures differently from men. Moore (1995:42-43), however, has taken the investigation of women's roles further, relating urban migration and gender conflict to the emerging class divisions and their consequences for women.

Women contribute largely to the formal economy of cities, and their position in the rural sector is improving as they play a dominant role in selling 'street foods'. A number of authors have noted that women from the rural areas visit their husbands in town (city) during slack periods in the agricultural cycle to collect money and purchase necessary items; these women might also bring food from the rural area for consumption by the urban household (Agbasiere, 2000:32-34), so there is some experience of urban environments for many wives.

Recently, according to Afigbo (2005:299), two important developments have directly enhanced market women's role in trade, namely the expansion of the trade from the coast to the hinterland and the proliferation of imported commodities from the coast to the urban markets.

When migration increased again, the demand for food increased, leading to the most profound impacts of urbanisation on the rural economy derived from the vast increase in food demand generated by the growth of cities. There was a significant increase in cassava planting and processing, largely done by women as a cottage industry. Demand for and production of corn also increased significantly. In the early part of the harvest season, fresh corn, sold as roadside fast food, became a highly profitable venture. Some of this produce was transported to the cities, supplementing the traditional sorghum and millet production. The expansion of commercial chicken and egg production largely for the urban market further raised demand for corn as feed. According to Nwankwor (2005:21), these factors contributed to the independence of women in the supply of certain agricultural products. Most of the women participating in this research are, or have been, involved in some of these activities, but, as will be demonstrated, a history of such forms of economic activity does not protect them from traditional attitudes towards women without husbands or (male) children. Still most of them have very limited rights in traditional societies.

In spite of the military regime's efforts to return Igbo urban workers to the land, Ezeilo (2004:15) argues that throughout this period, the continued growth of urbanisation and expansion of transport in the late twentieth century were the major driving forces of agricultural production and modernisation that gave rise to the increase in urban population and the increased participation of women in the wage labour force. She further argues, 'the rural and urbanisation evidence in the modern era has shown a marked correlation between the rate of urbanisation and the increased role of women in education and economic activity greater in postcolonial times'.

Nigeria became an independent country on 1 October 1960, and in 1963, it became the Republic of Nigeria. The national and regional political system of Nigeria has been described as a 'multicultural society with different traditional attitudes and socio-political structures' (Nyiam, 2002:11-14). The contemporary situation is an aggregation of ethnic groups—the Hausa/Fulani in the North, the Yoruba in the West, and the Igbo in the East under tension or ongoing conflicts.

Regional politics constitute a variety of social forces expressed in the patriarchal institution. It demonstrates the way patriarchal and kinship system, such as local politics, hierarchy of lineages/families, and eminent people, are related to the way colonial appointments of warrant chiefs and elders influence the laws and policies over the decades.

Political and economic conflicts represent two major factors—first, the marginalisation of the Igbos in the south-east and Warri in the south-south, and Ijaw tribe in the oil-rich delta state, which is an outcome of the differential allocation of the national fund to the development of the regional states as Dokobor-Asari reports (*Vanguard*, 11 November 2005). Besides, the effect of oil extraction and lack of funding to the local community in the Niger Delta has contributed to the underdevelopment of the local community in terms of poor infrastructure—roads, electricity, and pipe-borne water as well as a lack of hospitals and schools. The wealth generated by Niger Delta oil is not being put back into the development of the infrastructure of that community. This is because of struggles over oil exploration in the region and the distribution of profits to western regions; individual politicians and their clients are contributory factors to the ongoing regional conflict in the Niger Delta. According to Njoku (2003), the struggle for regional secession, especially by the south-eastern region of Biafria, started in the late 1960s and the unstable political situation in these regions continues to this day with the current problems of the displacement of the Igbos in the Muslim north and the ongoing political instability of the Niger Delta region centred on Warri and Port Harcourt (Uzoigwe, 2004:59).

The regional rivalry and hostility are relevant to the study as it looks at the internal and external forces as the immediate cause of the war to secede from the Nigerian Federation and to establish the independent regional republic. Although the war affected the whole country, the peoples of the former south-eastern region bore the heaviest toll, and at the end of the war in 1970, not only had they lost a significant proportion of their population but, in many cases, all their material possessions. It is pertinent to note, however, that in some respects, according to Murray's report (31 July 2007) the Biafrian war had serious repercussions on the status of women in Igboland. For example, during the war, many women were forced to assume new responsibilities; often they were the sole breadwinners of the family when the men were too scared to venture out for fear of being conscripted into the army. After the war, according to Anameze (1996:30-32), they asserted independence hitherto unknown to women in some communities. For example, many male informants stated that it was difficult to relegate women to their former, docile and servile status, and this caused the implementation of strict tradition on women in Igboland. The post-conflict situation in this region, together with the effects of military government, the exploitation by multinationals of the oil in delta, the corruption in politics in general, and with the diversion of income from the oil to politicians in particular, set the broader context for the study.

Women's participation in socio-politics has been problematic. Anifowose (2004:93) remarked that women's non-involvement in politics has been a hindrance to effective participation in modern Nigerian politics. Agbajajobi (2009:75-80) further adds that men, to further their political aims and ambitions, have used politics to manoeuvre their advancement. The participation of African women in the political processes of their respective societies is an area that has attracted much scholarly attention. It suggests that colonial domination and other emphasises on the political subordination and invisibility account for women's discrimination in the region. Since the return to democratic governance in 1999, the participation of women in politics especially in Igboland has been increasingly constrained (Nwankwor, 2002:4). At a national level, women are extremely poorly represented in government. In the House of Senate or National Assembly in 2008 and 2009; only 3 women were selected senators out of 109 members. In 2008 12 women were elected to the House of Representatives out of 320; their number increased to 21 in 2009. In recent times, there have been 28 women in all the state houses of Assembly, which means that some of these assemblies do not have any women out of 109 seats; women MPs had only 4 seats.

The regional and federal powers in relation to the position of law are still problematic, despite the fact that power resides in the local state government, which controls the appointments and backs judges or other administrators of the law. There is discrimination against women in the legal process both at regional and federal level. Ewelukwa (2002:440) argues that widows are reluctant to seek redress in court in terms of inheritance issues because they believe that the courts are inherently prejudiced towards them. Overall, the courts still appear to reinforce patriarchal practices.

Hitherto, local politics in traditional Nigerian societies exert power and influence and places particular emphasis on the manifestations of patriarchal power (Ezeilo, 2005:35). For instance, the politicised ethnic rivalries in Nigerian societies have economic effects on the region and that at local and national levels, politics proceeds on a patron-client basis. From this perspective, the uneasy relationship between federal government and regional governments, particularly with the unstable political situations in the delta and the north, still represents a problem in contemporary Nigeria.

At the national level, there has been anti-discrimination legislation; there is a framework of rights, but gender discrimination continues to exist, at least at regional and local levels. Using the judicial, executive, and legislative systems in traditional societies as a focal point, Nwankwor (2002:15) argues the interplay between cultural forces, the manifestations of patriarchal power, and the pluralism that characterises the Nigerian legal environment in perpetuating the subordination and subjugation of women especially widows. According to her, there are no national laws which specifically protect the rights of women. Where they exist, they are often inadequate or limited by virtue of the undue burden placed on the women. Sometimes, women are not aware of this legislation during court proceedings. The criminal code and penal code provide punishment for violent acts, but the system (e.g. police) refuses to deal with violence in the home as crime. In the case of domestic abuse, the burden of proof is so high that survivors rarely succeed in securing a conviction of the accused persons in court. Section 55 of the Penal Code encourages wife beating as a corrective measure. Similarly, Ezeilo (2005:17) asserts that there is no federal law prohibiting harmful traditional practices such as widowhood practices, female genital mutilation, and child marriages. In other words, religious laws are often manipulated and misinterpreted by institutions to suit them and to the detriment of women. The difficulties encountered by widows within the traditional sphere are exacerbated by the fact that official legislative and judicial organs of the Nigerian state are also predominately male in their composition and inherently patriarchal in their outlook (Ewelukwa, 2002:441).

The political participation in traditional Nigeria societies, according to Nwankwor (2005:32), reflects a mostly male character. Men are thus accorded a dominant position by virtue of their exercise of authority and power, which not only frustrate the advancement and protection of women but also marginalises them in political activities. Women who stand for elective positions more often than not have bitter experiences. This accounts for the universal belief that politics in Nigeria is characterised by corruption. Having indicated the increasing participation of women in the labour market as opposed to limited participation in the legal and political arenas, in this section, the status of women in legislative terms is briefly reviewed, and I give consideration of how effective current legislation is in terms of women's status and gender relations, and how their status is related to kinship. The Convention on the Elimination of All Forms of Discrimination against Women (CEDAW) 1979 was adopted in all West African states. In respect of this section 1, African Charter of peoples' rights demonstrates that all citizens should merit equal treatment (Nwankwor, 2005:12). Anambra State Passage of two bills at the House of Assembly on malpractices against widows A.S.N. Law No. 5, 2005 means that 'dehumanising treatment' or humiliating acts, which deprive widows of the fundamental rights and freedom, which she would otherwise be entitled to under the constitution are forbidden. Some of these 'fundamental rights' and directive principles are of vital importance in improving the status of women. The right to freedom from discrimination is closely connected to the statement on social objectives and directive principles of state social policy (Fox, 2005). In furtherance of the social order, every citizen shall have equality of rights, obligations, and opportunities before the law. However, women's rights and opportunities are severely circumscribed especially in the courts of law, as discussed below in relation to inheritance law.

According to Rothman (2005:22), the term 'gender' refers to the social characteristics that distinguish the sexes (males and females). It implies that social construction of gender is a subtle and complex process that includes tangible presentations of people, a sexual division of labour between women's and men's work, and subtle behavioural and attitudinal expectations. Gender is embedded in the social and cultural heritage of a group, and individuals are introduced to it as they encounter differential expectations and are exposed to dissimilar treatment that tends to emphasise differences at the expense of similarities. The above definitions are analysed through a sexual division of labour, which has significant implications for gender and kinship throughout the colonial and post-colonial and the contemporary period. Marriage, inheritance, and property rights are the determinants of women's status in kinship practice. Therefore kinship practice remains discriminatory towards women, as customary practices have dictated in the social and ethno history of Igboland.

Women's involvement in the political process of the country is nowhere proportionate to the 50 per cent of the population which they represent in the society. The nature of national, regional, and local politics is paternalistic. Thus, through structures and processes created by patriarchy, colonialism, capitalism, and gender inequalities, women's exclusion in the social and political life of the nation evolved intensively self-consciously masculine than most other social practices (Anyabolu, 2003:45). Nwankwor (2004:7) and Ezeilo (2003:15) add while inequalities may be exacerbated by particular social structures and traditions, it is mainly rooted in unequal power relations. These arguments, which focus on power relations, indicate women's marginalisation. This will be investigated in Chapter 2 as relating to the power of patrilineages, property relations, and the dynamics of marriages, and this will be further explored in the investigation. The whole episode of violence had its origin in the political structure that the British imposed on South-Eastern Nigeria.

Nwankwor (2005:13) argues that the political status of women relates to their economic position and points out that, 'women suffer from marginalisation in political and economic activities and the correlations between poverty and gender'. In local kinship, with reference to hierarchies of lineages of families, the compound head who is a senior, or eldest man, is in charge of political affairs within the governing structures of the kin groups. He settles disputes and supervises the productive and reproductive activities of the lineage. The patrilineal extended family is the central domestic unit of everyday Igbo traditional life and of collective economic enterprise where eminent men (clan heads, titled men and paramount chiefs) represent the major political players and take decisions in customary law, for example, inheritance and marriage law. The line of succession travels through the male line, which means that a woman can gain status on the basis of the birth of a male son. Kinship practice in this context determines women's right of inheritance, especially for women in general and more particularly widows. Nevertheless, the role of women in the hierarchies of lineages of families is still limited in terms of political and legal participation in the kinship system. Over the past decade, women have experienced a minimal improvement in terms of their participatory rights in the political and legal process. With this gradual improvement, it could represent the beginning of a more sustained improvement in widow's political, legal, and economic rights.

Similar to this, according to Mezue (2006), Achebe's *Things Fall Apart* (1994) illuminates how the pre-colonial social structure of 'village republics' and hierarchy of lineages gives explanations on the position of women and impact of marginalisation. Thus, both authors conveyed in the study the understanding of pre-colonial and contemporary Igbo practices, rural-urban ties, and desire for high fertility (reproduction). Local kinship ties represent a key means by which people gain access to economic, political, and social resources and also to privileges or favours. The reliance of Igbo people for access to social and economic resources run through extended families and communities of origin which represent an important component of the context for understanding human reproduction and specifically the continued values of marriage, parenthood, place of origin, and relatively high fertility (Smith, 2004a). Achebe's ethnographic research on the Igbo patriarchy was a useful source that emphasised the way communities grounded in rituals and symbolic power demonstrated the cosmology of the Igbo male authority. A more literary approach to this phenomenon was articulated in the work of Adichie (2006) in her novel *Half of a Yellow Sun*—a female perspective and the conflict situation in the Biafra War.

The 'caste system' or 'hierarchy of kinship groups' is the basic structural feature of traditional Igbo society. Gender and generation are key elements in the power structure. Women leave their family of origin and, therefore, their patrilineage on marriage and are integrated into their husband's lineage only after they have fulfilled their wifely duties by bearing a child, especially a male child. Marriage is usually patrilocal, that is, the bride moves to the village of her husband's lineage. Edholm (1982:167) argues that when anthropologists talk about marriage, it is primarily concerned with the ways in which mating (marriage) is socially organised and regulated, the ways in which parentage is assigned, attributed, and recognised; descent is traced; relatives are classified; rights are transferred across generations; and kin groups are formed. Such relationships are seen as constructed within the basic constraints and imperatives on the organisation of human life: production and reproduction, mating, dependence, the need for enculturation, and the life cycle.

Within families and kinship systems, the elders have more power than younger men and women, and male elders have more power than all females, demonstrating distinctions of hierarchy. It is argued that the elders in the kinship determine the status of authority in the political, legislative, and executive organisation of the village government. In some areas of patrilineal and kinship, the government of eminent people-clan heads, titled men, chiefs, and elders represent an instrument of social control.

The reputation of eminent people as members of the higher-ranking lineages rests on the identity of the lineage and that is the basis of the symbolic knowledge—maintaining the memories of ancestors from whom they derive power and from the myths and rituals which support their position.

The material or economic status and power of the eminent people are derived from all forms of wealth and influence or, in particular, the 'land'. According to Afigbo (2005:235), in traditional Nigerian societies, agricultural-based system has favoured male ownership of productive property resources and agnatic-kin cooperation gave prominence to men, both as economic actors and as representatives of the household. It is argued that the most common occupations held by eminent people are agricultural activities. Some of the eminent people living in the villages have gained access to education through affiliation of the missionaries. Afigbo (2005:298) claims that 'Christianity has been integrally related to the social and political development of Igbo society from the beginning of the colonial period'. The eminent people are included in the sample of the group in the study based on their knowledge and cultural information related to this study. With their current political status and ideology as custodian of the culture, only a few of them can read and write English or any other language, and their consultation makes the study more reliable and authentic. Kinship ties are the crucial means by which resources and favours can be accessed and are, therefore, the means to political influence and material gain.

The village republicanism provides the social structures of the family and leadership. The compound 'Obi' is characterised as the centre of the family where social and spiritual contacts of the family head is established (e.g. village politics and meetings), and each compound is fenced with a wall made of red mud, and the principal building belongs to the head of the family. Within the compound, each house constitutes a separate household meant for unmarried sisters and brothers and their wives and children. It is argued that the compound represents the way families try to actualise their inborn and natural inclination in a dynamic interaction with their environments.

The Igbo village can be described as 'a small face to face society'; Ugorji (2009:60) described it as a number of closely clustered compounds; families form the geopolitical parties, and several villages make up towns. Patrilineage defines a group, whose members claim to be descended from the men of a common ancestor. Ugorji (2009:55) traces the Igbo traditional lineage according to five different fathers namely (a) the *umunna* of the father (paternal patrilineage), (b) the *umunna* of the mother (the maternal patrilineage), (c) the *umunna* of the mother of the father (the patrilineage of the father's mother), (d) the *umunna* of the mother of the mother (the patrilineage of the mother's mother), and (e) the *umunna* of the spouse (the patrilineage of the spouse). His observation shows that the Igbo world view and philosophy of life-in-community is captured by the clearest expression of *igwe bu ike*—unity or strength is power or solidarity embodied in the kinship concept. No Igbo man would like to disappoint his ancestors by breaking the lineage. For this reason, to have family, and children has assumed a social and religious significance, they indicate success in life and social worth and communion with one's ancestors. They also indicate virility on the part of the man and fertility on the part of the woman. So in addition to boosting one's self-esteem in the society, marrying and having children are significant factors that enter into the definition of both sexual and gender identities. The word 'obi' signifies not only the architectural pattern of building but human relations in general. Kinship forms a strong interaction with the social organisation through which households and compounds are structured.

In the traditional Igbo society, marriage is 'arranged' and 'bride price' paid. Marriage can be monogamous or polygamous; it may be an enduring relationship entered into after much negotiation, or it may be a relatively informal arrangement. Christian missionary activities have affected the residential pattern of marriage with the married couple often moving to a new conjugal home, rather than going to live with the husband's kin. Second, according to Mann (1985:51), Christian marriage, in some cases, radically altered traditional Igbo inheritance practices. It gave spouses rights to each other's estates; it made Christian wives and their children sole heirs to a man's property, and through the marriage ordinance, it disinherited a man's siblings and any children by customary wives or concubines. Monogamy and concepts of individual rights have therefore been introduced into the traditional kinship organisation to varying degrees. It argues that the political elite and missionary activities contributed in the educational opportunities to read and write in a particular language.

According to Moore (1995:119), the relationship of bride wealth or bride price to women's economic security and independence can be difficult to unravel. However, Nwankwor (2004) and Ezeilo (2005:37) indicate that polygamy was practised in traditional Igbo families as the material base for transferring private possession of goods to male authority while providing at the same time tight control over women's freedom. While polygamy is still practised, monogamous marriage may be a preference for some, according to Nwankwor (2003), because it provides civil and canonical security especially in terms of property relations. However, marriages under the ordinances are not common because of the restrictions they place on plural marriage and easy divorce. Marriage is perceived as crucial for individuals and for the reproduction of the kinship-based social organisation. Afigbo (2005:257) puts the Igbo case as follows: 'Marriage enables individuals (man/woman) to live together and co-operate in an orderly social life'. Traditionally, kinship and community not only condemns women who cannot have children but unmarried and divorced women as well.

Reproduction and particularly the birth of a son are keys to both male virility and power and the integration of women into their affinal villages. A series of rituals are incorporated into everyday life. The head of the household—husbands of the family—regularly offer kola nuts in morning prayers everyday'[1]. Symbolically, the kola nut signifies unity and life; elders use it for prayers, for prosperity, and as blessings; it is used in ritual offerings to the earth goddess and the goddess of fertility by women. According to Ndiokwere (1998:47-50), if you ask the ordinary Igbo man and woman why he desires to marry, the spontaneous answer will be 'I want to marry in order to beget my own children, to get a family like my parents'. In the local view, 'every family maintains a successive line of male representatives, stretching from the land of the living to that of the ancestors. When no son is there to maintain the link, it is assumed that the lineage is virtually moribund. Therefore, it signifies an omen and the worst calamity that can happen to any Igbo family. Nzomiwu (1999:41), on this, writes, 'It is on this world view that political, social, economic,

---

[1]   Kola nut is a seed in a pod that grows from a tree. It is similar to a cocoa pod seed. Symbolically, kola nut in Igbo culture signifies unity and life; elders use it for prayers (blessing) and prosperity. It shows hospitality and sense of communion. Apparently, Igbo people value land where kola nut grows because of the cultural tie with agriculture and ritual sacrifices to the earth goddess.

cultural, moral, legal, and religious aspects of existence form a continuum'. The next section focuses more on the Igbo 'world view' or cosmology, which may explain the social functions of such a world view are addressed in Chapter 3, and the relationship between this theory, local practices, and women with *Ariri* (emotional distress).

Cosmology shapes the way Igbo people view the world and things around them in terms of the sacred beliefs and cultural taboos. According to Afigbo (2005:484), cosmology represents the interaction between people and cultural and religious world view. It implies that according to the laws of the Igbo, which reflected their views of religion, patrilineal kinship is predicated upon the goals of Igbo existence: to preserve and nurture life. Core values are derived from the need to maintain moral and religious order, which are embedded in the world view and in religious beliefs and practices. This is a Durkheimian view of the function of religion in a mechanical society. According to Afigbo (2002:75), Igbo traditional religion is a way of ensuring good fortune for their people. In other words, it is out of hope and need that the gods were created, and the Igbo people were only bound to their religion because of their own need to survive and a widely accepted belief is that this religion kept them alive. In the three-dimensional perception of space and the cyclical perception of time, the human world, *uwa* (world) is dominated by the Earth-goddess (Ala). Human beings share *uwa* (cosmos) with a number of patron deities, human spirits, and nature deities as well as a number of evil spirits, especially *ogbanje* (diabolical force) and *agwu* (shrine). There is also the spirit world where ancestral spirits dominate.

Traditionally, the Igbo perceived their world as created by 'Chukwu' (Supreme Being), who is manifested in a variety of ways especially in the fertility of the earth, animals and human beings. Furthermore, the Igbo concept of authority is connected with the concept of *Chi*, which is a transcendental power (Obiora and Edozien, 2001:20). In Igbo cosmology, *Chi* (spirit being) confers a sacred authority on the relevant man. This is still manifested in the social recognition of authorities and hierarchies of custom and cultural practices. *Chi* is, according to Metuh (1985:12), central to the cultural life of Igbo society. Metuh claims that '[i]t gives central focus to the indispensable component of male social status'. Igbo believe that life is determined by *Chi*, which shows the manifestation of infinite essence given to each man separately and uniquely. This suggests that kinship relations are shaped by patrilineal, male authority and are sacred institutions.

Belief in a supreme being imbues all of life and there is no split between faith and daily living. Equally, belief in the ancestors and spiritual forces is accepted in many and various ways (Obiora and Edozien, 2001:19).

The issues of conceptualising status, class, and the social position of women in the context of the tensions within the rural areas, in particular, between traditional beliefs and practices and the modernisation of urban life, with increasing access to wage labour and trade for women still affect the multiculturalism in Nigeria.

One key feature, which is to be noted in status of gender, is the level of education among girls and boys. According to Acholonu (2001:31-37), education increases the aspirations of women workers, which provides women independence and autonomy in the labour market. In contrast, Umar and Adoba in the local newspaper *This Day*, 6 June 2010, reports that the delivery of education in rural and urban has suffered from years of neglect (degradation of education facilities at all levels and strikes in universities and schools), compounded by inadequate attention to policy framework within the sector. The result was declining literacy rates in both local (state) and national level. It is argued that gender issues and sociocultural beliefs and practices inhibit access to basic education in communities. According to Nigeria Millennium Development Goals 2005 Report, literacy level in the country has steadily and gradually deteriorated, especially within the 15-24 age groups. By 1999, the overall literacy rate had declined to 64.1 per cent from 71.9 per cent in 1991. The trend was in the same direction for male and female members of the 15-24 years age band. Among the male, the rate declined from 81.35 per cent in 1991 to 69.8 per cent in 1999. The decline among the female was from 62.49 per cent to 59.3 per cent during the same period (Millennium Development Goals Report, 2005).

Statistics from the *ActionAid* published in 2003 indicate glaring imbalances against girls in enrolment, attendance, and completion rates in all levels of education, particularly in the South-Eastern Nigeria due to a variety of sociocultural and religious factors. It means that the educational status and rights of children, especially girls, are violated. However, regardless of the incontrovertible evidence that education is crucial for development of the society and the nation, there remain inequalities in access to education and poor people, and their children are excluded from the processes and outcomes of education, and the majority of school-age children out of primary and secondary school are girls, and such deprivation affect the levels of female literacy in general.

Hitherto, the beliefs on the 'impurity' of menstruating women lead, in some cases, to girls withdrawing from school when they reached puberty. According to Douglas (2003:30), menstruation is perceived as polluting and contagious and 'impure' women constitute a situation of sexual power and danger. Female sexuality evokes defilement and uncleanness, and menstruating women are restricted from certain activities and places, including sexual relationships, and participation in various rituals are segregated to avoid contamination of the other persons (Garg, 2001; George, 1994). There also a belief that infertile, 'childless' wives would conceive should they bathe at a particular river while menstruating.

The precariousness of a woman's membership of the lineage into which she marries, which is contingent upon the reproduction of male children to continue the kinship line and, in some cases, especially those of patrilocal marriage, the cutting of ties between a married woman and her family of origin demonstrate the social marginality of women except as a means by which men can form alliances through the marriage of daughters and as successful wives and mothers. These traditions are strengthened by the inferiority of women and the importance of their control by men in beliefs about kinship and society (lineage hierarchies) and the centrality of issues of fertility in ideologies of both femininity and masculinity.

In the life-cycle rites of passage girls are subject to ritualised forms of recognition. It is believed that young children, especially girls, are encouraged to participate in the numerous rituals such as circumcision that emphasise family ties. The age at which circumcision takes place varies according to the cultural and religious practices. For example, in the rural areas, girls participate in domestic chores while in urban areas, girls learn household duties, and boys are encouraged to take agricultural labour. The initiation rituals suggested that boys are more favoured than girls in religious communities and lineages. At puberty, girls move away to live with her husband's relatives with fewer rights attached with her dowry. In these cultural processes, actual biological events are subsumed and transformed as evidenced in the initiation into adult world. However, boys remain at home and take control in the family as well as care for the elderly parents.

Histories of female genital mutilation (FGM) represent the interests of sexual purity, which refers to various mechanisms of marginalisation of women. According to Whitehorn's (2002) study on FGM, cultural and social implications explain different cultural contexts that have led to quite different understandings of FGM and why it is carried out. He argues that not only do the reasons differ between culture to culture, but also individuals; age and status are also considered important. Additionally, Heger (2001) try to explain that female genital mutilation is a practice deeply embedded in culture and profoundly implicates culturally rooted notions of female roles and feminine identity. According to the World Health Organization (WHO 2008 Reports), there is growing evidence that approximately 138 million African women have undergone FGM worldwide, and each year, a further two million girls are at risk of being subjected to the practice. However, many girls and women suffer physical and mental ill health as a result of it. Infection, bleeding, pain, incontinence, and even death may occur.

There are more school dropouts among girls than there are among boys, so that the position may be much worse that reported. According to Umeora (2009:6), the lack of education given to girls in rural areas may indeed be due to the low status given to them and to adult women.

Besides, the rural community is composed of age sets, whereby individuals born within a decade are grouped into the same age grade (young adults fully initiated into the community), older and eminent men (clan heads, chiefs, religious leaders, titled men), and eminent women (heads of the women folk). Though there are some trade and intermarriages, each village is relatively independent of the others.

Customary law in this region constrains the economic and social independence of the women. There is a striking contrast to women from other tribes like Yoruba. In the study of Taiwo and Adeleye amongst 'Yoruba women', Barber (1995:83) indicates that Yoruba women have a greater independence and involvement in some socioeconomic and political activities than Igbo women. For instance, the Igbo women are not well exposed to education like the Yoruba women who belong to the dominant group among Nigeria's educated elite.

Achebe (1994) is a well-known twentieth century fictional writer, and the study used his narratives of patriarchal culture in *Things Fall Apart* to demonstrate the cosmology of the Igbo male authority. Conceptually, authority is a highly developed sociopolitical and religious structure whose sustaining ethos is that it enables the Igbo to establish a physical relationship and communion with the spirit world of their ancestors. Afigbo (2005:158-60) puts it that our traditional culture holds that the man is the head of the family and that man is the symbol of authority—the strong staying hand on the possible excesses of the child. Male authority in Achebe's literature shapes the way patriarchal society and culture is developed. The Igbo concept of authority suggests that kinship-based organisation, patrilineal, and sacred power are clearly manifested in the social recognition of authorities and hierarchies of custom and cultural practices in Igboland and also based on property relation.

One cannot study Achebe's work without being heavily conscious of the issues of gender. Igbo society is structured into class distinctions clearly marked by the societal standards. His first two novels—*Things Fall Apart* and *Arrow of God* present a traditionalist view of how things were; the men were warriors representing *Di-mkpa*, prosperous farmers *Di-ji*, hunters *Di-nta*, wine tappers *Di-ochi*, upholding clan and communal prestige. Each town and village had a list of titles, which every legitimate man is allowed to take provided he has a moral reputation. Politically, these titles provide the legislative social order as well as maintaining the traditional consciousness.

According to Afigbo (2005:28-53), male authority as representation of eminent men and the concept of master *Di* among the Igbo people demonstrate leadership and clearly shows political source of identity and achievements. In traditional Igbo society, the title *Di* is an effort to ritualise the process of transformation of personal achievement into social status. It indicates that a person has distinguished himself in a particular sector of life so as to be socially recognised as 'authority or master' in order to gain respect, dignity, and honour. For example, the classification of social status that demonstrates areas of men's authority and efforts as *Di-mkpa* reckoned with his personality in the household and *Di-ji* (master of yam) which justifies his mastery of farm work by possessing many barns of yam, as well as wives and children, which he shares not only with the nuclear family but the extended one. A *Di-nta* (master hunter) has demonstrated his expertise in dealing with animals so that meat is available to his people. A *Di-ochi* (master wine tapper or winemaker) is known for his special palm wine. *Di-mgba* (master of wrestling) has distinguished himself in defending the pride of his family and community in a recreational show of strength.

Achebe failed to address the status of eminent women in Igbo traditional society. Mezue (2006:18) hypothesises that the social and cultural changes that have taken place in Nigeria in the past thirty-five years have significantly contributed to the stress experienced amongst Igbo women. The social and cultural changes affect the patriarchal society, such as colonial imperialism, the growth in political awareness, and policy formulation since the end of the Nigerian Civil War in 1970. These sociocultural changes are significant in addressing the level of gender sensitivity in the Igbo patrilineal system.

In some respects, patriarchal Igbo society resembles social stratification and class system (see Weberian idea of class structure in Chapter 2). This explains that patriarchy forms the Igbo philosophy of 'authority' that makes kinship and the family important in sociocultural, economic, and political affairs. In Igboland, patriarchy provides a network and security, which every household needs for their social welfare, although it functions to exclude certain categories of women, notably widows and women without an heir, that is, a woman who cannot bear sons.

Achebe (1994) in his writing brings out the concept of compound—'obi' as a way of authenticating the village republicanism—'the central prototype of the culture and symbolism of male authority'. In Mezue (2006:20) the male authority determines the political representations and strength of leadership in *obi*. Thus, village structure maintains the level of political power demonstrated by the authority. In order words, village structure is a metaphor for virile masculine headship—to enter a man's compound or village and attack its members, one practically has to go through the sacredness of authority and figuratively through the man himself. One significant belief in African traditional religion is connected to the belief that the spiritual head of community is a mediator between the kin groups and the ancestral world.

Achebe restates the obsession with female chastity that characterised the fertility and dignity in 'motherhood'. Achebe's fiction evokes communities grounded in rituals and symbolic power, which make its characters famous. Mezue (2006:23) notes the patriarchal dimension in his narratives and points out that woman in Achebe's world occupy a marginal position full of inequalities: polygamy, fertility, sexual purity, and marginalisation.

This sociocultural and ethno-history outline of features provides the local context for the review of the literature in relation to concepts and theories of kinship, patriarchy and relations of property, and for the primary research.

Summarily, people continue to hold their traditional beliefs even though marginalisation and subordination of women demonstrate low status, which represent the key points for the research in relation to *Ariri* (prolonged grief). It is important to have some cultural knowledge about the social context and ethno-history of Igboland. The following points should be considered:

The centrality of kinship for identity, reputation, and access to resources and favours in a region with a history of politicised ethnic conflict and an unstable relationship with the federal government.

- The tensions between contemporary economic opportunities for women in towns, the low rate of women's political participation and their social status, which derives from the patrilineal kinship system and a patriarchal cosmology which adversely affects women's access to resources, particularly to land and control of valuable products.
- The dominance of the traditional patriarchal cosmological system which links male status to the ancestors, the land and the continuation of the kinship group through male children, and the corresponding marginalisation and subordination of women who are not 'successful' wives and mothers.
- The exposure to 'new', modern ideas, such as rights for women through trips to town and kin and by visitors provided strong connection to urban social interaction and educational awareness and challenges to traditional cosmologies.
- The patrilineal system is ranked according to the material wealth and the reputation of the clans and lineage; internally, status is organised by kinship position, age, and gender.
- Male authority is strong and cemented by cosmological beliefs such as *Chi* and ancestor worship.
- Rites of passage shape customary law on marriage, inheritance, and property which gave rise to situational conflict where widows and childless wives in their family of origin are likely to be subject to multiple forms of marginalization, stigmatisation and neglect.

ACKNOWLEDGEMENTS

I would particularly like to thank Dr Lon Fleming and Prof. Rena Papadopoulos, Dr. Rueben Ezeaka and Revd. Dr. Peter Ryman, Bishop Patrick Lynch ss.cc (Director Migrants/Victims of Human Trafficking, Bishop's Conference of England and Wales), Rt. Rev. Dr. Paulinus Ezeokafor (Bishop of Awka) for their tremendous support, encouragement, and guidance that kept me on track during the production of this academic work.

I also acknowledge the help and support of Dr. Michael Marrinan Chief Medical Director King's College Hospital London, Prof. Tibor Hortobagyi, consultant neuropsychologist and senior lecturer, Department of Clinical Neurosciences, Dr Dele Olajide, senior consultant, South London, and Maudsley Hospital NHS Foundation Trust, Dr. David Ndegwa Lecturer on Forensic Psychology King's College University London.

Appendix 1 and its uses in extract materials are from Women's Aid Collective (WACOL) and 'Women for Women' from non-governmental organisations (NGOs) in Nigeria dealing with women's rights and health-related issues. Their official website is www.wacolnigeria.org. I would personally like to thank Barrister Joy Ezeilo, the executive director of WACOL for the permission to use the material from the women's strategic legal studies centre.

Appendix 2 and its uses in extract materials are from Civil Resource Development and Documentation Centre (CIRDDOC); it represents the plight of widows and childless wives and highlights gender-power inequalities in the context of patrilineal kinship and low status to adult women. For example, widowhood practice demonstrates the long-term impact of violence, abuse, neglect, and the links with economic dependence. I am in debited to the Executive Director of CIRDDOC Barrister Oby Nwankwor for permitting me to use materials from their organisation.

Materials of Appendix 3 are extracted from the study of Barrister Nwankwor on inheritance law court procedure.

- Enugu state government in South-Eastern Nigeria enactment law entitled 'Prohibition of infringement of a widow's and widower's fundamental rights law'—Enugu State Law no. 3 of 2001.
- Report from Nnewi customary law case no. 7 'Oli-Ekpe' inheritance law landmark cases of *Muojekwu* v. *Muojekwu* (1997) 7 NWLR (Pt.512) 28, Igbo customary law on property inheritance.
- Report extract on exhibit (111) Nanka Mayhem: 'Afu Afughi Ozu' from Ugochukwu J. O. (1998) and a similar episode in Amaokpala 'Ichu Iyii Iri' Nwankwor J. (2001) associated with oppressive practices on widows and the low status of women.
- Extract from the Edo State Assembly, 29 November 2001 'Lauded over Widows Bills', prohibiting harsh widowhood rite and female genital mutilation (FGM).
- Extract from (Article 5) Convention on the Elimination of Discrimination against Women (CEDAW) Sections (c) and (d) in accordance with internationally recognised standards to provide of legal, judicial, emotional and psychological support to women from all forms of violence, abuse, and intolerance.

Appendix 4 and its uses in extract materials are from the Government of Anambra State, Nigeria—Ministry of Women Affairs and Social Development. Thanks to Dr Mrs Ego Uzoezie, executive commissioner, for providing materials on the legal and public complaints procedure related with disinheritance of women in the south-eastern region of Nigeria. This relates not only to the gender division of labour and the servicing activities of wives for their husbands but also to customary law of property inheritance and ownership of land.

Appendix 5 extracts materials from the Kleinman Explanatory Model (EM) (2006) representing the ethnographic 'semi-structured interview and participants' method for data collection and analysis. Kleinman's study in the development of a health explanatory belief model has led to a series of questions that can be used to elicit information (2006). In this way, he has suggested a way of looking at the process; by which illness is patterned, interpreted, and treated. The ethnographic approach to the explanatory model is an attempt to help individuals have an insight into thoughts, behaviour, feelings, and a general attitude to their culture specific illness (pathology) or other misfortunes (problems), and how they weave the answers to the questions connected with their problems into the story or narrative of their illness. As supportive literature, it is an interpretation of prolonged grief (long-term violence and abuse) associated with traumatic life events and their consequences.

This book is a representation and acknowledgement of the lives of countless men and women who are working towards the empowerment of women's rights and health care in the developing countries, especially in Nigeria.

INTRODUCTION

This book aims to examine the impact of patriarchy on the psychosocial condition (*Ariri*) of specific groups of Igbo women in Nigeria. It investigates the extent to which the effects of patriarchal practices may exacerbate mental distress amongst the widows and married women without children and analyses them in terms of patriarchal kinship structures underpinning customary rights of marriage, inheritance, and property relations.

The research methods and analyses adopted in this book are based on an ethnographic model. The research methods have three components: a semi-structured interview, questionnaire, and analysis of documentary sources. Ethnography, with its roots in anthropology and social psychology, is the most suitable study design for this work as the focus is on gaining an in-depth understanding of insiders' observation related to patriarchal practices and socio-economic deprivation leading to *Ariri* (mental health problems).

Analysis of property inheritance suggests that Igbo women suffer severe economic hardship and poverty, and they lack power over their social environment based on certain customs and traditional practices. These marginalise or exclude women from the kinship group into which they married, and these factors contribute to mental health problems. Local customs and traditions operate to restrict and prevent women from ownership of land and equal rights to own property. The cumulative effects of stigmatisation, exclusion, and deprivation result in a breach of women's human rights—civil, political, social, and economic, and also contribute to increased violence by men against women in the traditional society.

The aim of this book is to facilitate the dissemination of knowledge on the risk factors of violence and abuse of women with *Ariri* and promotes women's human rights and health care in Nigeria.

CHAPTER 1

Introduction, Aims, and Objectives of Study

1.1 Rationale for the study

This study seeks to investigate and explain the psychosocial determinants of women's health issues with reference to *Ariri* (mental distress) of particular groups of Igbo women—through a study of patrilineal kinship and related social, cultural, and economic patriarchal processes in South-Eastern Nigeria. It investigates this condition and its causes in connection with the widowhood and childlessness (infertility as a result of culturally specific problems and seeks to suggest how best this condition can be improved. Through such investigation, the study seeks to relate *Ariri* to the impact of certain patriarchal forms and practices on certain groups of the Igbo female population, widows, and childless wives with the struggle for gender equality and women's rights issues. The concept of *Ariri* is discussed in Section 1.4 below as a specific mental health problem that arises due to the culture.

Another study has explored the vulnerable condition of women, but there has not been sufficient research in understanding the impact of patriarchy on the psychosocial condition of Igbo women in Nigeria. According to the World Health Organization Report (2002), violence against women is a major risk factor for anxiety disorders and suicide. Further mental health issues include depression, increase in alcohol and drug abuse, aggression, violence towards others, risky sexual behaviours, and post-traumatic stress disorders (WHO, 2002). This study is therefore designed in response to the need to contribute to our understanding and experience of the impact of discriminatory practices amongst the female population.

1.2 Aims of the research

- To explore the impact of gender-based power on the female population of the Igbo Nigerian society and, in particular, two categories of women—widows and childless wives—through a study of the incidence of *Ariri*
- To critically review cultural stereotypes and stigmatisation of women
- To develop a theory which explains *Ariri* and make this available to health professionals as a complementary approach informing their practice.
- To examine how patrilineal kinship and patriarchal ideologies and rituals of control can lead to the extreme form of sadness (*Ariri*).

The current practices of isolation and social exclusion of widows and wives without children in Nigeria indicate that traditional institutions lack the flexibility of implementing changes designed to achieve gender equality. Therefore, the study investigates the relationship between traditions, custom, local cosmology, including beliefs, rituals, and law to assess how greater inclusion of women will create social change and improvement of gender in relations.

In addition, there is an apparent 'gap' between the new policies of the social integration through a decentralisation of power relations in patriarchal society and the everyday reality of gender relations. This book aims to highlight the issues of gender and power and in conclusion proposes an anti-discriminatory policy on women's rights.

Although there is much literature on Nigerian people as a whole, references to widows and childless wives are incidental and insignificant to discussions of and about men (Nwankwor, 2001:36). It is in the scarcity of any previous comprehensive study on women in marriage and after marriage that this study finds its justification. This study was undertaken in order to provide up-to-date information about customary laws and practices in relation to women's inequalities and mental health problems.

This study provides evidence of the psychosocial condition of the females with *Ariri* and those still with this condition, and it concludes with suggestions for future research. It is argued that certain patriarchal and kinship practices and ideologies can be identified as key factors in mental health problems in Nigerian women. Additionally, the book hopes to aid the making of future legislation and social policies, which could influence a change and contribute practically to anti-discriminatory practice and a reduction in harmful traditional practices on women.

The study includes an empirical investigation, examining the link between cultural forces (customs, rituals, and sanctions) and the manifestations of patriarchal power in relation to social exclusion of women from property rights and women's vulnerable position. In view of the cultural, economic, and political conflicts in inheritance and property relations in South-Eastern Nigeria, this study demonstrates what the customary rights of inheritance entails and how these can increase women's vulnerability, reflecting the extent to which patriarchy has affected them.

The general form of my argument, however, is to reassert what anthropologists have long held, at least at the level of rhetoric, that property is not primarily a relation between people and things, but a relationship between people and people, a social relation, or a set of social relations (Whitehead and Kabeer, 2001). It is argued in this study that women demonstrate, above all, the social character of inheritance and property, particularly land. The specific aim is to show how customary law and ideological practices, which are very often located within kinship and family structures, construct men's and women's ability to act as fully independent subjects in relation to property relation quite differently.

The investigation looks critically into the vulnerability of women and challenges the widely held assumption that they cannot own property in a situation where there are no male heirs in the patrilineal system. Most indicators of the patriarchal practices according to Okaro (2008:25) suggests that two-thirds of women, especially females in mid-life, live in the rural community and have access to limited social-network services or support that meet their needs. Sossou (2002:207) argued that widows in Sub-Saharan Africa are generally the poorest and most vulnerable and the least protected by law. According to Ilika (2005:65-75), 'widowhood and childlessness represents a "social death" for women, robbing them of their status, and consigning them to the very margins of society where they suffer the most extreme forms of discrimination and stigma'. Aguwa (1997:20-30) further explains it in this way that 'the colonial and postcolonial effect on discriminatory practices and customary law indicates where a woman cannot inherit, claim ownership, or dispose of property'. This statement suggests that female adult survivors are accorded very few rights and are faced with severe cultural forces.

The relationships between property relations, local implementation of customary law, and the patrilineal kinship system are analysed as key aspects of the patriarchal structures which produce the marginalisation of women in these categories and which renders them susceptible to *Ariri*. In traditional Nigerian societies, the conditions of female adult survivors (widows and childless wives) are regulated by an array of customs, rituals, and practices that have evolved outside the state sector and have not, for the most part, been explicitly sanctioned or endorsed by the state legal system. According to Iwobi (2008:37-86), most of the traditional practices on women are harmful, and the results explain the inequality, poor health, and social life of women in communities. As a result of these social problems, numerous scholars have used the consequences of inheritance law and property relations in marriage to demonstrate women's lack of social control over their environment and mental health problems.

This study draws on some of the social, theoretical framework to examine the subjugation of widows and childless wives in relation to their 'right of inheritance' and to examine the cultural rituals that produce psychological symptoms of stigma, fear, and anxiety, leading to the particular outcome of emotional distress. The impact of patriarchy was found to be a common factor among adult women with *Ariri*, and this points the investigation towards the factors that lead to the socio-economic differences amongst the female population. Above all, the study seeks to find the connections between the violation of property rights, indices of depressive complaints, and other sets of factors, which connect deprivation with stressful life events. Other variables included in this study aimed at clarifying some of the complexities which include psychological differences, cultural integration and social support, level of education, socio-economic status, and health measures affecting women's development.

The study argues that patriarchal control identified in the social exclusion and marginalisation of the women in households and local communities is a key element in *Ariri*. It encompasses not only material deprivation but also more broadly the denial of opportunities to women to participate fully in social and civil life. What the study will deduce from the scores of theorists is that the root of women's mental health problems may be a result of their exclusion and marginalisation. As Wilkinson (1996:12) puts it, 'There is clear evidence in relation to health that the extent of inequality is itself a major cause of social exclusion amongst the disadvantaged groups'.

Of these, the study raises the awareness of marginalisation as a significant factor in demonstrating the implications in women's living conditions. It investigates the experiences of two categories of women (widows and childless wives) with extreme social exclusion, stressful life events, and illnesses. Amongst the marginalised groups, who are not represented in the legal and political bargaining process, social improvement is mainly undertaken through policies that support peoples' rights to influence social change. There are various theories that people who are totally excluded from their community and participation in social activities lack a voice through which to express their related grievances.

Moreover, alienation from institutions and processes has been accompanied by emotional distress and incidents of violent disturbances.

1.3   Study setting

Primary investigation is carried out in the three villages of Awka South province of Igbo-speaking South-Eastern Nigeria, where I have worked and conducted this study since 2006. The community is about 35 km away from the Awka capital territory, Anambra State, and everyday life is increasingly affected by the close range of an urban centre. The local community is reliant economically on a combination of farming, trading, and remittances from migrants. Despite significant changes over the past several decades that have placed strains on traditional practices, ties of kinship and community remain powerful among the village residents and their migrants' relatives in overseas. For example, events such as widowhood and childlessness (infertility) in the villages can have extremely negative effects on the lives of women. It shows one of the major areas for subordination of women (e.g. social exclusion, marginalisation and stigmatization) in property relations and is still problematic in Igbo patriarchal and kinship. This is the objective of the study.

The research methodology adopted for this study was an ethnographic model with a descriptive approach. The research method comprised three components such as semi-structured interview, participant observation, and document review. The purpose of using an ethnographic method of research is the empirical motif based on involvement of different stakeholders with different motivations. Ethnography, with its roots in anthropology, is the most suitable study setting and design for this study as the focus is on gaining an in-depth understanding of 'insiders' (Robson, 2004:186). Perspectives on how traditional, ritual, and cultural practices contribute to mental health problems through semi-structured interviews and non-participant's observation will be demonstrated.

The main method for data collection is a semi-structured interview organised by Kleinman's Explanatory Model (2006:160) and informed by ethno-history and ethnographic sources. The model elicits and analyses the stories that people construct to make sense of an illness within the context of their culture. It stimulates researchers with interaction dynamics in being effective in gathering information for the study. Its flexibility makes it possible for researchers to invent new tools or techniques which are appropriate to the research context (Becker, 1998). In this study interviews with forty-three women, some of whom claim to have *Ariri*, are structured by six questions designed to elicit individual and collective perceptions of the condition (see methodological sections in Chapter 3).

From this study which focused on women in rural areas, I have attempted to establish that in Igbo patriarchal practice and ties of kinship in relation to marriage and inheritance not only disadvantage women but also increase their low status and prolonged grief. Poverty in rural communities exceeds the rates found in urban areas. Factors such as high unemployment and poverty rates increased the psychosocial condition of women. Significant barriers to seeking stability of socio-economic life in rural areas are marginalisation and decreased gaining access to social network services and support, while infrastructure and social amenities contribute to problems associated with welfare.

Most of the women in the area are farmers and petty traders and lack any formal education, but a few of them who are educated occupy teaching positions in primary and secondary schools, whilst others are administrators and secretaries in the public and private sectors.

I have chosen a specific town in the south-eastern region of Nigeria as part of this study primarily because of the geographical structures and landscape of the Igbo area. Part of the problem in this region is because land tenure is scarce and tension related to inheritance and property rights of women is perceived through hereditary and ancestry of male lineage.

1.4 Study organisation

The study is organised in the following. Chapter 1 considers the rationale for the study and seeks to investigate and explain the psychosocial determinants of women's health issues associated with *Ariri* (mental health problem).

Chapter 2 reviews the relevant literature and the discussion of social structures, kinship, property relations, and the cultural and symbolic control of Igbo women.

Chapter 3 presents the research methodology: with an ethnographic semi-structured interview implemented in the fieldwork, the researchers were able to gather information depicting property relations and the psychosocial condition of women. It also aims to provide the missing link to understanding the impact of patriarchal and kinship practice on women and linking the theory to the research.

Chapter 4 presents and analyses the data and discusses the research findings in relation to the literature and theoretical frameworks discussed in Chapters 1 and 2. The results suggest the pattern of customary law and practice as an extension of women's exclusion, cultural stereotype, and stigmatisation. Gender inequality has favoured economic dispossession of women's inheritance and property relations, a key factor in leading to 'women's *Ariri*' (mental health problem).

Chapter 5 is a conclusion which summaries the key points and relates issues of customary law and property relations to the statutory law and proposes legislation and policy intended to enhance the civil protection of women's rights and health care.

1.5 The position of widows and childless wives, inheritance, and socio-cultural related factors

Inheritance and property rights are issues which have not been examined in relation to gender to any great extent. In the field of law, little substantial work has been published on Nigerian women. There are two articles on the legal status of women by the Civil Resource Development and Documentation Centre (CIRDDOC) and Women's Aid Collective (WACOL). The first is on 'Fighting the Scourge of Stigmatization' and the second on 'Widows Denial of Inheritance Right' (Ezeilo, 2005:17). The implications of these on the maltreatment on women without children reinforce the authority of the patriarchy. They suggest also the invisibility of women as property owners under customary law in Igboland. It is in the absence of any comprehensive study on women, inheritance, and property rights, therefore, that the present research finds its justification. Whatever the reason may be for women's exclusion on property rights, the fact remains that it is tradition[2] in relation to inheritance and property rights which keeps women's oppression intact in the society, leading to the psychosocial condition to which the marginalised categories of women are prone.

What is important in this study is that women's exclusion in relation to property rights has left them without protection and security. It also demonstrates the complex problems inhibiting the actualisation of women's rights and health issues in relation to the strict tradition and cultural practices common in rural Igbo society.

Another problem is that women have less access to inheritance and property than men. Inheritance status has defined men's control over women. This exclusion of women, according to Nwankwor (2005:15), widens gender difference and hierarchy in patriarchal institutions. Whitehead and Kabeer

---

[2] The 'tradition' in this study will refer to the historical period before 1900. Traditional laws and relationships are, however, found existing at the present time with little or no change in certain rural communities and often underline the pattern of living of many urban societies. Anthropologically, 'tradition' includes the pattern of society and mode of social conduct as it still exists in rural areas of Nigeria.

(2001:121) claim that women's position as the property of men (husbands, fathers, brothers) with no rights to own property, ensures the status of women as not full political subjects. 'It is because women are property-less and are not construed as political subjects; it is because they are not accorded the status of subjects that they hold little or no property'.

Inheritance and ownership of property have a symbolic and spiritual dimension. This places widows in a difficult position by excluding them from this dimension. Among the Igbo patrilineal and kinship system, inheritance is passed on to the male heirs and/or male relatives of the deceased. According to Sossou (2002:147), widows could only benefit from these properties if they have grown-up sons or are forced to remarry into their deceased husband's families. All the same, the customary laws and rules, which determined the system of inheritance of assets and property, have remained relatively unchanged. Korieh (1996:34-9) argues that land allocation is regarded as temporary, since the land belongs to the children as a right. Although women or widows are not prevented by customs from buying land, they could only do so through a male proxy or adult sons.

Women referred to as 'childless' may have no children or simply no son and are excluded from participating in the rituals based on land and other forms of inheritance of property in Igboland. Kinship ideology and religious practice consider male heirs an important social phenomenon in the patrilineal system. According to Nwankwor (2004:36), 'there is a social and cultural belief that a male child appears to carry on the family name'. The reproduction of the patrilineage is crucial. Married women who have not produced an heir feel powerless as childbirth gives women the title of 'mother' in the family. In approaching marginalisation among vulnerable women, it is important to emphasise the moral value attached to marriage, fertility, and inheritance in the traditional Igbo society. In many cases, childless marriage loses its value. What this means for Africans, especially the Igbo people, is a concern for women's fertility and childbearing, which is embedded into their socio-economic life, since control of property and its use fall outside the areas of women's domain.

The relationship between economic dispossession of property and vulnerable women is a major contributory factor to poverty and hardship in household and family-related issues. This is critical for widows, considering the limited access to resources, scarcity of land, and pressure from the inheritance law in Igboland. Furthermore, given their dispossession of land and the means of subsistence, trading becomes an important supplementary source of income and, in some cases, even an alternative to family.

Urbanisation supports the economic life of women. Most women engage in trade and other businesses, which remain attractive for many women. From my investigation, I found out that a large percentage of women who were engaged in long-distance trade today were widows. For example, some of the women, who are local farmers, transport their produce to market in the urban cities. There are always groups of women, for example, urban women in formal employment or women in rural areas who grow food for city markets, who may have accumulated enough resources to support their families. Certain factors are responsible for this urban social network, such as loans from the banking system, other charitable organisations, and friendly societies, which help women to be economically independent. In this regard, wage earners have become an important part of urban economic life. Socio-economic life reveals significant differences of household characteristics associated with migration from rural to urban areas.

I had the opportunity to conduct this study, both as 'an insider and outsider'. I was an insider because I was of the same cultural background and religion as the participants. Conversely, I felt like an outsider because I was a male, a researcher, and had not lived in the society for many years.

Within my investigation and my observations as a local Igbo man, both provide an insight towards women's fundamental contributions in their households as well as to their lack of social status within the local community. As a priest, I was aware of the deprivation of certain groups of women and the ways in which this affected their mental health. As a researcher, I became aware that the customary law constitutes a major area where patriarchal practices maintain women's dependency. However, my status as both an 'insider' and 'outsider' raised issues in the course of this study. I am an 'insider' because I come from the same region, share the language, and I am familiar with many cultural and social practices.

However, although I share the same religion as the participants, I am a priest and therefore assigned a higher status by villagers. This contributes to my 'outsider' position as a researcher and a man and from a chiefly lineage. While this study benefits from my 'insider' local knowledge, it became clearer to me that I also needed to scrutinise my own position in a patriarchal kinship-based society and examine the culturally specific gender assumptions I may have derived from my culture and my religion, and their effects on the research sample, the participants, and the analysis and interpretation of the data.

As a priest and a male researcher, my research is influenced by the sample population obtained through fellow priests and the female assistants who interviewed the women. The co-pastor was contacted through correspondence in order to enable me to gain access to the three villages of the interviews. As a local priest in charge of the area, he provided me with the necessary information and arranged the meetings with the eminent people who are custodians of the culture; in this way, he influenced the research.

Understanding my limitation as a male researcher and the barriers in interviewing women, the female assistant was recruited from the local community in order to enable me to gain access into the women's world view. Additionally, the female assistant is a member of the local community and conducting interview as a secondary school teacher and works with the Justice Development and Peace Commission (JDPC) and is familiar with the issues being investigated.

The later supplementary interviews were conducted by a different woman recruited by the co-priest. The female assistant was married with two children and working as a graduate with the CIRDDOC. She had some degree of research knowledge in her higher education and works under the community and social section of the organisation.

The recruitment of the female assistants, through the help of the co-priest who is well connected in the local community, became a useful step for the selection of the participants (interviewees) referred in this study. In conducting the interviews, the research assistant read the consent form aloud in a local dialect to the participants, and those who freely volunteered to participate were selected; their confidentiality and anonymity granted. Importantly, as a male researcher and priest coming from the same cultural background as the participants, I did not use my position to persuade women's participation in the study, rather their freedom of participation allowed me to explore different and comparative experiences relevant to my questions. In this regard, I become aware of my role as an 'outsider' who represents the principles and practices of ethical issues associated with the current study to focus on my participants views and experiences without influencing their answers. In this way, I become aware of the cultural sensitivity and competence in reporting objectively the whole situation of the participants in the study. It helped me to think about myself as an 'insider' from the local community and not to be too emotional or judgemental in representing my participants. The reflection is considering how to represent 'gender' in an advanced academic study. Additionally, no psychological pressure was mounted on the non-participants as their personal views and beliefs were respected.

I have also investigated Igbo women's own efforts to organise and articulate their concerns and make their voices heard, most often in urban areas. At local, state and national level, more women's associations were formed during the 1990s, taking advantage of the new political openings to assert their leadership roles. They are also pressing for an expansion of women's economic and social opportunities and the advancement of women's rights. By improving their own positions, they are simultaneously strengthening the traditional Igbo society as a whole as well as enhancing the continent's broader development prospects.

My investigations on patriarchal practices on women were developed as a result of pastoral experiences working with people in the local parishes in Nigeria and contributing to the aims and objectives of this study. It shows how socio-economic deprivation and neglect have exposed some of the sociological issues which affect women. Having some familiarity with local traditions and customs, I know that certain topics have to be avoided, and certain questions were not asked in order to avoid fear of embarrassment. This personal history and local knowledge helped me as a researcher to avoid using my position or power to exploit this already vulnerable section of the population.

In relation to these issues, I wanted to know more about the women who have been subjected to decades of customary law and who could still be culturally stereotyped as responsible for bringing bad luck to the family. The social condition of the adult survivors of *Ariri* draws together the most vulnerable state of unresolved or repressed emotional pain and suffering. The problem is that much of the scanty information available on widowhood practices in Igboland is what may be described as unprocessed information. Understanding psychosocial factors associated with women's deprivation of rights shows that the patriarchal system and attitudinal behaviour on property rights of women with stressful life events, poor living conditions, and lack of control over the environment hastens prolonged grief in support of Ewelukwa (2002:481) who reported that deprivation amongst the excluded group lowered the level of their self-esteem, increased their levels of anxiety, and also showed a greater degree of perceived pain.

1.6 'Ariri': A culture—specific mental health problem

The study of *Ariri* attempts to demonstrate the way in which economic and political agendas are impacting rural livelihoods in Nigeria and to show how people's attachment and functions of inheritance and property in rural households are linked to inequality of women and their vulnerable position in society. I will attempt to show how these contribute to the way *Ariri* is interrelated and interpreted in the light of women's low status when dealing with culturally specific problems. However, *Ariri* can also give rise to new forms of how customary rights of women weaken women's access to property through household discriminatory inheritance and land ownership against women, especially widows and childless wives, within patriarchal and kinship practice. Women's centrality to diversified livelihoods and their interests in property (both as wives/daughters) within male dominated households and as members of vulnerable social classes and groups that face the risk of socio-economic deprivation and neglect have become more politicised in recent times. This study provides a discussion of cosmological beliefs, rituals, and gender-power relations and link with alternative explanations that leads to *Ariri* (e.g. sorcery, witchcraft, superstitious beliefs, and associated fears (phobias)). To this end, it raises the awareness of vulnerability that reflects social stigma, isolation, and prolonged grief associated with mental health problems in women and suggests coping strategies for the challenges they generate.

Aetiology

The term 'Ariri' is attributed as a cultural specific disease designating 'wider varieties and a generality of "disturbance" that explains emotional abuse and trauma related to unhappiness, sadness, or despair' (Ebigbo, 1981:84-91). Iroegbu (2005:78-92) focused on the social context and views of *Ariri* as a state of disequilibrium and disharmony between the individual and his or her environment. *Ariri* is a long-recognised phenomenon but has only been defined as a concept contributing to female mental health problems in recent years. This situation gives further explanation to the experience in cases of distress and prolonged grief, which represent two contributory circumstances related to female disadvantage in society. This implies, according to Udemezue (2010:9), that the majority who are poor and vulnerable are regarded as people who are profane or cursed. Consequently, they suffer not only from poverty, but also from social exclusion and lack of basic human rights. The previous study of Zack-Williams (2006:10-11) on blacks' mental health together with current research observes, 'Women with low moods met the criteria for anxiety and/or depression. Low self-esteem correlated with high level of anxiety and depression'. Thus, *Ariri* aimed at explaining varieties of social events that might cause a rise in women's mental health problems. Although mental distress is a widespread social circumstance, half of the Igbo widows affected are poor people with prolonged grief and are more likely still to be affected than the general population (Akaolisa, 2005:6-7). An explanation of *Ariri* is connected with sociocultural, economic, religious, and political factors that imply discrimination in relation to women's health issues. Furthermore, the idea of learned helplessness as it relates to women's perception and behavioural responses are best described as the *Ariri* concept (Nwankwor, 2003:27). Simply put, it suggests low status, esteem, and dignity. Perhaps this explains to some extent the indication of 'dependency' on how patriarchy can negatively affect women as observed in many parts of Nigeria. This is where victims feel emotional distress caused by social injustice related to neglect, rejection, and abandonment. These social stereotypes related to injustices simply drive women into greater depths of insecurity, stressful life events, and also emotional distress (Maritikainen, 2002:1091-93).

The social condition of women suffering from *Ariri* is born out of discrimination and marginalisation. The word certainly appears in many Igbo proverbs, *anya di gi ka onye n'akwa ariri* (you look like someone who is frustrated, depressed, or suffering from distress. Or it sometimes refers to a vulnerable state-prolonged grief.) Occasionally, this may be said to a man, but in the majority of cases, these words would be addressed to women. This phenomenon of *Ariri* brings vividly the expression of unresolved pain and suffering related to social and psychological harm. The disturbances of the marginalised and afflicted are also experienced by those whose lives are influenced with hardship and neglect. I shall attempt a general understanding of these psychosocial characteristics in the light of mental health problems, which have emerged from the research conducted on the vulnerable from anthropological, sociological, and psychological perspectives. This crucial research illuminates our understanding and cultural knowledge of *Ikwa Ariri*.

Conceptual frameworks

For South-Eastern Nigeria, the sound of words is of great importance. The very word *Ariri* itself expresses anger, frustration, tension, and the imposed inertia felt by the disadvantaged group of people. The onomatopoeic value of the word strikingly expresses the low status within the desperate condition.

The concept of *Ariri* is an everyday discourse with widely varying meanings depending on the context in which they are spoken. Tew (2005:216) suggests, 'The language used is attributed to traumatic experiences from social perspectives'. It can often substitute for 'suffering' deriving from the society, and owed to how tribes express their social problems leading to a depressive mood (Ewelukwa, 2002:436). Returning to Tew's observation, language evokes cultural interpretation of the feeling of *Ariri* in everyday circumstances of life. The concept, in general, comes as a product of many factors: physical, psychological, sociocultural, economic, and political perspectives.

Onomatopoeically, *Ariri* describes negative feelings (symptoms) through its sound that responds to sadness or despair. The sound of distress—*ihe nwute* (lamentation) in a local dialect (language) could depict an extended emotion, which is expressed in many ways. For instance, the sound *Ariri egbonam* signifies intensive or deeper emotion that describes lamentation. Thus, the social phenomenon describes *Ariri* in different responses that emerge and forms an amorphous mass that identifies a traumatic experience explained in a variety of possibilities. The study sought to find connections between harmful practice indices of emotional distress and psychosocial complaints and three other sets of factors, one connected with social exclusion and stigmatisation, a second set consisting of stressful life events, and a third set associated with lamentation (*Ariri* or emotional distress). Sociocultural predictors are included to seek the clarification of these variables: social exclusion, marginalisation, socio-economic status, level of living condition, and aversive life events.

Apart from this, onomatopoeia is a sound word, which describes post-stress and post-traumatic suffering or affliction associated with worries of heart or/ and frustration—*ihe ufu di n'uwa. It is* commonly perceived to be a 'foreign' phenomenon that evokes emotion and feeling. For example, the word *ihe ufu* is used as onomatopoeia to show the characters of mental distress. In a similar case, *ihe nwute* displays the characters of pain. Thus, the words *ihe nwute* or *ihe ufu* represent a homogenous language for interpreting a specific social pathology or disease such as *Ariri* (mental distress) amongst the Igbo people. However, 'emotion' recognised in the precolonial and postcolonial Igbo language that arises out of marginalisation is perceived to expose victims, particularly widows to certain levels of indignity. For example, the death of a woman's husband or the state of childlessness explains sadness, frustration, and worries over the grieving (bereavement). A further factor could include unfair loss of inheritance and property, which would have been dealt with justice and fairness but is completely ignored and/or overlooked as a result of women's ambivalent condition.

Afigbo's (2005:298) study of colonial and post-colonial times suffering could be given an explanation to misfortune such as terminal illness, death, childlessness, hardship (poverty), whose beliefs are linked with *Chi ojoo*—supernatural forces, witchcraft, or sorcery. The feelings of misfortune evoke grief occasioned by the levels of emotional and practical dependency engendered by loss which, despite confounding facts, individuals look at suffering or illness as originating from Supreme Being.

Attempts to understand what constitutes *Ariri* may be compared with attempts to understand the controversies that restrict women from gaining access to property as the core of women's livelihoods and other community services. Just like certain culturally specific problems, harmful practices might generate social stereotypes, and people would rather connect their frustration and suffering to human destiny—*akaraka ojoo*—interpreted as bad omen. Cosmologically, the perception of bad omens in human existence and suffering exposes the individual to painful memories, which exacerbate symptoms of stress. Iroegbu's (2005:87) study of misfortune attributed to witchcraft, and the experiences of people with constant accusations and allegations, especially widows and childless wives indicate prolonged grief and sadness, social withdrawal, and excessive anger. Widowhood practices provide the perception of constant accusations and allegations and period of confinement and restriction of widows from social contact. There is a cultural belief and social structure that a widow and childless wives are regarded as untouchable, profane, 'witch', 'outcast', 'defiled', and *onye ruru aru*. These social characteristics are stigmas used to demonstrate loss of social status. The stigmatisation has potentially negative health implications for the individual's mental health status.

Some believe that being alive creates a special bond that connects us to the Supreme Being—*Chukwu*—thus providing an answer to the unforeseen circumstances that create human problems. These factors persist in the way people experience and respond to the feeling of *Ariri* (mental distress). Consequently, *Ariri*, which is grief and expression of inner pain because it acts as an intensifier of low status, is internalised and preserved in memory. This is due to the fact that grief presents a situation in which one loses the power of negotiation, since it is beyond human control. The victim's helplessness is made worse as is the case for many rural Igbo widows in a way that integrates their experiences into their personalities in order to gain control of their destinies. Nwankwor (2004:8) adds that the degree of expression of negativities depends on the communities' culture, religion, and economic systems.

Ebigbo and Ohaeri (1990) argue that the goal of a man's life (fate) is to achieve his *akara aka*—the destiny imprinted on his palm. For both men and women, there is a strong sense that events are preordained and palms are often read to try to foretell future events. This explains the way culturally specific problems related to suffering could be interpreted. In other words, the destiny of a woman and a man is drawn on the traditional gender norms. Within this broad term, the male behaviour encompassed power and dominance. The dominant behaviour explains the religious circumstances that demonstrate women's subordination. Umeora (2008:109-15) argues that the destiny of most of the widows and childless wives are likely to reflect their weakness, powerlessness, and insecurity. Ethno-historical evidence on cultural and religious practice shows that discriminatory practice has influenced cultures, behaviour, beliefs and attitudes of widowhood since precolonial times.

The Igbo cultural belief associated with *Ariri* helps to throw light on the Igbo idea of how grieving could link different ways of given interpretation to pain, suffering, and affliction, which raises questions about individual excessive fear, worries, frustration, and despair. In other words, the negativities that surround widowhood practices are clouded in anxiety that creates worries, insecurity, and tensions in most of the social and cultural beliefs. For instance, the anxiety, which survivors perceive over the rite of cleansing, linked with sexual intercourse exposes fear of contacting Human immunodeficiency virus (HIV) infection. Acquired immune deficiency syndrome (AIDS)—*Obirinajaocha* evokes feelings of lamentation and sadness. Although widowhood rituals are intended as ways of showing respect for the dead, the cosmological evidence of the inconsolable sadness of isolation, loneliness, and loss of status of a widow exacerbates emotional distress and physical indignity. What this fact explains is that traditional practice is not reflected in the issues of harmful practices in order to accommodate women's social problems. Brown (2004) indicates that when looking at the incidence of per 100,000 populations, females in the community are at the most risk of sexual abuse.

Anthropologists have raised many issues about the impact of an oppressive culture and consequences amongst the disadvantaged group. A study by Eboh and Boye (2005:324) explains the vulnerability of women, especially widows and childless wives, on how religious circumstances structured their lives. According to Ilika (2005:77-88), lacking the right to own or inherit land and property leaves women with increased domestic abuse and violence, which increase their prolonged grief. These injustices simply drive women into greater depths of insecurity, poverty, and also emotional distress (*Ariri*).

Although various studies consider the effects of vulnerability on the marginal groups within the rural areas, Nwankwor's (2004) study focuses on disinheritance and women's emotional distress per se. Both of the studies adopt the diversity approach explaining that the impact of systematic inequalities and discrimination compounding to exacerbate traumatic events such as severe maltreatment, lack of shelter, and food. These factors are associated with a high prevalence of mental health issues such as anxiety, concentration problems, nightmares, and reoccurring memories (Loutan, 1999; Palmer, 2007b). The environmental deterioration, such as socio-economic deprivation (poverty) and other environmental degradation that places a disproportionate burden especially on women largely because of socio-economic differences exposes them at risk. Nwankwo's studies carried out on domestic abuse in the South-Eastern region (2004) inform that there are large numbers of violent incidents against women in rural communities, and access to appropriate treatment on property is less frequent.

It has been argued that social stereotypes and stigma, the effects of trauma, stressful life events, the influence of cultural practices, and individual negative image have played a significant role in a psychosocial explanation to mental health problems. Thus, *Ariri* provides a frontline perspective of the specific needs of the vulnerable groups, complexities of needs, and difficulties in gaining access to social network supports, among other concerns. From these explanations, one can see the importance of law, custom, and culture as a set of guidelines (both explicit and implicit) that individuals inherit as members of a particular society, and it relates to how people perceive their maltreatment, humiliation, social neglect, and other related abuses as well as their view of the world, how they experience it emotionally, and how they behave in their suffering in relation to others to supernatural forces, dominant views, and to the social environment.

Igbo women suffer lifetimes of violence in varying ways that are expressed in *Ariri,* and in other contexts, which might be readily recognised as a form of domestic abuse. This explains how rural women increased the extent to which widows and childless wives accepted traditional practices. It provides a way of looking at traditional issues, the long-term abuse, and the links with economic dependence. The painful experience is perceived to explain certain levels of indignity as victims live with face to face suffering or affliction in the natural world. However, the conflict between the will to deny abusive events and the will to proclaim them aloud is the central dialectic of mental distress. This explains the social and psychological experience of people who have survived abuse in their stories that is highly emotional, contradictory, and fragmented. However, secrecy frequently prevails in the abuse, and the story of the traumatic event surfaces not as a verbal narrative but as a psychosocial determinant to mental health problems.

Over recent years, there has been a resurgence of interest in the social aspects of women's abuse and trauma, in terms of seeking to understand what may contribute to how mental distress may be expressed and dealt with differently in sociocultural contexts. This interest, as a result of social and psychological experiences of *Ariri,* has formed the interface between gender-power relations, women's lack of access to inheritance and property, and links between trauma and distress amongst the female population. However, *Ariri* must be seen as inherent within a continuum of everyday-lived experience of alienation and what people may have to say about their own stressful life events and the meanings and histories and aspirations that they attach to them. A wider recognition of *Ariri* (mental distress) should figure within the overall social exclusion—the impact of socio-economic differentiation, discrimination, and social stereotype, which defines *Ariri* as a culturally specific problem of mental distress.

1.7 Review of literature

The relevant literature about women's psychosocial condition in South-Eastern Nigeria is quite limited. The scholars of West African societies, especially Igbo authors like Nwankwor and Ezeilo (2001:35-37), have long recognised the plight of women in kinship and property relations which carries with it political implications which are dominant. They both examined women's economic marginalisation under the influence of international literature, basically giving a theoretical review. Ewelukwa (2002:9) identified other research which reveals that social stereotypes, vulnerability, and stigma attached to women's disinheritance are common to poor health outcomes of women. In this regard, women's property relation is investigated, along with perceptions of the public about their economic dispossession, which increases poverty for women who were not provided for by men. The area within which women's property relation and abuse in this study has mainly been investigated is under social exclusion and marginalisation of women.

Okoye (2005:102) revealed the plight of Igbo women with regard to her work on widowhood practices. She observed the rise of cultural stereotypes as damaging to women's self-esteem. Okonkwo's (2003:4) observed the patriarchal and kinship system and found that another major factor affecting widows and childless wives is the low status accorded their gender. This leads to less access to sources of health information, less contact with the services needed to safeguard their health, and less power to obtain services as a result of poorer economic status and cultural barriers. Whitehead and Kabeer (2001:23) rightly indicate that women's disinheritance could have highly disempowering implications for rural African women and their participation in economic resources and assets to land law and practice. The main problem, as they argue strongly, is that women have too little political voice at all decision-making levels that are implied by the inheritance and property relations, not only within formal law and government, but also within local level management systems. What this literature implies is that the customary law is still inadequate with respect to the identification and prosecution of the above breaches in abuse cases on property relations in Igboland.

The reason I chose these local theorists is because their ideas underpinned the concept of gendered property relations. The relevant literature shows the significance of the vulnerability of women in socio-economic deprivation and neglect, which raises the impact of poverty and stressful conditions amongst the female population. For instance, Weber and other feminist anthropologists similarly argued that property relation is structured by domination through which power relations are governed on a regular basis and through which a system of inequality is established and sustained (Weber, 2005:20-36). Additionally, NGO reports have been used as a supplementary material as they provide relatively contemporary insight into gender-based issues and so complement local theories already mentioned. Furthermore, newspapers were used as they represent a relatively common medium for discussion of women's subordination and inferior position from the perspectives of widowhood and childlessness. This topic is also a common theme in Nigerian film industry, but this representation will not be discussed here.

The term kinship illustrates a social unit in an extended family. It consists of a group of families with a common ancestor, who ratifies their leadership order in the community. Anameze's (1996:18) description of this patrilineage highlights vividly the positive impact of the oldest man as a spiritual head of the kindred whose communion with the ancestors and social network contact with them is still upheld. According to Sossou (2002:206), kinship provides a key source of social and economic power and influences most of the cultural practices by which people in a society reckon kin relationships. Most anthropological and sociological studies of Africa, especially amongst Igbo people, deal to a certain extent with some aspects of the kinship system, which governs marital customs and regulations, determines the customary rights, and influences inheritance and property rights through patrilineal system. Afigbo (2005:247) confirms this by indicating that almost all the concepts connected with human relationship can be understood and interpreted through the kinship system.

CHAPTER 2

Theoretical Frameworks: Kinships, Patriarchy, and Property Relation

2.1 Introduction

With the various literatures on property, this chapter aims to evaluate the theoretical material available on kinship, patriarchy, ritual, material, and symbolic subordination of women leading to prolonged grief—*Ariri* (mental health problem). In this chapter, I intend to discuss major factors that reflect gender-power inequalities contextualised by patrilineal and other forms of customary law that reinforce women's lack of access to property under intestacy law. I aim to show how women are perceived as subjects and objects in property within patrilineal practice.

This chapter is developed with the help of Max Weber and other feminist anthropologists as they were most useful for the analysis of the women's property relations. Patterns of social stratification or class situation distinguished people from the division of labour, resulting in domination and loss of status in relation to assets (inheritance and property rights), their protection, and livelihood. I will conclude by maintaining that kinship remains a fundamental determinant for gender, ideological, and customary practices, which construct male and female subjects with differential power and socio-economic differences.

2.2 The centrality of lineage, marriage and parenthood, and attribution of status

The centrality of lineage in the traditional Igbo society identifies marriage as a social investment and attribution to the achievement of status. It has both an important practical function in cementing alliances in and between many families and communities as well as serving as an economic factor in increasing a man's available labour (Dehen, 2005:30-45). Uchendu (1965:16) claims, 'The Igbo world brings the living and the dead into a system of inter-relationship in which lineage continuity is a co-operate enterprise between the two and the marriage system the chief institution to bring it about'. Smith (2005:40) explains, 'A married woman in the Igbo society is regarded as a wife to the whole family'. This explains why most of the women married in the lineage and family at large are addressed as 'my wife'—*nwunye anyi* by adult males. Under customary law, marriage created a family unit within which the wife seemed to occupy a unique position. Smith (2005:30-45) remarked that patrilineal system marriage transfer gives to the husband exclusive sexual rights and claims to the domestic services of his wife and the right to support her and her children. The economic rights of wives and children consist essentially in their right to maintenance, accommodation, and socio-economic welfare.

The rationale associated with marriage in the traditional sense obviously will have implication for widows and childless women. In the case of a widow, it may limit the chances of remarriage outside the husband's family, since it may be viewed as breaking such alliance or bonds. However, many aspects of kinship ideology and customary practices in rural areas are still determined by customary law. This explanation will draw together other important aspects of the legislation in statutory law marriage and customary law marriage and practice.

Wife succession, central to customary law, raises the question as to the legality of the husband's alleged 'marriage' with his deceased brother's wife. Is inheritance of a wife under such circumstances considered to be a valid customary marriage? If it is, the husband's purported second marriage is void (Marriage Act, Cap 115) but that between the husband and his deceased brother's wife would be a valid customary union, falling short of the status of marriage (a sort of concubinage). It is argued that 'wife inheritance' is a marriage, and what the inheritor inherits in such a case is not a wife but rather the dowry the deceased husband paid for the widow, which entitles him to be considered as a prospective husband of the widow if they both consent. In line with native law, refusal of wife inheritance in some communities is considered a serious breach of familial obligations or tribal political tradition, and considerable pressures would be exerted on an individual to secure compliance.

Statutory law marriage is a monogamous type of marriage, which is found in customs law, equity, and relevant statutes of general application adopted from the British legal system in the eighteenth century colonial period. Suffice to say that in Nigeria, the British Marriage Ordinance Act influenced social kinship-related practices especially where polygamy was considered repugnant to the Christian faith (Mann, 1985:44). Polygamy is where a man may be legally authorised by tradition to marry many wives. Under these marital social statutes, women are used to boost the agricultural strength of men's economy. Moore (1988:126) further noted, 'The changing effects of the contemporary processes of socio-economic differentiation, new ideologies and forms of state authority on the organization of domestic life also affected the nature of gender relations. Feminists from various disciplines have consistently argued that the "family is the central site of women's oppression in society"'.

Bamgbose (2002:13) stresses, 'Major differences as a result of social changes may occur in the women's right of inheritance at marriage because of the dowry system on the death of the property holder or owner'. This view shapes the social structure, the body of rule, which governs customary law and gives it direction. The rights of inheritance are still deep-seated cultural trends in African societies, especially in Nigeria, which affect certain groups of women in the Marriage Ordinance Act. This of course extends throughout the social relations of the marriage partner and sometimes influences what options are available to a woman on the death of her husband. There is evidence of oppression in the social network of public and private systems where discrimination against women is a barrier to access social support. In this study, the forms of marriage described so far, therefore, are part of the Igbo social and structural system, which can influence the widowhood option in her domestic and affinal relationships. I shall discuss other options on widow inheritance and remarriage, explaining how far they are a viable alternative for the widow to satisfy the marriage need to be under a man.

Wife succession (levirate) under customary law

In many African societies, especially in the precolonial era, Igbo people made provisions for a widow to be inherited by her deceased husband's kinsman. According to Ewelukwa (2002:424), kinship-related practice means that 'widowhood inheritance' is designed for a widow to be 'taken over' or 'to be inherited' in a more general sense by a brother. A 31 May (2005:8) Amnesty International (AI) report states, 'Some customary law systems prescribe that a widow be "inherited" by a male relative of the former husband. The widow is seen as the "property" of the former husband's family'. Korieh's (1996:57) study on 'Widowhood in Igboland' notes, 'All these customs of preferential marriage can be seen to be continuations or renewals of the existing structure of social relations. All of them are also examples of the unity of the sibling group since brother replaces brother'. Levirate marriage (wife inheritance), where a family member inherits a married woman whose husband is dead, continues to be practiced under various customary law systems in Nigeria. It explains some of the implications in polygamous marriage for co-wives. In a different study, Anameze (1996:34) explains, 'Conflict of interest amongst co-wives could result to hostility. Although polygamous life opens opportunities for co-wives, most of the women are likely to end up with socio-economic constraint. Ownership and control of family resources is another possibility, which is usually allocated to men on marriage. This explains how property is protected by customary law and custom controlled by the family head'. Thus, sons have a right to inheritance. With this arrangement Ezeilo (2005:30-47) remarked, 'Childless wives in a polygamous marriage may be only allocated a portion of land for agricultural purposes. But she cannot dispose of such land since, theoretically, such land belongs to the sons of the deceased husband'. Apart from the allocation of resources, a widow in either a monogamous or polygamous marriage is likely to face social and economic marginalisation. It means that tension still exists amongst women in both marriages which is experienced and lived out in the household. It is argued that many aspects of kinship ideology and customary practices perpetuate discrimination against women. For instance, practices observed on the death of the common husband are the same for all widows and sonless wives in relation to survival strategies. Chiegboka's (1997:33) study on 'Women's Status and Dignity' remarked that the status of women in marriage and property demonstrates the social position of women in terms of their rights and obligations in family and local community. The legal status of an individual, at a given moment of time, may be defined as the totality of all his rights and duties as recognised in the laws and customs of the society to which people belong. In marriage, according to Igbo customs and tradition, an individual has a duty to exercise their rights and obligations in the family and the rest of the community. These are gendered, and the social and economic status of women depends upon their relationship with male kin that is as daughter who achieves a good marriage, the wife of a husband, and mother of a son.

2.3 Kinship and concepts of patriarchy: An investigation on the Issues of property of widowhood and childless wives

Kinship is an important concept that is central to anthropological practices and theories with regard to the level of the household and residence in the Igboland (Ebigbo, 2005:73-87). During my investigation, I learnt about widowhood and women without sons by observing their level of interaction and composition in the villages. It is thus apparent that kinship and marriage in South-Eastern Nigeria is still a discriminatory practice to widows and childless wives. Chiegboka (1997:33) rightly observed, 'There is no partnership in this relationship and women are overlooked and marginalized evidently in marriage'. Again, in monogamous unions as well as in every other marriage union in Igboland, women suffer in the areas of childlessness, gender of the child, and ownership of the child. Ola (2009:285-91) captured the plight of a childless woman in these words, 'Children were seen as the glory of marriage but that glory was first and foremost the glory of man. The barren woman was considered of no value and useless to the community. In some communities she was scorned and at times labelled a witch, although one would only hear discrete whispers about it. A childless marriage was considered meaningless and the man was pressured into polygamy'. Uchendu (1965:57) complements this in these words, 'Children are a great social insurance agency; a protection against dependence in old age; to have a male child is to strengthen both the social and economic status, for it is the male child who inherits the father's compound and property'. A woman, and worst still a man, who has no male child contemplates old age with particular horror. The fact that a woman only procreates children of the female gender, leading the man into polygamy, could also generate a household dispute. This brings to focus in widowhood and childless circumstances the incident of customs and traditions in the Igboland as having a lot of interplay in the plight of women. The biblical evidence, such as Genesis 3:16, reflected the plight of women in what God told Eve, the first woman, 'Unto the woman he said I will greatly multiply thy sorrow and thy conception in sorrow thou shall bring forth children and thy desire shall be to thy husband and he shall rule over thee'. This biblical statement justifies a kinship structure where a husband has been mandated to rule over women. The anthropological fights against the structure of subordination in the traditional religion or custom did not spare the widow in her plight over her husband's death. She is normally ushered into widowhood with all sorts of dehumanising ceremonies or sanctions. According to Sossou (2002:214), 'The debilitating psychological impact of widowhood has a common manifestation in various stages, such as grief, sadness, anxiety, confinement, loneliness, fear, general uneasiness, torture and oppressive denials and constraints'. In this regard, the issues of widowhood and women without sons remain an investigation of theories of kinship and concepts of patriarchy in the traditional Igbo society.

Parkin and Stone (2004:222) defines kinship as a cluster of positions to and through which an individual traces family links with others through birth (descent) and (marriage), which give people rights and positions across generations. Kinship, from the definition, is above all concerned with relationships which are socially constructed. The aim of the definition is to demonstrate the close connection of the social and cultural ties related to the patrilineal society, including those based on different traditional varieties of the institution of marriage defined broadly as a 'conjugal contract'.

A return to a polygamous marriage is principally done either because of search for male progeny, expansion of lost immortality, economic benefits, duty to ancestors, and control of male infidelity. Moore (1988:42) noted, 'Kinship as an anthropological way of identifying the tradition and institution of marriage where the family intersects with the division of labour through the patrilineal society'. In a patrilineal society, succession is from father to his children or father to his brothers. For example, in the Igbo law of inheritance, on the death of an intestate father, his eldest male child inherits the property of the deceased father, and he holds the property for his own benefit and that of his younger brothers as well as the wives of the deceased. If the deceased has no male child, the brother or uncle or cousin on the paternal side inherits. This ipso facto enhances the concept of inequality and subordination of women to men (Chiegboka Ibid: 33). Polygamous households of this kind described the common social characteristics in West Africa, the economic determination, and crucial productive units as well as authority of those males who are in control of the household. The marginalisation of women in this polygamous union is readily evident since one single man can have many wives, and women are not empowered.

The emphasis on what women and men do inevitably raises questions about gender relations with particular references to the division of labour, comprising women's activities, and men's social role. It is an interesting fact that scholars who maintain that women's subordination is not universal tend to approach the problem of gender relations through a consideration of what women and men do, rather than through an analysis of the symbolic valuations given to women and men in any society (Moore, 1995:30). In this regard, there will be an examination of sociological approaches to the study of gender as it concerns a social relationship in marriage. Moore (1995:31) further indicates that 'in household labour and production is where women reclaim their "identity" through domestic chores and reproductive activities'. This is designed in the way women express themselves more independently in the household activities. Thus, families are identified in practical considerations and flexibility as keys to equitable divisions of household labour and the construction of gender relation through negotiations and boundaries within sex division of labour; how divisions of labour influence gender perceptions of self and other and how it conceives gender-appropriate behaviour. Nevertheless, the social construction of shared parenting illustrates how more equal domestic gender relations arise and under what conditions they flourish. Rudduck (1982:76-94) on this adds 'the everyday aspects of child care and housework help share ways of thinking, feeling, and acting that become associated with what it means to be a mother'. However, 'maternal thinking' suggests that in domestic activities what develops in fathers, too, as the social meaning of gender begins to change. This de-emphasises notions of gender as personality and locates it in social interaction. To treat gender as the 'cause' of household division of labour overlooks its emergent character and fails to acknowledge how it is in fact implicated precisely in such routine practices.

In this anthropological perspective, kinship constitutes the mode of classification of kinsmen. Therefore, what kinship meant for Morgan is all about a people grouped and classified as compared with real biological ties of consanguinity and affinity. Hence, the facts of consanguinity mean that those persons are related by blood descent from the same ancestor. Thus, affinity according to (Parkin and Stone, 2004:35-37), shows the sexual and reproductive relationship between male and female. In a different view, Parkin and Stone (2004:251) sees 'kinship in a practical way as living and thinking about relatedness—a process of becoming complete persons. However, the core substance of kinship in this study demonstrates the significant meaning of affinity and consanguinity'. Schineider (1984:175), from an anthropological perspective, explains kinship in the light of procreation as being formed by bond and cultural ties between persons. These ties are considered to be inherent in the human condition associated with social and cultural relations. Evans-Pritchard and Fortes similarly develop a more sociological relationship in kinship ties, which generates a familial bond.

The term 'kinship' has been dominated by various opinions of the social anthropologists like Parkin and Stone, Fortes, Kroeber, and Radcliffe-Brown. For the most part, 'kinship' was considered as a basis of family relatedness. According to Radcliff-Brown (1950), kinship systems can be typically traced from both matrilineal and patrilineal descent. Levi-Strauss (1971) compares this idea with Radcliffe-Brown's choice of the nuclear family of parents and children as the irreducible social structure in kinship system.

The kinship is traceable from the household, which constitutes the parents and children within a particular patrilineage. The aim here is to demonstrate the close connection of the social and cultural ties related to kinship, including those based on different varieties of the institution of marriage. Beside this, Schneider's ideology on 'kinship' began its revival in feminist anthropology where it was closely linked with gender. Historically, there are many shifts of emphasis about 'kinship' in different epochs. In our time, 'kinship' has moved into the area of political economy, in line with wider concerns in anthropology with social inequality, power, and history (Parkin and Stone, 2004). In the controversy of the past and of recent times, according to Anameze (1996:31), kinship highlights a special mode of denoting relationships. Hence, there is a strong tie and relatedness in kinship that accounts not only for biological aspects but connects the social and cultural relations of the members of the household and the lineage.

2.4 Patriarchy

Weber explained patriarchy in the context of gender inequality as a form of male domination that had its origins in the sheer physical strength of men (Rothman, 2005:27-29). According to Weber, domination as a patriarchal system of social values and belief legitimised the subordination of women in the family and other institutions and the economic system (Rothman, 2005:35). He further remarked that one of the consequences in a patriarchal family is that gender can become the basis of the formation of 'social groups' that result in the exclusion of women from male-dominated groups (Ibid: 35). My aim in claiming that many of the theoretical assumptions of the nineteenth century are still within the post-modern patriarchal society is to show that the concerns confronted by the anthropology of women have a necessarily long history in the feminine study.

The term 'patriarchy' is polysemous, with a multiplicity of meanings—the assertion of male power, dominance and control. It designates also male head (authority) of household. Filmer's (1680) theories known as 'patriarchal' aims at the *arche* (rule) of the *pater* (father) which explains a set of power hierarchies.' Similar to this is patriarchy as 'hegemony', which is derived from the Greek term *hegemonia,* meaning authority or leadership, from *emenon,* leader, and demonstrating position of authority. Generally, the two terms *patriarchal* and *hegemonia* illustrate the same social role. It denotes the maintenance of social power structures through the compliance of the subordinate groups, who accept and help to support these structures. Filmer built his argument to consider the authority of the father as born into families, which have a hierarchical structure.

Whitehead (1984:189-90) remarked that 'it is kinship/family system, which constructs women in such a way that they are more restricted than men in the patriarchal society'. Within the feminist movement and feminist writings, the term 'patriarchy' has been and is widely used as a method of describing societies where women do not have equality with men. For Weber, patriarchy is formally defined as a form of domination characteristic of the household group or clan organised on kinship and property rights. This provides the basis of the claim to power (Weber, 2002:119). Tong discusses patriarchy in many different ways—as a 'system characterised by power, dominance, hierarchy and competition' (Tong, 1989:3) and one with legal and political structures and social and cultural institutions. Rich (1977) defines patriarchy as the power of the fathers: a familial, social, ideological, and political system in which, by direct pressure or through tradition, law and language, customs, education, and division of labour.

Patriarchy, as a sociological theory highlights, is a relationship of dominance and subordination, a systematic domination of women by men and domination of men by other older men (Champman, 1995). The terminology suggests the significance of patriarchy in relation with authority and power in the family. It suggests that, throughout the history of class society, patriarchy has posed its value as institution of class rule and dominance. Moore (1995), Walby (1989), and Whitehead (2002) argue that it functions in all societies where social stratification is based on property ownership. Thus, 'power' is seen as the main instrument of authority in patriarchal societies, where the male head of the household takes decisions based on family matters, production, trade, and property. It denotes the maintenance of social power structures through the compliance of the subordinate groups, who accept and help to support these structures to a greater or lesser extent. Mann (1985:53) throws more light that patriarchy refers to particular organisation of the family in which fathers have the ultimate power over family members; a weaker version points to the father's right to exact obedience and punish disobedience. Mann, in his definition, shows that power is the main instrument of authority in the patriarchal system where one person takes decisions on family issues. 'It implies the recognition and exercise of the hierarchical position where patriarchy is held together to form male authority'.

The Igbo kinship and social organisation support this view. The social network of Igbo culture would reveal the extent to which men and women bring different things into a marriage and acquire different things through marriage. In Nwankwor's (2001:34) view, 'kinship and family systems construct the social status of women and men in patrilineage through which the Igbo culture is being led to the understanding of a fulfilled human existence'. Ebigbo (2005:76) further notes, 'kinship is considered as an ethnographic way of identifying the tradition and institution of marriage where the family intersects through patrilineal'. It is suggested that the features of the ethnographic situation in African societies are perceived through a kinship system that is determined by the existence of the larger group *umunna* as basic units of descent, conjugal and familial. Within this social context, the extended family system is widely spread. This implies that the sociology of the traditional Igbo society sees the family as a corporate existence. At its simplest, kinship refers to the ties which exist between individuals who are related, through birth (descent) and through mating (marriage). It is thus primarily concerned with the ways in which mating (marital relationship) is socially organised and regulated; the ways in which parentage is assigned, attributed, and recognised; descent is traced; relatives are classified; rights are transferred across generations; and groups are formed. Such relationships are seen as constructed within the basic constraints and imperatives of the organisation of human life—reproduction, mating, dependence, the need for enculturation, and the life cycles kinship (Edom, 1982:167). Drawing from the two definitions, this study demonstrates that kinship descent structure is designed to explain the domestic units or cells of patrilineage with the relationships that are socially constructed.

This takes us into kinship relationships based on descent and established tribal affinity. What is being examined here is the notion that individuals have their existence, and claims of rights are demonstrated through kinship. This illustrates that kinship gives an ontological explanation to intrinsic human coexistence in understanding family and social relations. This, as a central maxim, defines traditional forms of marriage, with the characteristics on the material, social, and psychological level within the domestic domain. Fortes (1970) argue that kinship ties are particularly binding, creating for the most part inescapable claims and obligations. Radcliff-Brown and Forded (1979) maintained that in African societies the kinship system provides a channel through which almost all the rights and obligations of individual members are mediated.

2.5 Social theories on property relations

The influence of Nwankwor (2001) and Ezeilo (2005) into Igbo customary practice on property and functions explains not only gender inequality, but also subordination of women as a setback to women's access to socio-economic livelihood and causes mental distress. Lack of access to property under colonialism and during the postcolonial period provides a setback for women, leaving women in a state of even greater insecurity with poorer prospects of accessing land and inheritance. This is likely to be because inequality in a woman's position in patriarchal and kinship practices encourages customary land laws and other injustices, which control conjugal, political, economic, and other social activities as a result of women's vulnerability. Sossou (2002:201) revealed deeper inequalities, with increased commercialisation of land and problems of land scarcity. The kinship systems have failed to protect the interest on property rights of women and, in doing so, have left women with even greater constraints and despair. These arrangements have included bride wealth, widow inheritance, and dehumanising rituals pertaining to widows and keeping women in a lower social status.

Social theories relate concepts of patriarchy to property relations, noting that as Whitehead (1984:176) argues, 'property relations are social relations and always bound up with issues of gender and power'. Moore (1988:199) argued that the issue of marriage to women's economic security and independence had been a difficult one to undo. Dowry was often thought to indicate a woman's right to inherit a share of the patrimonial property and gave her greater economic security, status, and independence within the marriage (Whitehead, 1984:187). In Moore's (1995) analysis of a Greek village, she argues that women have considerable power within the domestic sphere because of the land women bring to marriage as dowry. In the community studied by Whitehead (1984:186-89), women maintained control over this land, which could not be taken away by their husbands without their consent and, in some cases, not without the consent of their fathers, brothers, or guardians. Hitherto, anthropological discussions in this context tended to look at property in terms of the relationships established between kinship groups, family units, or households. Women were frequently subordinated within such systems, and their concerns and interests with regard to marriage and inheritance of property had not had sufficient analytical attention (Hirschon, 1984:188).

In Igbo society, traditional gender division of labour shows greater value attached to men's ownership of property (land) and less value to women's work except childbirth, child-rearing, and domestic activities. Whitehead (2002) argues that, on the important part, 'property' played in the explanation that gives rise for differences in kinship behaviour. She pointed to the link between the economy and stratification through the system of patriarchal inheritance, which organises the transmission of property from generation to generation, at death, at marriage, or at some other point in the life cycle.

Looking at economic materials, distribution, and inequality of resources that demonstrate the relationship between control of economic resources and power and/or status around property, she argues that 'in all economies it was the ownership, command and control of material resources which were the most significant aspects of property' (Whitehead, 1984:183).

Whitehead's further explanation shows that the differences between men and women in the number of properties owned or access to properties might show a significant aspect of gender relationships. Properties are not primarily a relation between people and things but a relation between people and people. Evidence from women's studies suggests that '[w]hatever the nature of the economic system described in terms of the nature of its production and exchange relationship, women's capacity to act as fully acting subjects in relation to objects (property) or the aspects of persons which may be always more circumscribed than that of men' (Whitehead, 1984:186). She further argues that it is kinship or family system which serves to construct women as less able to act as subjects than their male counterparts are able to do so.

As the basis for her argument, Whitehead uses what are technically non-developed peoples through anthropological studies of Africa, Australia,

New Guinea, and parts of South America. Here, the group owns land. In such groups, men and women have important productive roles and have acknowledged rights to communal property, including land. However, her study of the Kusasi of North-East Ghana shows that despite this, land is distributed unevenly, with men having several acres for every one acre owned by a woman. Equally, there was a disparity in the power wielded by both. For example, an adult woman does not command the labour of an adult man, but the man does that of the woman. Essentially, she argues that despite a national equality, there is de facto inequality because of gender in non-developed cultures.

In more developed cultures, the legal systems confirm a similar inequality. This applied, until recently, to the relationship within marriage. In the Kusasi, women who are in polygamous marriages cannot initiate cases in the local system and also are not eligible to try cases. This is not so different from the British system until relatively recently, although polygamy was not a normal practice.

In speaking of property, it is important to note that Whitehead does not speak of physical property only, but man and woman as property. Thus, she describes women as property in marriage rites, both in what they bring to a marriage and as property within the marriage, so women are considerably less than full-acting subjects than men. For instance, she uses the 'dowry' as a form of female property but argues that, in fact, women act merely as conduits for the transfer of property from man to man.

In bringing her thesis up to date, Whitehead describes the present construct of marriage in Britain as one in which women can own property within the marriage and have enforceable conjugal rights. However, her argument focuses on the inequality between the sexes on dissolution of the marriage.

As an analysis of the roles of men and women, her article ranges from non-developed cultures to present-day Britain to show an inequality between men and women both in respect of physical property and subject-property, that is, the power of each and either in society. She identifies the kinship and family system as important sites for ideological and legal practices, which construct male and female subjects with a differential power relation. As such it is far-ranging, but she does not expound on the reasons for this. For instance, the place of childbearing in the subordination of women appears to play no role in her argument. Her arguments are important in understanding women's role in modern society but only as a socio-economic model.

A major problem posed by women and property is the criticism levelled against the theory of stratification, which demonstrates the social exclusion of women or gender blindness or inequality. Stratification or status is a term used by sociologists to analyse political influence (power), economic status (wealth), and social status (prestige). This is how gender inequalities can be understood clearly in modern times. Class divisions are so marked in some modern societies that there is no doubt that they 'overlap' substantially with gender inequalities. According to Whitehead and Tsiakata (2003:101), the material position of most women, especially in property, tends to reflect male dominance/control. Parkin and Stone (2004:14-15) has explained it in this way: 'female status certainly carries with it many disadvantages compared with that of males in various areas of social life including employment, property ownership, income and so on. However, these inequalities are associated with sex differences. This is because for the great majority of women the allocation of social and economic rewards is determined primarily by the position of their families and, in particular, that of the male head'.

Central to this study, Whitehead explores different ways of understanding of women's vulnerability and compares them to lack of access to property and patriarchal domination that match up with local experiences of women. According to Razavi (2003:31), patrilineal kinship reveals gender inequality. A woman's kinship status as daughter, wife, mother, and widow or childless, is important in the application of full legal inheritance and property rights. In addition, in kinship terms, women are subordinate, 'inferior', and less-than-fully-acting subjects. It is a socially recognised institution where a widow is taken over on her husband's death by his male kinsman, usually a brother, in a sense as part of the deceased's property (estate). As a consequence, women may be more exposed to the risk of lack of protection and low status in relation to forced marriage or other forms of violence (e.g. exclusion, discrimination, and marginalisation). Additionally, Agarwal (2003:27-36) explained the complexity of women's deprivation of inheritance and associated it with what she sees as 'social obstacles' or lack of access to services especially in claiming landed property.

In many rural communities especially in the south-eastern region of Nigeria, the legal dimension of property relations is far from simple. This is because different legal traditional (both written and unwritten) laws may coexist. This creates complex situations so that women's and men's access to property may be subject to controversies. Customary law conspires with civil law to create inequality, which is rooted in traditional systems that have a cognate element. In patrilineal kinship system, property relations investigate the discrimination and constraints, which determines kinship belief and practice within the current customary land tenure system. According to Riche (2003:420), gender relations are not fixed, and social relations and their corresponding actors are living, dynamic and, thus, recreating gender inequality and that gender inequality is based on unequal distributions of power. On the other hand, Cornwall (2002) explains that gender is but one aspect of social and power relations. Understanding power relations underpinning the acquisition or claim of land

and inheritance, and how these affect women improves the awareness of how the kinship system works in practice.

Theory on property and women's access to land and property inheritance so far provides this study a pattern of marginalisation and constraints faced by women in kinship and customary practice as central to the proposed analysis. However, the effects of deprivation and socio-economic neglect have been shown to produce patterns of exclusion, especially with regard to women and the disadvantaged (Whitehead and Tsiakata, 2003). Women losing access to land upon the death of their husband is a striking illustration of gendered exclusion. Concerning women, the assumption that women owning landed property in their own rights would contribute to better investment and efficiency (ultimately contributing to reducing poverty and stressful life events) has not adequately taken into account women's own interests (Whitehead and Kabeer, 2001). On the theoretical perspectives, gender discrimination across rural areas is one of the most important concerns and plights of women because of the economic differences related to material resources to which people have access to determine a great deal about their lives. To describe inequalities in property relations, sociologists speak of the existence of 'social stratification', which can be defined as structured inequalities between different groups or class of people. It is useful to relate stratification in this chapter in order to examine how authority in patriarchal institution is structured in property. The idea motivates this study by looking at 'social status' or the position of women (widows and childless wives) who are marginalised as the lowest position with regard to diversity of beliefs and practices. In this practice, there is a strong taboo (or sometimes legal prohibition) preventing women access to property. The 'status' is applied here is in order to explain how strict customary law discriminates women and control of material resources. Max Weber in *Economy and Society* provides information on how inequalities create not only controversies in ownership of property but also maintained exclusion of women in agrarian societies. With regard to the property issues and women's problem with access to land, this chapter looks critically on how inequalities affect women in general and the role kinship institutions play in shaping their domination and subordination of women.

Hirschon (1984:46) writes a classical feminist critique of women's literature, showing how different writers have been one dimensional when considering women's roles in relation to property. In contrast, she quotes Beechey (1978) in suggesting that it is essential to treat the interrelationship of production and reproduction as a 'single process'. Hirschon's (1984:41-47) agreement of this concept is shown here: 'Property relations entail social mechanisms of transmissions. Resources whether productive assets or personal valuables, are transmitted through inheritance and marriage transactions'.

Hirschon's argument in this study raised anthropological insights into women's subordination. Prior to this, she had agreed with writers quoted by Whitehead that the term 'women' has to be subjected to analytical scrutiny as 'women' and is not to be used as a catch-all phrase. However, in subsequent sections she goes further than Whitehead in describing how females are used as 'property', that is, the 'giving away' of females, the provision of dowries, and how their subordination in many cultures represents unequal inheritance rules and division on divorce.

In setting out her views on the anthropological insights, Hirschon claims, correctly in my view, that existing views on the role of women must be critically challenged if effective feminist action is to be undertaken. As examples of the contradictions that arise when such a challenge is not mounted, she cites the role of women in Alto Minho (Portugal), India, and Accra (Ghana). In the former, women own and are perceived as morally weak, greedy, and polluting. In Accra, similarly, market women control much of Ghana's trade and command considerable economic wealth. Yet they are characterised as deceitful, irrational, and inferior and cannot hold political offices. On the contrary, whilst in New Guinea, Hagen women are considered spendthrifts; it is the men in Daoulo who are cast as irresponsible.

Both Hirschon (1984) and Whitehead (2002) identify the insubordination of women through the notion of property, both as subject property and object property. Hirschon, however, argues that this is too broad a statement and that the issue revolves at the center around the relationships of men and women and their relative power and that this is the basis for examining how power is conceptualised.

The materials that Hirschon add to Whitehead's theory are that of the domestic/household sphere, which all feminists agree has been severely devalued. Until this area is subjected to more rigorous examination, including the effects of ritual and religion, the study of the insubordination of women remains incomplete. In this thesis, what Hirschon does is to draw together the various anthropological studies and to point out missing matters. She does this analytically and in a way which highlights the different cultural models and the similarities contained therein.

Adichie's (2006) postcolonial experience on *Half of a Yellow Sun* provides another understanding of situational conflict as the civil war deprived women of their social status and rights. Adichie (2006:73) further explains the social and economic importance of production and reproductive decisions, which can be better explained in relation to subordination and marginalisation of women in politics and social life. According to Akoma (2009:86-96), colonial observation brought forward the consequences of language barrier that relate to colonial cultural and political dominance. Her experience, like rest of the other authors, shows the difficulty in understanding the British district commissioner and his warrant chiefs and translators on political and social issues such as inheritance law. According to Ezeilo (2005:8), authors' perspectives indicate that indigenous authority and private corporations in Igbo community became interested in the production of agriculture and the acquisition of land. Thus, the marginalisation in production and reproductive activities brought problems for women: women were particularly disenfranchised in the governing process and challenged their decision-making roles in the economy.

Since the majority of women's property rights are defined by their marriage in patrilineal system, it follows that their class position is most often governed by the husband's class status. In attempting to raise a definition of class status, Aniagolu (1975:96) remarks, 'To determine precisely what a "status" is, is in my opinion the most difficult problem in the whole science of jurisprudence'. However, status and class derive from inequalities in possession and control of material resources that have traditionally been male-oriented.

Central to the Weberian analysis of economic exploitation is the belief that the idea of private property created a basic cleavage between those who translate economic resources into the political sector by control and those who are subordinated (Rothman, 2005:8). Hence, property rights are a major shift in women's exclusion in household production, characterising male dominance (Stanworth and Siltanen, 1984:69-90).

2.6 Max Weber: Class status, property, and their relation to political power

Class status and property relations are central in the discussion of Weber's theory of patriarchy and most useful for the analysis of the patriarchal customs and gender relations and their centrality to status and power (Weber, 1994:656). Within the social sciences, recent attention to property is evident in anthropology and economic sociology. Property here provides widespread views and applications of theorists in the analysis of private property rights. Weber is considered as the father of sociology, and his work is conceived to include the civil and political rights that arose following the revolutions of the eighteenth century, and the second essay on society and economy is applied to the economic, social, and cultural rights that respond to the social questions of the nineteenth century on property relations.

His book *Economy and Society* prefigured class status emerging from property relations, which may form power and political affiliation related to authority/hierarchies and people's socio-economic life experiences over property rights (Weber, 2002:77-128). Considering the 'social inequality' and economic exploitation through property relations as possible ways to analyse the disadvantaged groups in the patriarchal traditional family, Weber became interested in the idea of people's rights as applied to property relations. In similar circumstances, Gerth and Mills (1958:181) note, 'The power of those with property compared to those without property gives the former great advantage over the latter'.

According to Weber (2004:72), the genuine place of 'classes' is within the economic order; the place of 'status groups' is within the social order that is within the distribution of 'honour', living in the house of 'power'. Their action is oriented towards the acquisition of political power, that is, to say towards influencing communal action.

Weber argues that class status and property demonstrate the inequality of social status among those who are without significant capital resources. His attempt here is to deal with the question of the emerging middle class, the bourgeoisie, which shows that 'class status' is based upon the ownership of property and their opportunities (social roles), which are articulated by power relations (Weber, 2005:195). With this ideology, Weber does not differ substantially from Karl Marx on the issue of 'class consciousness' (Weber, 2002:60). In simplified terms, he developed a broad view of the modern capitalist system, which is an economically dominant class to secure continuing economic exploitation and political control (Rothman, 2005:5). Weber believes that most individuals in the organisation are subject to some form of bureaucratic control, whether industrial, political, or religious. In the traditional society, in a similar way, local customs and traditional practices reinforce men's control over landed property, for example, land ownership and agricultural produce. Evidence of inheritance rights within the patriarchal institution, therefore, is perceived through male lineage, kinship, and gender. This trend serves as a way of understanding the traditional Igbo pattern of looking at the patriarchal practice towards women, which this study uses to demonstrate marriage and property rights of women.

Class differentiation in Weber's school of thought is making a valuable contribution to the understanding of the situation of property relations and how it influences people in the patriarchal traditional household. Weber's ideas on the family (*oikos*) are defined as a set of sexual and economic relationships regulated by political power (Rothman, 2005:35). Thus, socio-economic status is used to visualise society as a hierarchy of 'social groups'. His model of social phenomena encompasses a broader view of economic classes and also includes status groups and parties, thus allowing individuals and families to be located on three hierarchies of inequality: inequalities of lifestyles, prestige (social status), and power.

Property in Weber's theory is regulated within a social class. For Weber 'classes', 'status groups' and 'parties' are the observable phenomena of the distribution of power in a community (Weber, 2005:192). A social group is grounded in the prevailing values, beliefs, and ideas of society to mark a difference on socio-economic status, which may be based on income, ethnicity, ancestry, education, and occupation. Because those in a status group are aware of their shared interests, they are likely to attempt to develop mechanisms for maintaining and protecting their social position and that of their children. Most of his thought indicates that "those with the most economic resources also tend to have the highest status' (Rothman, Ibid: 35). In addition, Weber acknowledged that those in a higher social class would selectively interact only with others whom they consider to be their social equals by socialising with them at the same level. Hence, outsiders viewed as 'social inferiors' will simultaneously be deliberately excluded from such level of social network connections. Significantly, class-based disparities exist in the Weberian traditional society to highlight distribution of wealth, prestige, and political power (Rothman, 2005:37). Many factors such as gender, race, and ethnicity account for this situation and have the potential to exaggerate these patterns of inequality. In other words, differences in the level of households are apparent, but class status has more invidious implications which include the quality of health, access to quality education, access to the social network system, psychological well-being (self-esteem), and exposure to violence.

Weber's (2004:33) analysis of bureaucracy thus noted that modern state institutions are based on a form of rational-legal authority. He distinguished the three types of political leadership, domination, and authority as follows: charismatic domination (familial and religious), traditional domination (patriarchs, patrimonalism, feudalism), and legal domination (modern law and state bureaucracy).

Weber recognised that enormous power is concentrated in the hands of the people who head the large organisations that dominate those in a lower social group (Weber, Ibid: 192). Most of his thoughts address the most extreme cases where status groups evolve into what he called 'castes', where distinctions of social status are maintained by rigid social conventions, or even laws that prohibit property rights and marriage outside the group (Weber, 2002:199-209). Moreover, even physical contacts with caste members can be considered degrading, as though physically encountering caste members might contaminate them. In this way, he felt that exclusionary practices were usually associated with class position, but other bases of exclusion were race, language, and religion' (Weber, 2002:109). Much of his sociological work took the form of a critical response on class status and property as a contemporary idea of dominance and control in the social organisation. Weber's ideology has the same phenomenon with the hierarchy of Igbo kinship groups, the eminent persons, and the rural households in relation to class status and controlling of the local customs and cultural practices, where village women in the categories analysed may be susceptible to *Ariri*.

Weber advanced the study of women's oppression by considering the impact of economic production as the capability of the owner's power to achieve his desired ends or goals (Giddens, 1995:48). Further, Weber indicates that power or domination is an expression of social control by individual decision-makers to realise their objectives in a particular range of contexts (Giddens, 1995:49). Worell and Remer (1996) added that women have been looked at in relation to the roles they occupy (e.g. daughter, wife, mother, and worker) the discriminatory practices that restrict their opportunities, the victimisation and violence they experience, the diverse groups with which they identify, and their psychological processes. We can deduce from this argument that patriarchal ideology is not an exclusive site for the production of women's marginalisation and thus that women's exclusion cannot be analysed independently of the economic and property relations (Gardner, 2006). Post-feminism draws such attention by arguing that social and political power attached to the tradition of patriarchal systems illuminates the way women's exclusion has been the main task in the analysis of patriarchy that has been ultimately beneficial to capital.

It became clear that 'women's concerns could be reinterpreted in the broader context of gender inequality based on a shared contextual approach to oppression' (Worell and Remer, 1996:9). Rollo (1972:23) noted with concern that 'women's alienation in capitalist and patriarchal societies has its breeding ground in impotence and apathy and that a state of powerlessness is the source of violence'. As we make people powerless, we promote their exclusion rather than control. Wallace (1990:17-18) explains it in this way that 'women's position in production could be what determines women's frustration. It is designed so that social class is determined by patriarchal control of the means of production'. And those who share a common relationship to the means of production—owners and labourers—should not share the same class position. Hartmann (1978) in addition maintained that in order to understand the subordination of women in patriarchal societies, it is necessary to understand Weber's economic exploitation in order to show the specific forms female oppression take in such societies.

2.7 Property rights of women and tension between customary and statutory laws

The examination of the Nigerian legal system will help us to illustrate the nature and social structure of the judicial system that shapes the law and its legal principles by which this legal system has dealt with either widows or married women without children in their right of inheritance. Parallel to this, customary law discriminates against women's succession of property rights and regards a female as a transient member in matrimonial homes. Customary law regulates over eighty per cent of the lives of Nigerians, and evidence to this fact can be appreciated when viewed from land tenure and marriage (Nwankwor, 2001:23).

Nigeria is an independent sovereign state and has been a full member of the British Commonwealth since her independence in 1960. Her legal system was typically British with the adoption of English law. This study demonstrates that there is a greater degree of application of the English legal system even in marriage ordinance (statutory marriage) in their territorial zones. The British law was effective during the colonial era, but some of the modification has brought changes to suit the local legislation.

Nigeria, like other colonised countries within the African continent, operates a dual system of laws, the statutory (common) law and customary law. The constitution of the Federal Republic of Nigeria Act 1999 provides in Section 21 that the state shall protect, preserve, and promote the Nigerian cultures, which enhance human dignity and are consistent with the fundamental objectives. The Evidence Act of Nigeria defines 'custom' in Section 2 (Article 1) as a rule which in a particular district, has from long usage, obtained the rule of law. Such a custom can be applied as part of the law governing a particular case if it has been noticed judicially or it can be established by evidence to exist. Subsection 2 stipulates the conditions under which the court would take judicial notice of a custom. Section 14 (Article 3) provides that even where a particular custom is proved by evidence, it would nevertheless not be enforced if it were held to be contrary to public policy or repugnant to natural justice, equity, and good conscience. Thus, the Superior Court of Judicature exercises jurisdiction over all matters both civil and criminal.

In Nigerian society, if a woman becomes a widow, she will be subjected to one of two legal systems: statutory law or customary law. According to statutory law, a widow is allowed to inherit part of her husband's property and estate including land. Section 36 of the Nigerian Marriage Act provides for the widow with the following support. 'A widow with children is entitled to one-third of her husband's estate; whereas the woman with no child is not entitled to any of her husband's estate'.

The above provision, therefore, indicates that in legal principles, a widow is entitled to inherit from her husband on his death under *mortis causa* (after death). Similarly, his children are entitled to inherit from his estate. Where both widow and children survive the deceased, the nuclear family is the sole beneficiary. But how is this applied in practice? This is where the sociologists have tended to draw our attention to the objectives of marriage both *inter vivo* (before marriage) and *mortis causa* (after death), where in many cases related to inheritance and property rights, the applicable rules are difficult to discern. Even where they are known, the provisions are not really subject to precise interpretation. Evidence suggests that the widow's rights of inheritance under the Marriage Ordinance Act are completely ignored by the deceased's relatives who regard the deceased's estate as their birthright. It is indicated, according to Nwankwor (2001), that '[c]ourts do not follow statutory law but customary law'. In the case of *Augustine Muojekwu* v. *Caroline Muojekwu* (1997) case no. 7 NWLR (Pt. 512) 283, a case of inheritance under Nnewi native law and custom Anambra State of Nigeria, the court held that according to the native law and customs that property can be allotted to a wife. Nwankwor (2001:7) remarked the difficulties in application of law. 'One rule, which most traditional African societies are unanimous about is that in the customary law of "intestate" succession, the widow has no place in the sense that she can never inherit from her husband'.

In the 1980 case, which Omiyi reported in her study, a widow under native marriage had three female children only and no son. When the widow made claims on the right of the estate, the brother-in-law objected and also maintained that the widow should be expelled from the late husband's compound. This position was held because the widow had no son and could neither inherit her husband's estate nor administer it. Parallel to this, in 1995, a town in Orumba North Local Government Area of Nigeria, another land dispute is demonstrated as follows: A widow had sold a piece of land. Her son challenged his mother's right to sell any part of his father's landed property. In his judgment, the traditional ruler of the town who was noted to be the custodian of the customs and traditions in no equivocal manner condemned the practice of purported purchase of land from a widow. Such purchase was disallowed by the customary laws of the town particularly in a case such as this where the woman, a widow for that matter, had a grown-up son who was the automatic heir to the estate of the deceased father. Thus, it is common knowledge in kinship-related practice in most communities in the Eastern region of Nigeria that women have no right of inheritance. For example, a woman cannot inherit property in her father's house because she has no locus standi to bring an action in respect of family property since she will soon be 'sold' off to another family nor can she inherit from her husband's house because of the possibility of divorce or remarriage[3]. Supporting these facts,

---

[3] Patrilocality—according to this Igbo custom, a woman has to leave her parental home at the time of marriage and join her husband in his home. Widows who may continue living in their husband's home, live a life of rejection, poverty, and deprivation of physical and emotional needs.

Ezeilo (2005:12) states, 'The estate of a man who dies leaving no male issue does not remain in his immediate family. His immediate brother is entitled to succeed to his estate. Where he does not have a surviving brother, the eldest son of his brother inherits the estate. It goes on even unto a distant cousin of the intestate, rather than to his daughters or sisters'.

In the above cases, the provisions of Section 36 of the Nigeria Marriage Act were overruled both by the courts and local council. A similar case reported by Omiyi from Ghanaian law shows how widespread kinship practice cuts across many African societies. In a follow-up customary law case, a widow sued her deceased husband's family, claiming one-third of her husband's intestate estate basing her claim on two grounds. First, she asserted that she helped the husband to acquire the property in question. Second, she claimed that she was a lawful customary law widow and therefore was entitled under customary law to a share of her husband's estate. The court dismissed her claims although it found that she actually helped in the acquisition of the property. It was held that under customary law, a widow does not become a co-owner of property she helped her husband to acquire. These examples demonstrate how customary law supports patriarchal practices in violation of federal law.

Metuh (1985:29) writes that land in Igbo custom is described as 'sacred'. 'If ever there was a supreme god among the traditional Igbo society, it is "land". The principles of the usage of land, inheritance and taboos associated with landed property must be understood in the light of the people's moral and religious attachment to it and not only its utilitarian value as a means of production'. This of course has implications for women, especially since the control of land is within customary practices which placed widows in a different position. However, many of the women in Igbo society presented the issue of property right as one of their major problems. This state of affairs is widespread for many widows and married women without children. The law is very silent on how the distribution of property should be done in the case of barren women. Women's disinheritance in the study involves a broader understanding of how sociocultural, economic, and political structure widens the psychosocial condition of survivors for this study.

2.8   Customary law and practice

In traditional African society, especially in Igboland, children are seen as the main fruit of marriage, highly valued and regarded as the fundamental component of an economically secure household. The first responsibility of a wife is therefore to produce children. However, patriarchal practice treats married women with male and female children differently. The Estates Act 1685 and the intestates Estate Act 1890 combined to demonstrates that a widow of the deceased would be entitled to one of her husband estates if he was also survived by children (Uzodike and Onokah, 2003:317-27). According to Western Nigerian legislation, Section 49 (1) sets out the order of distribution of the estate of a person who dies intestate. This inter alia states that nothing in this law shall affect 'distribution, inheritance, or succession of an estate where this is governed by customary law'. It is, however, stipulated in Section 1 (3) that customary law shall apply 'unless otherwise expressly provided for'. This stipulation brings into play Section 49 (5) of the law, which expressly provides that in certain specified circumstances if a person dies intestate 'any property of the said intestate shall be distributed in accordance with the provisions of this law, when a person dies, leaving a widow any issue of such marriage'.

The right of inheritance and property relation is determined by gender. The position of women with male children is a guaranteed inheritor of her late husband. This desire for children particularly 'boys' increases the labour force and inheritors of the property rights amongst the Igbos has not changed in its effect on the status of women. The importance of male heirs (sons) in customary law cannot be overemphasised. Male heirs of the patrilineage formed the nucleus of marriage, having collective rights to the land (Anameze, 1996:17). The adult ones are a powerful group since they are active agents of socio-political and moral control as a factor of leadership. In the words of Chiegboka (1997:32), male heirs become a representative of local custom (*Omenala*) because of their position of primacy among kinsmen. There are two ways of looking at male heirs amongst the Igbos: It is seen first as central in family and exercises a considerable amount of power in kinship system, and second, they become a unifying force among the communities. These dual characters are fused into the various ways by which religion binds the community and reinforces the activities of heirs together. All these socio-religious factors from male heirs distinguish the condition of childless wives and infertility.

The difference between the customary rights of male heirs from childless wives and infertility is based on the ground of culturally rooted gender discrimination. The inability to achieve pregnancy in marriage predisposes a woman to lack of rights over inheritance succession. Childlessness is one of the reasons for the exclusion, discrimination, and stigmatisation of women. Other reasons include pressure to prove fertility from the family, lack of socio-economic support, and frustration in marriage.

My observation of women and their cultural experience show areas of difference, especially where a widow without a male offspring loses her rights of inheritance and property of her late husband in a household. In another aspect, her fruitfulness of female offspring is unlikely to be valued. The stigma attached to barren women has been previously noted, and to this may be added disinheritance in the household. Since infertility is found to result in perceived role failure with social and emotional consequences, herbal treatment is seen as option for women, while for the man, the frequent option is remarriage. Survivors who cannot afford money for medical consultation and treatment find spiritualists (traditional healers) and prayer houses as the only options to their childlessness. Since women bear the greatest burden of being childless in Igboland because of their low social status and culturally rooted gender discrimination, their affliction and suffering becomes unbearable.

The alleged sterility of women has led to innumerable divorces and the separation of spouses, and it is a contributing cause of discrimination, deprivation, and stigmatisation. Luke (2001:32-45) traced an ideological association between female sterility and disinheritance and remarked, 'As the barren woman fails by the common standard of marriage and womanhood, she is attached by stigmatisation of barrenness. She would still be called a "worthless woman", it would be, as it were, overshadowed by and fused with the other paramount stigma of barrenness itself'.

The customary marriage, under property rights of women, during recent years suggests that widows who experience exclusion either had no male children or one male child only. It may still pose problems for widows in a situation where a deceased husband has been allocated family or kinship land and both spouses have then invested all of their life savings in building a family home that the husband thereafter bequeaths to his widow in his will. In such circumstances, it seems that whichever construction is placed on Section 3 (1), the widow will find it extremely difficult to rely on her husband's will to establish a claim to the property. On a practical level, even when the property in question is completely self-acquired, the difficulties awaiting a widow wishing to claim such property under the terms of her husband's will are compounded by the implacable hostility that she is likely to encounter if her claim succeeds in court. As Enemo (2003:305) explains, 'even if the court upholds the will, the wife is unlikely to enjoy quiet and peaceable possession and runs the risk of being ostracized and oppressed by her husband's family'. In such a situation, she usually takes the line of least resistance by relinquishing her claim to inheritance under the 'will' (See Appendix 6). Consequently, once a will runs counter to the customary laws of succession, the members of the traditional society will regard it as an aberration and ignore it in favour of the customary laws.

Mikell (1995:423) indicates that 'women said they wanted recognition of the married couple as an economic unit, which took into consideration contributions the wife made to existing property that was owned in the husband's name'. Conjugal, familial, and kinship systems appear often to operate so as to construct women as a subordinate gender, such that by virtue of carrying kinship (or familial or conjugal) status; women are less free to act as full subjects in relation to things and sometimes people (Whitehead, 1984:189-90). The problems women face when it comes to the eventual death of their husbands and when their status as a wife is questioned are because they are currently insufficiently protected by the law. The cases brought to court by women demonstrate women's attempts to change the situation. Moore (1988) writes that one must move decisively away from the idea of women as necessarily passive in their response to state oppression but begin to examine the many different ways in which women struggle; protest in the face of the state should be empowered.

Apart from women's challenges in Nigeria, some are fortunate in terms of slowly breaking down the rigid cultural and social norms. In recent times, resources like religious activities, education work, and wages are also leading to the enhanced control few widows have over their life. This is also resulting in better self-esteem. According to Dolphyne (1991), 'there were categories of women who commanded respect in their societies by virtue of the fact that they have attained a level of social recognition in education, profession in business'.

The Convention on the Elimination of All Forms of Discrimination Against Women (CEDAW), to which Nigeria is a part of, calls in Article 2 on state parties to take measures to abolish laws and customs that discriminate against women in local communities. Section 42 of the Constitution of the Federal Republic of Nigeria prohibits discrimination against any person on grounds of sex, religion, tribe, and so on. It is against this background that a customary practice that allows a distant male relation of an intestate to inherit his estate to the exclusion of his widow and female children offends not only the above sections of the local laws and articles of an international convention but also our collective intelligence and sensitivities.

2.9   Ritual

Religion and rites of passage in West Africa, with particular reference to South-Eastern Nigeria, is central in tradition and cultural practices. Life-cycle rituals cut across childbirth, marriage, death, and widowhood are practiced. In traditional Igbo marriage, asking the young woman's consent forms the initial ritual process and introducing the woman to the man's family and the same for the man to the woman's family, testing the bride's character, checking the woman's family background, and paying the bride's wealth (Agbasiere, 2000:114). Sometimes marriages have been arranged from birth through negotiation of the two families. In recent times, Christian marriages have changed the Igbo family since western colonisation. Igbo people now tend to enter monogamous courtships and create nuclear families, mainly because of western influence (Ezeagbor, 2004:34). Adopted western marriage customs have been incorporated—weddings in church are sometimes accompanied by a traditional wedding.

The ritual practices arise from the strong sense of the local custom and tradition between the living and the dead, which form a basic factor of the cosmology of the patriarchal Igbo society. The significance of the ritual practices connects the stages of widowhood in relation to reintegration of the survivors in the community. Different theorists had viewed ritual as reinforcing collective sentiment and social integration. Afigbo (2005) makes ritual a central part of analyses of the way societies cohere over time. Rituals, in conjunction with religion, form a prescribed set of traditional beliefs and cultural way of life. A ritual, like religion, is another word, which has posed many problems for anthropologists in establishing a definition. Goody (1961:142-64) indicates, 'The study of tradition and societies has always been faced with the difficult problem of defining what kind of phenomena can be called ritual'. The problem is even more complicated in the case of traditional societies because people in such societies have no concept of ritual as a distinct phenomenon. It still remains the case that groups for a variety of purposes use rituals and that these purposes could themselves be categorised to celebrate and maintain communities' social structures.

Eliade (1993:169) held the view that ritual recapitulates the mythical origin or beginnings of things. He further maintained that 'in the origins of things resides the paradigm, the powerfully generative archetypes'. Turner (1969:29), exploring the rituals of the East African Ndembu, remarked, 'Ritual could only be understood as conveying meaning by means of symbols'. Several scholars have expressed their views on the various nature of ritual that is performed in societies to have relatively fixed sequences of behaviour and communication. In attempt to expatiate the impact of ritual on certain disadvantaged groups, especially women in traditional societies, I use the case of 'widowhood' and 'childlessness or infertility' to justify how ritual and cultural taboos oppresses women.

Wallace (1990:61) illustrates different types of rituals such as those found in divination and curing rituals that seek to injure others, such as those in witchcraft, sorcery, casting the evil eye, seeking to prevent illness or misfortune, or preventing or curing illness; ideological rituals that symbolise and reinforce group values, such as rites of passage and taboos; salvation rituals that help individuals cope with personal issues, such as possession and trance; revitalisation rituals that seek to correct societal problems.

Tradition comes into the reinforcement of the ritual performances. The striking thing in the analysis of 'ritual' is how it connects people's activities in cultures or communities. Hence, ritual helps to understand the way characters or behaviours are enacted in narratives, stories, images, or the principles embedded in them with action. It is argued that ritual has been, and still is, an effective way of socialising with people to conform to values and way of life, which they have not chosen for themselves. Ritual behaviour can involve members of groups, small and large, and does so by working with the whole of a person—his body, reason, and unconscious needs and desires. It can appeal to symbols, actions, bodily movements, values, and beliefs and ideas and produce some momentary kind of unity. Various attempts have been made to classify rituals engaged in by people around the world. One classification scheme that encompasses the definition is cited in Wallace's work *Culture and Personality* in which 'ritual is designated to control the natural environment, reinforce group values and seek to correct societal problems' (Wallace, 1990:106-7).

Widows and childless women as noted are considered to be profane, unclean, and isolated. As Potash (1985:23) noted, 'cultural practice involves the expression of this belief in conduct and rituals'. As ritual occupies religious importance in African societies, widowhood and childlessness reveal the predominant patriarchal concerns for pollution and taboo (Douglas, 2003). Though variations in traditional mechanisms used in cultures might be different, research will consistently point to a high degree of correlation between tradition and women's response to ritualistic activities. The experience in which a widow and a childless woman capture the distress within the traditional Igbo society is generally referred to as *Ariri*.

The outcome of childlessness for a woman especially in the Igbo society is less status. My own experience about the condition of these women is that they are being maltreated in so many ways because of a suspicion of being witches (*amosu*) who are likely to have been married in the spirit world. Practically, the childless condition of women causes emotional distress to a husband and other members of the extended family. For example, Mesaki (2009:132-138) noted that in African societies accusation of witchcraft is rampant. The works of Ayittey (2001) and Harnischfeger's study (2008:56-78) are significant in demonstrating that witchcraft belief is the outcome of social instability such as poverty, intimidation, oppression, and economic distress.

Analytically allied to the ritual is the belief that the dead create a link between the living and the ancestral community in the spirit world. Since the dead are given a religious ritual into the spirit world, Igbo societies meticulously observe the practices associated with funeral or burial ceremonies to appease the death. If not, he/she would be considered to have been improperly buried and would be denied a proper rest into the ancestral world. Afigbo (2005:273) notes, 'ritual acts are performed by the living for the dead to cause the spirit to be settled in peace. The living had certain rites to carry out on their own behalf which if omitted would bring the displeasure of the ancestors upon them'. This paradox gives greater credibility to the past and thus helps us understand how ritual practices serve as a vehicle for enforcement and control of the deceased, especially the widows in the community. According to Okoye (2005:14-15), it is common in traditional Igbo society that a widow is seen as being in a state of ritual impurity until such defilement is removed. This fact agrees with what Mezieobi (2011) described in the Enugu, Anambra, Abia, Ebonyi and Imo state areas, that ritual practices show a genuine reaction to the loss of the husband, while others help to clear the widow of any suspicion of killing her husband.

Thus, it is necessary in every tradition that ritual is performed for the dead to enable the deceased to have no contact with the ancestral spirit of his wife or wives. Eboh and Boye (2005:348) suggest that the unhygienic ritual shaving of head, drinking of remains of bath wash from the husband's corpse, and not allowed to bathe constitutes women's health hazard. Nevertheless, it is important to emphasise that the men and women related to the deceased come under varying degrees of ritual. Men are also expected to mourn their wives, although the expectations would appear rather low-key.

2.10 Widowhood rituals and cultural practices

Ritual seclusion and general isolation of the widow for a certain period from the community is a widespread practice in Africa. This affliction basically creates a terrible experience for widows. It underpins the combination of power. The study of Nwadinobi, Oluyemise, and Bamgbose (2008:71) suggest that practices of widowhood are designed not only to restrict women, but also symbolises the widow's dethronement and her consequent reversion to her lower status. Additionally, Okoye (2005:88) in *Widowhood and Practice* writes, 'All other ritualistic activities serve the same purpose and any mystification of sanctions and superstitions geared to the oppression of the widows'. So each time a husband dies, there are a few women as *umuokpu* who administer measures to carry out rituals, which they have received themselves as widows. Nwankwor (2004:15) further indicated, 'Widowhood rituals in some Nigerian cultures provide for inhuman and degrading treatment of the widow by the extended family members'. Ezeilo (2005:48) believes that the most striking description of widowhood is captured in this comment, 'The guilt we feel as a victim will never leave us'. Ezeilo's observation represents widowhood practice as follows: 'Each morning after the burial my mother in-law took me out to the back of the house. I had a bath with very cold water. This was done very early in the morning when it was still very cold. As she did this, customs demanded that I must be crying and calling my husband the name I used to call him when he was alive. This lasted for four days. I stayed at home for the next three months mourning him without going out'. Exclusion of widows from physical contact with other people, based on ritual practice, is characterised by situations in which basic care, support, and other forms of affective needs of women are intentionally withheld. Such practice, in general, describes the state of widowhood as a common way of intensifying the marginalisation, neglect, and subordination of women.

Returning to the earlier argument, widowhood practice in South-Eastern Nigeria relates to property and patriarchal control. These rituals are specifically designed to establish so that a widow was not complicit in her husband's death. There is an ever present suspicion whenever a man dies that his demise is attributed to supernatural causes or the machinations of his enemies (including his wife). This belief invariably engenders an atmosphere of suspicion, which points to widow as the person who was closest to the deceased (Ibhawoh, 2002:127). This often involves keeping the widow in the same room as her husband's corpse, sometimes for several nights, obliging her to sleep at the burial ground, or compelling her to drink the water used to wash the corpse, while declaring an oath that she had no hand in his death (Korieh, 1996; Okagbue, 1995:201).

According to Korieh (1996:65), material on patriarchy and male control of inheritance and property is acquisitiveness, which basically controls treatment of widows. It is a common practice encountered by widows, such as looting of their personal and matrimonial property by in-laws immediately after the death of their husbands and even before the burial. In giving full rein to such acquisitive tendencies, these in-laws are emboldened by the knowledge that in matters of inheritance, 'the rights of widows to property remain circumscribed in many Nigerian cultures' (Okagbue, 1995:214).

2.11 Contemporary African perspectives

In contemporary African perspective, as noted, marriage and property have often proved remarkably adaptable to changing social conditions. According to Enwereji (2008:165-69), it has been observed that property and kinship practice relate the total social structure, which is linked to economic and political arrangements of the lineage ties, as mostly likely to reinforce women's exclusion of inheritance and property rights and poor health outcome. Ukpokolo (2007:41-68) remarked that pattern of land production and ownership of property depends upon the type of lineage and the ethnic and legal systems women participate in and had degree of control that husbands acquire over wives and their activities in considering socio-economic and political behaviour of marriage, property rights of women, and a kinship system. This explains clearly the problem of domestic rights of women in marriage, which can be best understood as overlapping basis of gender and social stratification in Nigerian situation in recent times.

Finally, any social perspective related to *Ariri* (mental distress) should be informed by principles of anti-oppressive and empowering practice. This involves an awareness of power relations and maintains a concern with those factors which may diminish people's sense of self-esteem or constrain their personal, social, or economic opportunities. It raises questions of discrimination, inequality, social stigma, and internalised abuse that may take place within a kinship system or in other social contexts. I shall attempt to deal with these in greater depth and detail in the following chapters.

This chapter summarily indicates the following:

- Central to lineage system, inequalities are deeply set in the structure of patriarchal and kinship practice. It is reinforced by where property and inheritance are involved.
- Customary systems of land tenure and administration for achieving gender justice with respect to women's inheritance and property claims receive insufficient attention in rural areas.
- Traditional widowhood practices and oppressive women's rights increases the level of their subordination and vulnerability and also 'Ariri' (mental health problem).
- Women's conjugal rights will provide support for socio-economic and political status of women under customary law and practice especially in administration of Estates laws where their husbands die 'intestate'.
- Max Weber's theories and other feminist anthropologists remain relevant for this study about the transformation necessary in the property rights of women in the patriarchal and kinship practice.

Chapter 3

Research Methodology

3.1 Introduction and study aims

The chapter will examine the way through which the researchers go about collecting data for this study. This illustrates the patriarchal processes towards women as investigated through the research instruments: semi-structured interviews with open-ended questions, questionnaire, participant observation, and documentary sources obtained from the accounts of widows and childless wives in the three villages of the Awka South region. My aim in this chapter is to present an ethnographic way of looking at the cultural practice and cosmology which represent kinship practice and customs—marriage, inheritance, and rite of passage and how it influences the social behaviour of women and their health and belief systems. This approach will enable me to gain a better insight of the interview content developed in every stage of the research process. These reflections would benefit from some references to literature on insider/outside perspectives and the position of the researcher's account of the fieldwork and local community. Finally, the extent to which this study offers an African voice and an Igbo African perspective on the world view is considered.

3.2 Research design and methodological considerations

The process of this study design started with the considerations of the themes that I wanted to explore. I knew that I wanted to look at an area that is relevant to this study, that is, on the impact of patriarchy and the psychosocial condition of Igbo women. I examined women's social condition, in the way their customary rights have been overlooked. I have investigated this area in order to generate information and knowledge about certain group of women in their vulnerable position, which forms the study aim through which my research questions and findings are focused. I started by using 'thematic maps' to consider these areas with particular interest. In this regard, I deduced that gendered property relations and their psychosocial effects advance the knowledge of marginalisation and stigmatisation of women by looking at the areas of inheritance law and how the NGOs direct their anti-discriminatory practice. The marginalisation indicates where an individual does not participate in key activities of the society in which she lives. It directs our attention to those living in a particular environment and refers to a lack of participation of women, which can be researched at the micro-ethnographic analytical level.

The study method will be testing first, whether patriarchy can negatively affect women's social status. Second, it will address the extent to which gender inequality could affect women's socio-economic deprivation and neglect. Consistent with this, the methodology uses an ethnographic approach to provide a way of studying a particular set of group within their social environment. It influences the way researchers generate knowledge of the 'insiders' account (narrative), using procedure, selection, and comparison as criteria for the study.

The need for empirical investigation is important since most of the studies conducted on traditional practices related to violence against women have been carried out with the use of secondary data (Nwankwor, 2005). Given the dynamism of culture and the complexity of variations of individual motivations for negative traditional practice on women underscores the need for method triangulation of study in this field. Furthermore, the study should be balanced by qualitative research approach of the depth of analysis needed to promote cultural awareness, education, and effective information for promoting anti-discriminatory practices towards women.

The study addresses both qualitative and ethnographic materials that provide basic knowledge on the social context of the community in gender and cultural terms. This implies that the qualitative research allows the researcher to explore and incorporate various perspectives held by different views and at the same time requires critical reflections of research in the research processes (Borkan, 2004). Cresswell et al. (2004) indicate that qualitative researchers maintain that reality is socially constructed and that an intimate relationship between the researcher and the researched is of a value-laden nature. Strauss and Corbin (1990) justify this statement that qualitative research can be used to understand any phenomenon about which little is known, especially in the context of widows and childless wives where few or scanty studies have been carried out in South-Eastern Nigeria. By contrast, quantitative research may work best in isolating and identifying the correlates associated with variation at specific moments in time. It is also considered as a possible approach, providing a way to measure how many participants feel, think, or act in a particular manner.

I discussed my initial ideas within previous studies on human rights and decided that by using a question that considered the perspectives of patriarchal and kinship practices on inheritance and widowhood, I could gain a more in-depth understanding of conflict situation on gender inequalities which could exacerbate harmful practice through ethnographic research model and how best to work with adult survivors (widows and childless wives) with these culturally specific issues. In this regard, I was also able to learn about using ethnographic materials to look at the vulnerable position of women with *Ariri*.

Atkinson and Hammersley (2007) define ethnography as forms of social research, having a substantial number of features such as a strong emphasis on exploring the nature of particular social phenomena, rather than setting out to test hypotheses about them. It works primarily with 'unstructured' data, that is, data that have not been coded at the point of data collection in terms of a closed set of analytical categories. It investigates a small number of cases—perhaps just one case—in detail. The analysis of data involves explicit interpretation of the meanings and functions of human actions, the product of which mainly takes the form of verbal descriptions and explanations.

This study is to provide a detailed ethnographic description of a particular set of circumstances, on discriminatory practices and their effects on women's roles and status in the south-eastern region of Nigeria and to encourage the reader to make their own interpretations. My aim in this study is that ethnographies are guided from the perspective of the participants' account. In this way, ethnographic research provides me with an opportunity to engage with participants and their narratives regarding how their problems are perceived, and why they had come to take part in the interviews. Ethnography is an area in which I have had direct fieldwork experience and have built up my expertise and knowledge. With the systematic and comprehensive information about the local community, the interview process is used to test hypotheses in my investigation, and it records all the necessary and detailed information useful for this study. Bassett (2004) indicates that the aim of the research method underpinned by the philosophy is to uncover hidden phenomena and meaning by interpreting frequently taken-for-granted shared practices and common meaning. The researcher develops a philosophical understanding to see what is otherwise concealed. A personal pre-understanding will be brought to the text by the researcher, since this cannot be bracketed out. Therefore, the researcher will participate in the interpretation process of the data (Holloway, 2005).

3.3   Advantages of ethnography

Historically, the ethnographic research is a product of an interpretative account, reconstruction or narrative about a group of people (in a community). It includes in this current study some historical material and paints a picture of women marginalised or discriminated over a period of time. In this methodology, the predominant viewpoints or paradigms that guide ethnography as a social science is its dynamic overview of study methods and design, including how to develop study questions, what to consider in setting up the mechanisms of a study, and how to devise a sampling plan. However, using the ethnographic method enabled the study to identify people's cosmology and cultural beliefs (influence of human behaviour) related to the plight of women as a wider concern in the Igbo society.

With reference to the essentials of ethnographic methods, readers are provided with an introduction to participant and non-participant observation, interviewing and ethnographically informed survey study, including systematically administered structured interviews and questionnaires. These data collection strategies are fundamental to the procedure of this research.

Thus, as an ethnographer, I made use of tools such as social structures, social events, cultural patterns and the meanings people give to these patterns to demonstrate the social phenomena under study.

Analysing and interpreting ethnographic data provide a variety of methods for transforming piles of field notes, observation, tapes, questionnaires, surveys, documents, maps, and other kinds of data into study results that will help people to understand the social condition of women and facilitate problem-solving. Importantly, ethnography assumes that we must first discover what people actually do and the reasons they give for doing it. In this way, the tools for ethnography suggest 'discovery' for data collection. They accounts for 'codification' of ethnographic study methods and 'replicated' version of data by other researchers even though the field situation may change (Shapiro, 1998:282-89). This format helps to produce valid and reliable data.

Areas of difference with other research methods

Scientific ethnographic research is conducted in a field setting where the researcher enters as an 'invited guest' to learn what is going on in the community. In this way, ethnographic approach cannot control what happens in their field situation of choice.

The ethnographic field situation is unlike 'clinic or laboratory-based experimental research', where most aspects of the environment are controlled where researchers can use the same instruments to achieve the same results if the study is repeated. Even when ethnographers use the same instruments, changing circumstances beyond the ethnographer's control may generate different results that they must be able to explain.

What is important to ethnography as a scientific instrument is the ability to adapt or create locally appropriate aids to data collection or instruments that are effective in building a picture, narrative, story, or theory of local culture that is predictive, at least in the short run, and produces hunches, guesses, and hypotheses that can be applied to the same situations or to other similar situations using the same research methods and data collection techniques (Ember and Ember, 2006).

Similarly, ethnographers are holistic in approach and do not shy away from surveys and other instruments that are used to test concepts and theories derived from other fields or from 'outsider' observations (Heider, 2001). But instead the ethnographer will take the position, consistent with their belief in the integrity of local cultures, that such instruments and the theories that usually direct their use should not be arbitrarily used without testing them locally for both practical applicability (i.e. do local people understand the language and ideas used by the ethnographer?) and theoretical applicability (i.e. do the theories that guide these instruments have meaning in the local setting?) Increasingly, this position is increasingly being shared by members of other disciplines who historically have held strong beliefs in the generalisability and universality of human behaviour, motivations, and beliefs. Growing understanding of the importance of local culture as the context for study and intervention has helped to increase the visibility and perceived value of ethnography research.

There are, however, limitations to qualitative research. Qualitative research rejects the scientific model and positivism in preference for an emphasis on interpreting insights, and instead of searching for truths, the investigator seeks valid and rigorous meanings or interpretations (Borkan, 2004). Thus, while the credibility in quantitative research depends on instrument construction, in qualitative approach, 'the researcher is the instrument' (Patton, 2002:14).

The application of quantitative notions of rigor to qualitative research provides a poor instrument for evaluating qualitative research (Dreher, 1994). Within this study, the aim for reliability in the data is based on consistency and care in the application of visible research practices and reliability in the analysis and conclusions that is reflected in an open account that remains aware of the partiality and limits of the research findings. It has been argued that the elimination of subjectivity in quantitative or qualitative research is impossible (Smith, 1987). Within this study, the researcher's actions will influence participants' responses, thereby affecting the direction of findings. Meanings are negotiated between the researcher and participants within a particular social context so that another researcher in a different relationship will disclose a different story. This study is thus a joint product of the participants, the researcher, and their relationship.

It could in fact be argued that it is even detrimental to research and ethical research practice to eliminate subjectivity (Davies and Dodd, 2002). When carrying out the in-depth interviews, rather than creating distance, efforts were made to gain the trust of the participants to enable them to feel comfortable about articulating their opinions, feelings, thoughts, and experiences on issues which were difficult at times. A degree of empathy and connection is necessary if the interview is to be faithful to the material and meaningful. As Davies and Dodd (2002) argue, knowledge can never be impartial or value free. Rather, they suggest a sense of responsibility, accountability, partiality, and subjectivity within the research. Instead of a standardised application of rules, they believe this can be achieved by careful attention to the research process through reflection, reflexivity, and by rendering visible the research process.

This study is informed by investigation of traditional harmful practice and its negative effect on women. The research is to promote the awareness of the existence of discriminatory practice in the south-eastern region of Nigeria and within patriarchal and kinship institutional structures (Nwankwor, 2003). This approach will inform every stage of the research process. The researcher is aware that the knowledge acquired from the study is not produced in a vacuum; rather, it is located within a complex set of social structures. My identity, motives, and agenda will impact the research questions, methods used, and the conclusions drawn. Instead of assuming a neutral, objective stance to work on the impact of traditional practice, I will be concerned with how the language of power, oppression, and domination is used to maintain and perpetuate traditional gender patterns. Additionally, I need to be aware that people who are the objects of research are often those in relatively powerless positions and who have no control over how they are represented in study reports (Truman et al., 2000). This explains that the researcher presenting people's experiences from the perspectives of dominant cultures and groups has to develop methodologies that are respectful, ethical, and authentic.

From the local custom and cultural perspectives, this study would have been improved if participants were enabled to have a part to in designing and carrying out the study, rather than only being interviewed. It would have been beneficial if the research had been negotiated between the participants and researcher, including the interpretation of any findings. Unfortunately, due to limitations in time, this was not possible. This would be something the researcher would strive to do in the future.

3.4   Research methods

This study used a multi-method approach. A mixed method can expand the understanding about certain phenomena from one method to the other and thus being more informative (Richardson, 2000). To answer my research questions, I used the interview process to generate knowledge from the women who suffer from *Ariri*. Additionally, it can give confirmation of findings from different data sources. A mixed methodology approach uses the philosophical assumptions of enquiring pragmatic knowledge. The strategies of enquiry within this framework can be seen as sequential, concurrent, and transformative (Cresswell et al., 2004). According to Lee (1993), mixed methods, or triangulated as otherwise called, are one of the best options to employ when researching any sensitive topic or a topic that is in any way 'hidden' and thus more difficult to study.

The samples of forty-three participants were chosen in order to maintain reliability and generability in the face to face semi-structured interviews. The forty-three participants included twenty-three female adult widows and twenty childless wives selected from three villages to investigate how patriarchal practice can negatively affect women's vulnerability. In addition, ten key informants that represent eminent people. Clan heads, titled men, and women (*umuokpu*), community leaders as custodians of tradition, and government and also NGOs—public health officials, social workers, and legal and human rights activists—were interviewed in order to ascertain perception on discriminatory and cultural practices. The documentation from a range of legal cases, both on customary and statutory law, national and international framework, and social-inclusion case studies represent further views on the themes and research questions. Finally, a female assistant was chosen because of my limitations as a male researcher in conducting interviews with females. The female adult survivors were selected based on the objective of the research investigation with range of cultural practices, disinheritance (social deprivation related to socio-economic neglect), educational profiles, and marriages in local tradition. The sample of women could be described as having low status and experiencing prolonged grief. Data was collected using a number of methods.

- Semi-structured individual interviews of widows with children and childless wives using Kleinman's Explanatory Model
- Questionnaire
- Five eminent men and five eminent women with informal conversations
- Five Informal conversations with different NGO directors
- Documentary sources
- Employment of female assistant

Kleinman's Explanatory Model

The data utilised in this study are analysed in terms of the Kleinman's Explanatory Model developed to address collective experience of social and cultural illnesses or disease within the local community. It focuses on gaining an in-depth understanding of 'insiders' perspectives on how tradition, ritual, and cultural practices contribute to mental health problems through semi-structured interviews and non-participant's observation. The explanatory model is an attempt to help individuals from different cultural backgrounds to have an insight into thoughts, behaviour, feelings, and a general attitude to their own problem. The ethnographic study method is a multi-method that enables the researcher to use multiple or mixed methods and reflects an attempt to secure an in-depth understanding of the phenomenon in question (Flick, 1998). Ethnography is useful in this context because it provides cultural information used in order to identify social problems and assessment, such as sources of information regarding harmful traditional practices, tensions survivors experienced during widowhood as well as cultural taboo, or restrictions associated with violence and emotional abuse in order to establish women's *Ariri*. There were six short questions in the interviews where the participants identified the cause of their illness or problems, which I used in the investigation on 'women's *Ariri*'.

1. What is your illness or problem called?
2. What do you think your problem does to you?
3. What do you fear most in your problem?
4. Why do you think this illness or problem has occurred?
5. Have you sought any help for your problem, and whom did you consult?
6. How do you think the problem could be treated?

The explanatory model helped to elicit information as participants were contacted and interviewed in order to look at the connection between participants' condition, the new ideas, and the meaning that their mental distress or social pathology brings to the study in response to cultural and religious practices, domestic abuse, and post-traumatic stress disorder (PTSD). In this context, explanatory model proposed two core concepts to illustrate a change in women's coping behaviour: first, in terms of socio-economic well-being and, second, in terms of religion and spiritual support. Prayer fellowship and counselling forms a bridge of supportive mechanism towards trusting and setting boundaries for vulnerable groups and moving away from the stressor and social environment. The victims felt and hoped that they had more control over their lives and thus the sample was both adequate and comprehensive.

The authority and power in kinship-based Igbo societies are connected largely on informal authority of the ancestors. With regard to the interviews, 5 eminent male clan heads and 5 eminent women (*umuokpu*) who were respected figures in the local community were contacted. The two groups were principally well known with respect to societal influence and represent the political roles of the local custom and traditional practices that provided access for the interviews.

The interview provided the opportunity to appreciate the conflicts resulting from the traditional practice on women. For example, widowhood practice and their tensions speak very strongly in the painful experience of survivors, and this in turn has continued to influence their human rights and health issues. Women who were over 60 are not exempt from these regulations, but modifications of the rites were easily made where failing strength and health demanded them, especially with regard to rituals conducted in the 'forest or stream' at midnight. This explains that even in a polygamous family, all the deceased's wives fulfilled these rites. The interview also allowed close contact with the adult survivors and understanding of the conditions in which they live. This is necessary for an objective appraisal of the consequences of the negative impact of tradition and cultural practices associated with ostracism.

Interviews were conducted in three parts, generally in two sessions; each lasted for 45-50 minutes in order to maintain the approved and standard time frame. All participants agreed to participate after being presented with the objective of the study and protocols for informed consent approved by School of Health and Social Sciences Ethics Committee (SHSS), Middlesex University. All interviews were tape-recorded and transcribed, and the interviews were coded using NVivo 7 ethnographic software. The first set of data examined, in greater depth, the overall experience of women identified as suffering from *Ariri* caused by serious deprivation and stigmatisation. The second section focused on the role of eminent people within the local community in order to gain information about how the local culture and practice affects women's inheritance and property rights. These eminent people are made up of two main groups, the custodians of customary law and members of NGOs who support an equal-rights agenda. The method utilised to collect the data is the ethnographic approach, using semi-structured interview, questionnaire, and documentary sources representing both a quantitative and qualitative perspective. The interview location was also important as it constituted a relatively safe environment. The village hall represented the sole option in terms of location for the interviews, as it was impossible for the interviews to take place in the participants' homes. This is because if the researcher had been seen entering the homes, it would have caused a potential source of scandal and suspicion. The neutrality of the hall was therefore perceived as the most appropriate location for the interview. I believe that when interviews took place in the participant's social space, their position of power is reinforced, but in practical terms, it can be difficult to arrange interviews in 'neutral' venues. I requested all interviews to be taped in which almost all the participants agreed on without exceptions. However, some expressed the feeling that most of their comments would be disclosed or misrepresented, but I reassured them on the confidentiality of the interview. As I was from outside the community, they appeared to believe that I would not betray their confidence. Furthermore, they appeared to trust me because of their strongly held beliefs of the trustworthiness of members of the clergy, which are an inherent in the belief system within the Igbo community.

In the absence of written records of traditional ways of life, oral tradition is the only source of information. Eminent men and women, who are the more dependable sources of the tradition, are the first category of our interviewees. Those who were important, based on their experiences and the functions they exercise in the community, include religious specialists and NGOs. The principal persons in the case study—married widows and childless wives—are also important sources in the ways their experiences embody the realities of the past and how they overcame these issues. The groups interviewed were prearranged, but they proved extremely useful in the way answers given by individuals were corroborated on the spot. This was helpful in determining the reliability of some of the information. Structured questions were prepared for the interviews; these were adhered to, and interviewees were allowed to express themselves without restrictions.

Related documents of cultural and religious practices of the area are few. However, the willingness of the eminent people and NGOs to make them available for the study shows the concern of many.

Questionnaire

The questionnaire was administered to the participants in the study and the following categories of clinical sub groups which represent the Igbo terms for indication of 'Ariri' (a cultural—specific mental health problems) were identified:

Exclusion	igupu mmadu
Self-isolation	mmadu inoro onwe ya
Discrimination	nkewa
Marginalisation	ikpa oke

Oppression	imegbu mmadu
Neglect	ileghara mmadu anya
Humiliation	ileda mmadu
Intimidation	iyii mmadu egwu m'obu ujoo
Blame	ita uta
Stigma	oru ejiri mara mmadu
Stereotype	isi otu akuku ele mmadu
Ostracism	isupu mmadu n'obodo

'Ariri' is a linguistic translation of 'low status', which reveals the mental health problem among the female population. Each participant was asked to complete a questionnaire, which provided additional quantitative and qualitative data on *Ariri*.

Conducting In-depth interviews

In the process of conducting the interview, I wanted to take particular care in the planning the process of interviewing. I wanted to make them semi-structured to enable me to have a specific framework to follow but also to allow further discussion around the subject.

The semi-structured interview by Kleinman's model helps in initiating conversation which allowed participants to express their views, beliefs, experiences, and feelings, including how to unearth the range and depth of the participants' undersatnding on particular issues. Full details of this model are explained in (Appendix 1).

The participants were asked what it meant for them to be disinherited and why women's expectations and disappointment evokes the feeling of emotional distress (*Ariri*), and also what they can do to improve their normal lifestyle. Another factor through which participants were approached is their observation of ways their health, beliefs, and social life differs in their social status in comparison with the rest of the women in their local community. Women tended to be less evasive in their responses when they are asked questions that touched them emotionally—affecting their real-life situation. In this regard, they tended to give less 'designed to please' answers to questions if they had very strong views on the issue. Thus, the probing techniques helped to ensure that the answers to the range of questions were directly relevant to the participants.

In this study, I found verbal responses very rich and informative; however, during one of the interviews, some participants were reluctant to voice their views on certain issues for fear of being misunderstood. So I devised a probing method whereby the same questions were presented in different ways to elicit a fuller response.

Importantly, there were occasions when I was quite 'up front' about the limitations of my knowledge, for example, the complexities of women's gestures (nodding of heads and looking strange and unusual to me). The female assistant offered an explanation of this for example—that it reflected a 'painful experience'.

I discovered throughout the interviews that this ancient tradition is practised across all socio-economic classes by a range of ethnic, cultural, and religious groups. There is assumption that the practice has no health benefits for the women. This explains the 'strong' feelings of women being vulnerable—marginalised, humiliated, and stigmatised—which may have contributed in influencing attitudes, especially in those from a low socio-economic background. Any indication of 'change in attitude' towards women's empowerment, such as community support, would encourage them.

Semi-structured interviews enable the participant to bring up issues, which they feel are important, whilst at the same time ensuring that the researcher's 'core' questions are covered (Fielding and Thomas, 2001) when time is at a premium (Duke, 2002). Furthermore, semi-structured interviews are thought to be more effective than highly structured or unstructured ones when interviewing people as they encourage more open sharing.

The interview schedule was drawn up after the review of literature, the examination of documents relating to the study, and informal discussion and personal contact with knowledgeable personnel. The schedule was piloted and revised accordingly. The questions asked were aimed at eliciting information about the participant's social condition and the lack of access to social network services. Participants were asked to give their account of their involvement, experiences, hopes and aspirations.

Within my planning, I also took into consideration the need for a suitable private location that would be undisturbed as well as my need to enable my interviewees to focus on their opinion and experience without influencing their answer. A good interviewer, according to Leedy and Ormond (2005:149), is above all a good listener who lets people say what they want to say in the way they want to say it.

With the participants' informed consent, I tape-recorded the interviews and produced written notes. The notes were not verbatim transcripts but contained sufficient details to enable a careful analysis.

Eminent men (clan heads)

The clan heads were contacted through a letter, explaining the nature of my research and possibility of conducting interview, with the help of the local priest, and to obtain permission alongside with *umuokpu* (heads of womenfolk) to refer widows and childless wives to us (this was done by the female assistant and myself). Access to these men and women are important because of societal influences. The authorities are well respected in the role as the elders of clan and kinship ascribed in traditional practice based on the research investigation.

However, 5 eminent men and 5 eminent women supported the conduct of the interviews. Women (widows and childless wives) who consist of my local contacts formed the first wave of the semi-structured individual interviews. Interviews were held with the clan heads/women such as village chiefs, native rulers (traditional rulers), faith leaders, and other eminent women who had the knowledge about the customary laws of the area in order to determine whether strict patriarchal culture on women's inheritance and property rights can lead to psychosocial factors that lead to their mental distress. The opportunity was taken at these interviews to pose controversial questions around marriage, symbolic rites of passage, and customary rights of inheritance.

The main anthropological point here is that every survivor fundamentally feels insecure because male behaviour is rooted in the control of land and property in Nigeria. The difference and attitude towards customary rights, which Igbo tradition exhibit towards women, show that the traditional belief is more restrictive. Traditional widowhood rituals are particularly negative for women in general as the underlying assumption is that the widows are somehow responsible for their husband's death and must exculpate themselves by swearing an oath of innocence. Since women live in fear within the family, their struggle continues to manifest in various facets of strict tradition, which constitutes their subordination, rendering them dependent and property-less.

Eminent women (*umuokpu*)

Eminent women in the study are groups of women who must have contributed to household domestics, as a producer, consumer, and reproducer of the community. They depict the response to the psychological needs of their husbands and children, providing warmth and nurturing, as well as taking care of the household needs. In traditional societies where families are the basis for social organisation, many of the societal functions are carried out in the family with the advice of the eminent women to serve the community and not themselves. What this meant is that *umuokpu* are supporters of peace and consulted in cases of family conflict. However, as a principle in kinship political affairs within community, these women speak little when called, and as a category, they are jural minors. For example, no senior women are included in the company of chiefs and elders who try cases, and women cannot initiate cases on their own behalf. *Umuokpu* continue to intervene in women's and men's lives to ensure that communal values are adhered to.

From the interview I gathered from women, it provided an insight into some roles women play in family matters. But there is a limitation in women's exercise of power in comparison with their male counterparts. The issues of gender relations still indicate a lack of social security and feeling at home, in the traditional Igbo society, which seems to be the reason for women to desire men's companionship and protection (Field notes, 15 July 2006). It is interesting to note that eminent women come from different walks of life and are married with children. None of the members of the group during the interview mentioned that they were childless. The only widow among them described the 'traditional society' as rigid and governing social actions on a regular basis, and they establish and sustain patterns of inequality. For example, property, status, and organisations are embedded within authoritarian measures to maintain social control. The fear of authority can be considered to be essential barriers to women. Another female described 'authority' as an oppressive way of exercising dominance and control, which reinforces women's dependency (Field notes, 8 August 2006). This is where property rights still provide some limited access of family and lack the protective means of women's rights.

At the end of the interview, participants were asked to provide names of people who they felt would be important for me to interview, and in this way, the sample 'snowballed'. Some participants gave me contact names and numbers and some documents or internal reports which I would not otherwise have had access to. This strategy proved both useful and interesting. Personal recommendation did seem to help to open doors, and participants would often make remarks about the person who had suggested them; most times, people were happy to be included. Asking for suggestions not only generated the sample, but it was also a means of generating data about networks—who knows whom, who values whom, and perceptions of where and how an individual fits into the network. Comments often being 'you really need to talk to X about that' (e.g. local councillors) (Field notes, 27 June 2006). As the data collection proceeded, fewer new names were suggested. I had already interviewed or contacted many of the people or group who were suggested to me.

Informal conversations with five different NGO directors

All NGOs were cooperative in providing the following information. The NGO concerned is a coalition of eastern NGOs (CENGOs) working with the most devastated population who are deprived and neglected in the society. The local document and reports amongst others in the 'widowhood' and other incidents obtainable from the NGOs have shown that the consistent pattern of traditional practice on women is as a result of gender norms. The usefulness of the documents in the study reveals the negative attitude/perception in relation to cultural restriction and discrimination on women, which not only destabilised the psychosocial life of the people, but also affected the political system of the local community suggested for the study. In a face to face meeting with the directors, I discovered what is really important for the categories in the study by finding out how best to structure their problems. Interviews with the different directors left me with the impression of the marginalisation of women in rural areas.

The majority of the data collected was discussed extensively with five different professionals who represent a group of experts—stakeholders in the provision of information on human rights, health care, and social welfare of Nigerian women—in order to explore the traditional and self-care practices of the Igbo society and to formulate an accurate and reality-anchored picture of the nature of the health and social-care system operating in Nigeria. Such background information would help health and social-care professionals, both local and national, make sense of the needs and behaviours of Igbo women under patriarchal traditional rules. The information provided by them integrates the legal, financial, and counselling support offered to the vulnerable or disadvantaged.

Documentary sources

In order to address the research objectives which are related to the adaptation process of widowhood practice, it was decided to examine the way in which the NGOs and local state documents projects their issues, especially literature resources, where most of the evidence about cultural and religious practices in connection to women's deprivation of inheritance and health issue is published in South-Eastern Nigeria. The articles derive from diverse anthropological, sociological, psychological, and legal paradigms that share common roots. The purpose of using documentary sources is to compare women's experiences. Analysis from the documentary source is integrated from the main informants. I made use of the documents from NGO material sources to draw similarities and differences on how patriarchal practices affect women. NGO sources were utilised to provide a contrast representing a perspective from foreigners working on a practical basis within the communities described in the research in direct contrast to the theoretical African sources.

The usefulness of the documentary sources provided an understanding of the effects of subordination of women and the experiences and interactions in terms of how women's rights over inheritance and property are undermined. It has been necessary, however, to contextualise this information and to be able to explore the adequacy of memories and accounts. This has been achieved by undertaking a number of interviews, which allow one to compare the accounts given, thus allowing the detail of the picture to be built. A mixture of media sources, including newspapers, journals, and government documentary sources were utilised to provide a rich variety of sources to inform the analysis.

Triangulation has been achieved through the combination of interview data, literature review, and the use of documentary sources (Denscombe, 2003; Gomm, 2004). Ritchie and Lewis (2003:35) has argued that documentary sources are appropriate where '. . . the history of events or experiences has relevance . . . This is pertinent as we are concerned with how and why particular events occurred and these can no longer be investigated by direct observation or questioning as they are in the past'. The participants in the study have been interviewed, and the documents, which highlight most of the evidence associated with their social problems, were also examined, for example, policy documents of CIRDDOC, WACOL, WON, and FORWARD, including 'Women and Customary Right of Inheritance Right, 2003' (A publication of CIRDDOC), archives 2004 report on 'Women's Economic Rights—Bill Against Harsh Widowhood Rites', and 'Fighting the scourge of stigmatization, 2005' (A publication of WACOL and WON). The FORWARD (2006) provides information for women's health issues and endorses positive traditional values but promotes the eradication of practices that prejudices women. Contacts with these organisations helped me generate information on the way in which women with deprived inheritance and property rights perceived their 'experiences' and how such feelings affected their loss of social status.

The examination of documents was undertaken, mindful of the pitfalls of that process. Similarly, Denscombe (2003:167) urges mindfulness in the use of documents, setting four criteria for consideration—authenticity, credibility, representation, and meaning.

Hitherto, exclusion of women from inheritance is believed to be the sociocultural root cause to lamentation, sadness, and misery. In this case, women's social and cultural factors become significant for the data. Reports produced by the NGOs and other African journals in the study showed mapping out the sources, critical decisions, and barriers identification of NGOs, and agencies and their affiliations—how and when they became involved in women's projects, challenges that affect their work, and circumstances that led to certain changes in the social network services for the disadvantaged groups.

Employment of female assistant

The female assistant was recruited with the help of the co-priest working in the three villages of the local community, and she was not paid for her duties but received expenses for meals and transportation. The research assistant was recruited based of the information on the study. She was recruited for three reasons. First, her position would enable participants to feel at ease while sharing their life stories throughout the interviews. Second, she was recruited in order to support my role as a male researcher and also to provide the necessary sociocultural information and explanation around women's world view within the community. Third, her presence would minimise the suspicion of villagers as a result of the bias associated with male-female social interaction.

As I planned the interviews, the female assistant was given an orientation (training) on how to conduct ethnographic semi-structured interviews and also to be familiar with the items on the questions and the expectations at every stage of the interview. Completing the aforementioned training is a way of being focused and detailed in conducting the interview. In addition, the assistant had some degree of research knowledge acquired during her higher education. She was a married secondary school teacher in the community with children, and so she had experience of interviewing and/or helping people complete questionnaires. In addition, she was recruited for the study because of her community studies and working as part time with the JDPC based with the disadvantaged groups. The research assistant was asked to keep notes about the interview encounter. She recorded the place and time of interview and the context within which it happened. For example, if the interview took place in the village hall, she will be asked to describe the physical surroundings, paying particular attention to any cultural symbols and to note whether anyone else was present during the interview, whether there were any interruptions, whether anything unusual happened and to note other observations which she considered significant. This helped me as a researcher to gain a better insight of the interview content. However, the nature of my research was to familiarise myself with the study, and it was the best way our interviews could help generate knowledge and other research skills to achieve success. At the early stages of the interview, which I facilitated and handled, the female assistant offered insights and made practical suggestions in some of the areas on which I needed her attention. In this way, her role contributed to the success and facilitated the improvement of the data collection tools.

Transcribing, translating, and back translating the interview data

Almost all the interviews were conducted in the local dialect. The female assistant and I translated and transcribed the interviews from the Igbo language into English. In order to assure the quality of translations, my research assistant double translated randomly selected transcripts and was back translated again to vernacular, which is the local dialect. One of the supervisors of the study compared the two Igbo versions of each translation and was able to confirm their accuracy. It was found that although some expressions differed in the conceptual meaning, they remained true to the original transcript.

3.5 Research setting and sample populations

My visit to the three villages shows that patrilineal kinship systems, cultures, and religious practices were located at the centre of the people's world view. Evidence to the patriarchal rituals and belief is connected to *Ala* (land or earth goddess), according to religion, is sacred which represents to the 'fertility' of the community. The village republican structure is patrilineal and patrilocal, and hence family life is centred on the lineage (*umunna*) as defined through male descendants and reinforced by the inheritance law and practice. Upon marriage, husbands and families exchange bride price for the reproductive and productive capabilities of women. One of the best angles from which to see villagers as they are is that of people trying to actualise their innate inclination in a dynamic interaction with their environment and their neighbours.

The community is divided into three villages with different religious denominations such as Roman Catholic Church, Anglican, Pentecostal, and Animists. However, each village have specific attributes for which it is known, a specific contribution that it made to the overall well-being of the entire local community such as military prowess, maintenance of an oracle (traditional deity) and belief system. I lived in old Aguata Local Government Area where the town was carved out to join Orumba North (local government area). Geographically, many towns and villages, which surround the community, are agrarian oriented both in the west and eastern south of Awka. Parallel to this is one of the daily markets, which serves the entire community and its surrounding towns and villages. Alongside the market are the motor park, shops, and restaurants situated along the corners of the roads.

The people of this community are very hospitable, friendly and moderately enterprising. They can be regarded as a semi-urban set up. I see the local community as a busy area with roadside restaurants, shops, and places of worship. They could be very religious and often are prepared to die for what they belief in. Farming has remained one of the main occupations of the people, and their products have always been found in different markets amongst the neighbouring towns. The raw material for making local mats and baskets grows in abundance in the local community. The town is 35 km away from the northwest of Anambra state capital city. I began my day trip of the fieldwork (interview) in the evening because villagers attend to their businesses and farming usually in the morning hours. By evening from 5 p.m. GMT local time, everybody is expected to be at home, which is when I usually started off conducting the interviews. Part of my observation with the environment is the level of poverty, which is high amongst widowed families with children, especially those with a low-economic standard of living. There is poor infrastructure and lack of social amenities such as erratic supplies of electricity, pipe-borne water, and health-care facilities. However, mountains, valleys, and erosion sites highlight the scenic beauty of the town. There are no industries, and this presented the picture of migration of young adults into the cities to look for job and further their education. On one side of the road, you can spot an elderly woman carrying a large amount of firewood on her head from a farm or perhaps a smiling boy walking barefoot hawking peanuts, oranges, and ripe bananas. For instance, as a result of the low socio-economic situation, few of the widows could afford the fees to send their children to school, and this would affect the economic status of the family in a negatively.

The colonialism and post-colonial experiences such as early missionaries and civil war has had considerable influence on the social and political life of the community. Aside from this, cases of superstitious and ritual belief provide some of the explanations attributed to sorcery, witchcraft, and causation of certain mysterious death, misfortunes, illnesses, and diseases which raises fear and anxiety amongst the population. In order to ward off curses or suspected evil attack, traditional healers (local medicine man or *dibia*) are consulted. Communities in this region feel strongly that religion and spiritual resources are relevant to their coping behaviour than Western medicine.

Another observation encountered is the issue of ostracism or cultural restriction associated with widowhood. Such practice is perceived within a religious context and sanctioned by a religious framework. To say the least, women in this community develop fear regarding the cleansing rite, bearing in mind the unhygienic techniques from the sexual cleanser and unsafe sexual practices, which could lead to the spread of HIV infection. The prevalence of alcoholism in the community is another catalyst for unsafe sexual practices, which was dehumanising in that victims in most cases mask themselves by not wanting to talk about it because of feeling of shame of disowning their culture.

As I reached the interview site, I was worried about how to behave, especially when interviewing women. There is a stereotype that surrounds the male-female communication in the local community. This raises gossip, suspicion, and false allegations. It is a discomforting experience that male researchers go through. I handled this issue through the recruitment of a female assistant and conducted interviews in the village town hall rather than in private homes. This protected my position as researcher in maintaining boundaries and neutrality. The location of the village hall is important because of the participants' safety. However, the location was found very remote from the people's residence. The choice of the location provided room for personal privacy and respect to participants' safety. Additionally, I felt it is important to take such a decision in order to protect my integrity and safety as a male researcher from the unforeseen circumstances from the local residents.

The next step was to consider whom to include within my sample. This would be a purposeful, rather than random sample, as my priority was to include those from a specific background. Davies (2007:146) recommends that core samples should include a range of people that will allow you to explore different comparative experiences relevant to your question. Some, whom you know in advance, will present data that may challenge the assumptions you find yourself making.

Taking this into consideration, I knew that as I come from a sociological model of approach, I should include participants from specific areas for the study as well as those who have a more systemic knowledge of social and religious context and also cultural issues. I also wanted to include at least five NGOs who have lawyers, social workers, psychologists, counsellors and teachers as their participants' understanding could be particularly relevant to my personal theoretical perspectives and hypothesis. A special reference was made to the development of knowledge and experience from their suggestions and referrals over time. The research has therefore been undertaken by looking for patterns and associations derived from observations.

Many of the laws, administrative policies, actions and attitudes associated with widowhood and widows represent the areas in which NGOs such as WACOL and Legal Women of Nigeria (WON) operate in providing counselling and financial aid to disadvantaged groups. Thus, most of the NGOs had been involved in the implementation of 'Building a Better Life for Women' (WACOL Report, 2007) and the updated strategy. There are two non-profitable organisations—one concerned with harmful traditions on women and the other concerned with legislation, policy, and implementation. It has been equally important to pursue both areas and to ensure that each has been sufficiently considered and given equal priority in regard to their importance to women's rights. Rural communities are where violence on women still shows a social divide associated with disinheritance and women's 'dependency' also contributed to the selection. With this in mind, I feel my data collection might be valuable to the study. No additional interviews were undertaken once participants began consistently telling similar stories; it was felt at this stage that 'saturation' (Ritchie and Lewis, 2003) had taken place, and there were no further 'unexplained' areas to pursue.

Sampling can only be used when the target population is involved in some kind of network with others who share the characteristic of interest; in this case, many people were connected. According to Arbor (2001), there are both strengths and a potential weakness in this approach. One advantage is that it reveals a network of contacts that can be studied. Within this study, what was interesting was not just the participants who were nominated, but those who were not (areas of omissions are significant). The 'omissions' here are significant for me because it raised my awareness of tensions within the family and community. However, I recognised that these omissions could be because there are underlined psychological pressures. Although I bore this in mind and it informed my research, I felt that this aspect could distract me from the main focus of my study. The possible reasons for these omissions (e.g. the 'value' assigned to another individual's opinion or role) became more apparent as the study progressed and the nature of the relationships between participants was revealed. As snowballing involves personal recommendations that vouch for the legitimacy of the researcher, it is an approach frequently used when trying to find a sample of people with stigmatised behaviour (Lee, 1993). In this study, it was used to help open doors that otherwise may have remained shut. The study was significant and politically sensitive because participants vouched for my credibility to protect their interest as a 'proper' researcher. In this way participants were assured of confidentiality and anonymity.

It was important to include people who were involved from the 'outset' and could be instrumental in the research. Furthermore, it was essential to include people from different sectors or organisations, for example, stakeholders with strategic responsibilities and with an overview of the process, as well as those who were responsible for delivery. From the outset, it was envisaged that the majority of the participants were more willing to share their experiences. Initially, I thought I would go into the interview with more confidence and clarity as I was aware that I would only get one chance and wanted to be able to make the optimum use of it. Nevertheless, personal contacts and meetings enabled me to gather information needed for the analysis.

Recruitment and selection strategies

To ensure my professional position as a researcher, I wanted to use particular recruitment and selection strategies to identify my participants and also ensure the nature of information from widows and childless wives, eminent people and NGOs to generate cultural knowledge. In the selection also, I became aware of the inclusion and exclusion criteria in order to reduce the risks to participants. The following criteria were set.

Inclusion Criteria for Participants

- Participants from eighteen years upwards
- To have the capability to provide all the necessary information about the study
- Ability to give informed consent to researchers'
- Willingness to discuss their experiences and views to the researcher
- Willingness to be tape-recorded during the interview

Exclusion Criteria for Participants

- Under the age of eighteen years of age
- If it is too painful or psychologically intrusive to recall memories in accordance with the research topic
- People with learning difficulties who cannot retain conversation (stereotypical rather than experience-informed perspective may be given)

Thus, I felt conducting an important research of this nature requires taken these important processes of selection strategies. As a researcher, I felt that it would have been beneficial to the research to spend more time building up a relationship with the key participants. Due to time limitations, it was not possible to engage with each organisation for more than the period of introducing the research and carrying out the interviews. In this way, I wondered if there had been more of a long-term relationship, I would have heard different responses from the participants.

Once confirmation of willingness to take part was received, I was able to contact participants and organise meetings with them in order to prepare for the in-depth interview. The village was used to identify kinship and community and trace address or residence of participants for selection. The interviews were held in a village hall as I sensed the good atmosphere of the environment and area of location, which is more secure and allows room for people's privacy. As I arrived at the interview, the participants were as friendly as they were during the previous meeting. I was happy and relieved that they were still willing to take part. In this way, the interview could be successfully audio-recorded and would ensure the participants' and researcher's safety.

The audio-recordings were transcribed within two days of the interview to maintain accurate ethnographic information. Once the research project has been completed, a summary of the findings will be given to all participants.

After completing the first three interviews, the data gained was transcribed and analysed. By using the interviews as a pilot, I ensured that the questions I was asking were enabling me to answer the research question. As the data from these interviews provided me with the data I required, I was able to conclude that the interview schedule was satisfactory, and I could use the initial three interviews carried out to inform the results. However, I did modify the way that some of the questions were asked to ensure that clarity was provided to the participants. As I gained more understanding of what questions worked and which ones required further explanation, I amended the delivery of the questions accordingly.

As the interviews progressed, my confidence and ability as a researcher improved. In this way, I felt that the research topic was challenging in that I was engaging with a vulnerable population and discussing potentially cultural and sensitive issues. It is acknowledged that as this is the first time I have completed ethnographic research, I was learning and refining my skills during the process. At all times, I reflected on my role as a researcher to consistently maintain the integrity of the information.

Given that I wanted to obtain an in-depth understanding of traditional practices on women and wanted to be able to discuss these perspectives in detail, I decided that I should take an in-depth semi-structured interviews with participants from different works of life: widows, childless wives, eminent groups—clan heads, traditional chiefs and titled men and eminent women (*umuokpu*) and NGOs (e.g. CIRDDOC, WACOL, WON) working with vulnerable women in South-Eastern Nigeria. Bell (1999:70) indicates that '[a] major advantage of the interview is in its adaptability. A skilful interviewer can follow up ideas, probe responses and investigate motives and feelings, which questionnaires can never do'. For this study, an ethnographic semi-structured design was used. An ethnographic approach is well suited to questions that require exploration and where there is a need for a detailed close-up view for studying groups in their natural setting. It helps to create situations in an effort to understand how disadvantaged groups or individuals attempt to make sense of social events and the cause of certain behaviour (Lyons and Coyle, 2007).

Widows

A woman is pronounced a widow at the death of her husband and has an obligation to mourn her husband for a specific period of time (usually a minimum of six months). According to the classic customary law and practice, she may not adorn herself with jewellery, cosmetics, and all sorts of perfumes or scented oil or any other means that relate to her hygienic lifestyle. In Igboland, however, customs seemed to have triumphed over statutory law, and stringent mourning observances are imposed on widows. Additionally, cultural restrictions in inheritance and property relations have been a subject of much controversy around widowhood, and only through the rites of passage (*ime ajadu*) can a widow secure inheritance and protection of her children among other things. Thus, failure to observe the stipulated periods of mourning, which vary according to the circumstances, or to behave in the required manner earns the widow ostracism or hostility of the family and the local community, who may even accuse her of causing her husband's death.

Childless wives

A childless wife, according to the local custom, is socially perceived as barren. The issue of infertility is a sign of poor reproductive health, which prevents women from gaining access to family and community services such as inheritance and property relations. It is argued that childbearing in patriarchal and kinship system in Igboland determines woman fecundity (womanhood). Unfortunately, a childless marriage, which is usually a source of disappointment, is often blamed on women irrespective of the fact that the problem could be a result of male impotency. In many African societies, especially in the Igboland, 'male barrenness' is a taboo and not to be discussed.

To understand our motivation for this emphasis in the rural community, one has to understand the situation the vulnerable Igbo women face. Household tasks are extremely labour intensive and almost all of them fall to women. They cook over charcoal fires, wash clothes by hand, and tote water for drinking and bathing. Igbo women also play a central role in agriculture because they plant and harvest crops as well as raise livestock. Most Igbo women must also find ways to earn an income and find work in the open-air markets where the poor shop. Moreover, many women raise their children alone with little or no support from a man. Mothers go to great lengths to send their children to school, making sacrifices to pay fees as they want so badly to provide their children with a brighter future. Whatever wages they earn goes towards feeding and educating their children.

Eminent men (clan heads)

The clan heads are the custodians of the culture who interpret customary law and influence any decision-making in kinship practice. They are perceived as spiritual head or authority of the local community that must be respected in terms of social and political matters. However, cultural issues, especially marriage, land, and inheritance, as well as widowhood practices, are the underlying areas of specific laws that oversee the traditional practice in Igboland.

Eminent women (*umuokpu*)

In Igboland, women folk contribute to the welfare of the local community by exercising the roles through the maintenance of social and political rules. They serve as producers, consumers, and reproducers of the community. Similarly, through their social organisation, many of the societal activities in the household are carried out, and they could be advisors to the traditional chiefs and titled men in terms of women's issues. This means that the *umuokpu* are supporters of peace and provide counselling based on family conflict and resolution. It is interesting to note that eminent women represent different categories of women in terms of marital status, childbearing, education, and trading in their villages. *Umuopku* continue to intervene in women's and men's life in order to ensure that family and communal values are adhered to.

Non-governmental organisations

In this study, it is pertinent to highlight the roles of NGOs—organisation-based records, such as abuse complaints and records of violence and victim-based records, such as those complied by asking representatives samples of persons whether they have been victimised with issues that are derived from the existence of the vulnerable population within the traditional practices and the society and life in modern Igbo society. The data collected from the multi-agency will aid in the proper documentation of the analysis. It is essential to utilise these sources as they are generally useful within the context of a rigorous quality control process. Despite the fact that they are not traditional academic sources, they are often written by academicians and linked to other peer-reviewed journals as they share knowledge and provide more information from a comparative perspective on a particular social issue.

The NGO is a coalition of CENGOS working with the most devastated population who are deprived and neglected in the society. These organisations, such as CIRDDOC, WACOL, WON, and FORWARD have worked for more than twelve years within the south-eastern region and have provided documents and related information for women's right and reproductive health issues, and they recommend legislation and social policy on positive traditional values but promote the eradication of practices that are harmful to women, especially the widowhood practice. The documentary review provided me with an in-depth understanding of how traditional practices influence women's customary rights and interactions in terms of how women's rights over inheritance and property are undermined.

I made use of the selected documents from NGOs material in order to look at areas of similarities and differences for my analysis. It has been necessary, however, to contextualise this information and be able to explore the adequacy of memories and accounts of the experiences of the vulnerable position of women. I wanted to use a semi-structured model of interview, which is a face to face encounter, in order to engage, listen, and observe how my participants narrate their stories. The usefulness allows the representation of the accounts given and thus allows the detail of the picture of their experiences to be built.

I purposely chose widows and childless wives in the study in order to investigate whether patriarchy can negatively affect women's social status and also any other influence associated with their mental distress (*Ariri*) in Igboland. However, I was interested in the role of eminent people especially the way customary law is interpreted and how inheritance and also reproductive health of women have been overlooked. Additionally, social, economic, psychological, and human rights represent the way violations of women's rights were given priority. Another approach was looking at the documents in order to examine critical decisions of cases and barrier identification of NGOs in relation to how and when they became involved in women's project, challenges that affect their work, and circumstances that led to certain changes in working with the vulnerable population. From the personal contacts and meetings with different groups in the study, I came to realise the divergence of opinion on how women are treated, given that many feel that women now have the opportunity to express their abuse-related violence.

3.6   Ethical issues

The study gained ethical approval from the ethics committee of the School of Health and Social Sciences (SHSS), Middlesex University, before potential participants were approached and invited to participate within the research. The majority of participants have never had access to basic education, and so the researcher, accompanied by the female research assistant, read the consent form aloud in the local dialect to ensure full comprehension of the interview guidelines. However, ethics were not treated as a separate part of this research once consent was gained from the ethics committee. Ethics are integral to this research and are intertwined in the approach to this research in the way questions are asked, how answers are responded to, and the way the material is reflected upon. An implicit part of ethical practice thus involves the acknowledgement and location of the researcher within the research process. The British Sociological Association (2002) guidelines to ethical issues are used to account for participant protection and data dissemination of knowledge. The ethics summarise the basic principles such as consent and freedom of participants as well as safety issues in relation to reduction of the risk to researchers. However, research participants are protected by confidentiality and anonymity. This explains, for example, Data Protection Acts and Human Rights Act, which may affect the progress of the research. In this context, none of the participants were exposed to any physical harm. Similarly, Davies and Dodd (2002) perceive ethics to be always in progress and never to be taken for granted, is flexible, and responsive to change. They argue that there should be an emphasis on a sense of empathy and imagination, rather than on demonstrating a deductive and calculative reasoning.

The application and approval required me to be organised within the timescale. It was successful, and the guidance helped me in the preliminary interview in 2006 in south-eastern region of Nigeria. All tape-recordings for the purposes of interviewing were destroyed after twelve months of the interview period. The experience taught me the importance of starting the research process early and building in sufficient time to allow for significant delays. I became aware of the ethical importance of conducting a social science research by upholding public trust and confidentiality, and I felt that I was representing the ethics committee within the research capacity. On the part of the researcher, ethics involves truthfulness, openness, honesty, respectfulness, carefulness, and constant attentiveness.

The participants were identified by a co-pastor, having been previously briefed by the researcher as to the nature of the information required.

As part of this process, I developed field explanatory notes for my interviewees, informing them of the nature of my study and that all data would be anonymised and destroyed after my Ph.D. thesis had been submitted to the exam board and asking them for permission to make a tape-recording of the interview and to use direct quotes. From the outset, participants remained as informed as possible, regarding the study and ensuring that this was done in a clear, concise, and non-judgemental manner. At times, there was a balance between ensuring that participants knew enough about the study without providing too much detailed information that it became overly complex and confusing.

The construction of the sample of village women raises ethical issues. The status of the researcher and the authority of the eminent women involved in identifying and approaching the potential participants may on reflection have been experienced by the women, initially at least, as a pressure to participate. The research methods limited the gender-power aspect by involving the eminent women and the female assistants, but in the early stages of the research, the possible influences of the status differences were not addressed. Nevertheless, as noted below, the participants were informed of the subject of the interviews and were made aware that they could opt out at any time so informed consent was achieved.

In addition, the researcher was aware that because of his position, the participants may have given answers that they believed the researcher wanted to hear. The researcher achieved the collective salient points from the participants by letting the participants speak freely with a minimum of interruption to ensure non-value judgements on the part of the researcher. This, in turn, facilitated the analysis of data to ensure as much veracity as possible.

At all times, consideration was made for the sensitive nature of the study, for example, in terms of potential psychological intrusion from the interview. The questions used within the semi-structured interviews related to participants' experiences and thus the risk of psychological intrusion should be minimal. However, as participants may have been women with *Ariri*, the subject matter could be sensitive, and thus there is the potential for a misunderstanding of cultural and social boundaries. To minimise risk, the research was carried out into Igbo tradition and culture, and this information was used to ensure that a non-judgemental approach is taken, and introduction session on the subject matter of the interview is well explained to the participants. All participants were made aware that they could opt out at any time if they wished to do so. The researcher also acknowledges that he has a role to play: if the interview did become too upsetting or difficult for the participant, then the researcher was aware that he could terminate the interview. In addition, the researcher ensured that the interview questions were as straightforward as possible and were as least likely as possible to be misconstrued. Importantly, the researcher tried to ensure that he did not make cultural assumptions during the interviews; rather, if he was unclear, he tried to adequately probe to ensure that the true meaning was established. However, it was anticipated that as a 'male' researcher, it would be 'necessary' and 'advantageous' to include a female assistant during my interviews with these vulnerable women. It was necessary to ensure I was chaperoned and 'advantageous' because she would be able to open up and elucidate areas of their lives, which as a man, I may not be aware of.

Freedom from exploitation means that any new information gained from the study will not be used against the participants in any way. This is particularly relevant when dealing with such vulnerable people. It was therefore important that all participants were fully informed of the aims of the study and the extent of their involvement. With regards to the risk/benefits ratio, the researchers and the study's steering committee or advisory group agreed that such a study would provide important data, which will ultimately benefit the participants.

The principle of respect for human dignity includes the right to self-determination, the right to full disclosure, and the right of informed consent. A person's right to self-determination means that the person decides voluntarily and without any pressure or force to be involved and to terminate his/her involvement at any stage she wants without incurring any problem. This right is closely linked to the rights to full disclosure and informed consent. The participants of this study were provided with all the necessary information regarding their participation and their consent was ascertained prior to any involvement. As Duke (2002) notes that there are ways of using the physical space so that the researcher and participants are in more 'equal' and 'neutral' positions. Bearing this in mind, I ensured that, with my female assistant whom I introduced, we sat in similar-sized chairs, face to face with each participant, and no one else was present. I also mentioned that his was a confidential environment and that all information used in the study would appear anonymously. They were also offered the opportunity of being interviewed by the female assistant of the study team if they so wished.

The principle of human justice includes the rights to fair treatment and privacy. This was highlighted to the female assistant to ensure fair and non-discriminatory practice based on the requirements of the research. The existence of a semi-structured interview is aimed at fairness by ensuring that similar information was collected from each participant in a similar way. The right to privacy means that the information from the interview will not be disclosed to others. Participants were assured of their anonymity and confidentiality of any information they provided.

3.7   Data analysis and validation

Data collection and analysis are intertwined in qualitative study. Davies (2007) suggests that there are three main methods of analysing qualitative data—that of content analysis, a study of written materials, that is, diaries, thematic analysis, a look at the social meaning within a conversation or interview, and linguistic analysis, where the use of language is considered. My study question is based on a number of themes that I am particularly interested in, where violence and abuse are related to deprivation of inheritance and property relations. The data was obtained through the use of interviews—an analysis based on a thematic approach seemed to be the most relevant analysis style for me to use. Braun and Clarke (2006:97) write that '[y]our method of analysis should be driven by both your research question and your broader theoretical assumptions'.

The key themes at the beginning of my study were that I wanted to consider my participants' personal opinion and how there social status was influenced by patriarchal and kinship practice on inheritance and property relations. I wanted to look at the wider aspects of what is considered to constitute harmful practice associated with abuse and emotional distress (*Ariri*) and given their opinions on the above, what type of coping mechanisms for women with *Ariri* would different professionals see as being the most appropriate with their specific need.

Thematic analysis is a flexible way of reflecting on reality and untangles the surface of reality (Braun and Clarke, 2006). In this way, themes were used to analyse the data as it allows for the identification, analysis, and reporting of patterns within the data and ensuring that the researcher's own preconceived ideas do not bias the data (Braun and Clarke, 2006). Themes do not passively emerge from the data; rather, the researcher plays an active role in identifying patterns. Having read much into this area and naturally having views and opinions on the topic, the researcher acknowledges that without a fixed approach to developing themes, predetermined ideas would impact the results.

By ensuring that readers know how the data was analysed or what assumptions informed the analysis, clarity can be provided on the study. This means that throughout my data collection, a constant comparative process of defining and redefining any emerging themes in the light of new data was utilised with other studies on the topic and used to inform other research carried out in the future (Braun and Clarke, 2006). The emerging themes were then elaborated conceptually both from the data and by using theoretical and empirical constructions from the literature (Patton, 1990). The female research assistant and the researcher who conducted the interviews performed the initial analysis of the interview data. Their views, important issues, and themes after each interview were documented. Following this, all transcripts were being transferred into qualitative data analysis software (NVivo 7) and coded using emerging themes from the initial analysis.

In the process of analysis, the first fifteen transcripts were completed and random samples of six transcripts were printed out for independent manual analysis. The analysis was then compared for similarities and differences and a new, more refined coding framework was developed. This was used to code the remainder of the transcripts as they became available. The views of the researcher continued to be taken into consideration, and any new emerging issues were added to the coding framework.

Preliminary Mapping of Networks Concerned with Women's Projects

- Overlapping and interconnections (organisations and agencies)
- Identification of potential participant (marginalised groups)

The documentary review has identified a series of activities involving the NGOs with the disadvantaged groups in South-Eastern Nigeria. The organisations use seminars, conferences, and workshops on 'women's rights and health' to coordinate their publications. It is a forum where the organisation disseminates information on the impact of power and politics in tradition; local custom and religious practices become instrumental in looking at the many roles of women in Igboland. In the process, local customs of inheritance and property rights have succeeded in excluding widows and childless wives at the marginal existence. However, whilst most of the other traditional practices like killing of twins became inactive, land and property has managed to hold its own against the marginalised groups. The documentary review suggests that social exclusion is a vehicle for understanding the disadvantaged groups with less social status. It reveals how violence enables these groups of women to occasionally use moments of lamentation (*Ikwa Ariri*) to express their sadness, unhappiness, and miserable condition within the society. The information from the review is a useful in developing the findings and analysis of the data. The descriptive analysis will be used to demonstrate where possible relationships, associations, and explored differences. I will also be extracting the data from the interviews thus creating rigorous thematic analysis.

The documentary review and analysis were interconnected. The first reading of documents helped identify what issues need to be explored as part of the study analysis. The first step in identifying a potential organisation was to examine information about their projects and look into their working modalities with the disadvantaged groups. Personal contact and meetings with the executive directors of CIRDDOC, WACOL, and WON helped to ascertain how the organisations operate, what they have done, and what has not been done in relation to the social exclusion and marginalisation of property rights of these women. However, the key method I used to contact these groups was through interview and personal contacts to promote the aims and objectives in working with the female population. The major work of the organisations includes advocacy, counselling, developing their skills and education, offering confidential advice, and information on health issues. From the personal contact and meetings with the stakeholders of the managements, I learnt that the organisations have been established to support the changing roles of women in local communities. I believe this manifests itself in a wide divergence of opinion on how women are treated given that many feel that women have now had the opportunity to express their abuse-related violence.

By using structured questions to frame my interviews, I was able to clearly see the differences of the participants' opinions in their answers to these questions. I could then compare this to my expectations of each participant's perspective, having gained information from my literature search on different theoretical backgrounds of the NGOs working with the vulnerable population within a natural or environmental setting. Hitherto, what sustained and expanded the goals of the organisation was social inclusion and empowering women, which was important in a society where marginalisation and exclusion created social divides. It is suggested that people look for help when they are disadvantaged, and these groups provide the support and understanding they need. The NGOs recognised the violation of the inheritance and property rights and worked towards minimising all forms of violence towards women in families. With time, I became familiar with some individuals who introduced me to other networking systems to work with the vulnerable population in Nigeria. The organisations also provided practical realisation of the human rights of women with other forms of legal support to assist women in their marginalisation.

3.8   Verification of data analysis

To analyse the data using thematic analysis, after all the interviews were transcribed, a six-stage process was used (Braun and Clarke, 2006).

Gain Familiarity with the Data: This involved me, as a researcher, immersing myself in the data to ensure that I was familiar with both the depth and breadth of the content. I read and reread the transcripts, starting to mark ideas for coding as I went along.

The style of data collection and analysis were designed to enable me to obtain a deeper understanding of 'women with *Ariri*' for the study. The theoretical standpoints enable me to compare women's vulnerable position with the information that I had obtained from my literature, which show the predominant characteristics of the psychosocial condition evident in economic dispossession that advances low social status. Most indicators are associated with poverty, sadness, frustration, and despair, which increase rural exposure of cultural restriction on women that are common and evident in the traditional practice. Additionally, the relationship regarding gender suggests that women with *Ariri* lack protection. This leads to the most common ideology of women's subordination and inferiority associated with their vulnerability and low self-esteem.

On Each Interview Transcript Interesting Features of the Data Were Coded: This is the stage when more formal coding of the data took place. The researcher in the role of the analyst coded the data that appeared interesting. The codes 'can be regarded as the most basic segment or element of the raw data or information that can be assessed in a meaningful way' (Boyatzis, 1998:63). However, notably, codes differ from the themes, which were often broader. To highlight codes, I worked systematically through the data, trying to ensure that equal attention was given to each data item and that interesting aspects of the data items were formed on the basis of repeated patterns.

I was able to use Kleinman's Explanatory Model to influence how I organised my data for analysis. I wanted to use Kleinman's model because it provides the basis of eliciting and analysing the stories that people (participants) construct to make sense of a condition within the context of their culture. Factors/criteria selected respond to questions and queries from interviews such as: 'What does your illness or condition meant to you?' or 'Do you feel close to your family?' or 'Have you received any form of assistance for your condition?' or 'What do you hope to achieve from this condition?' It helps to stimulate researchers' interaction with the participants in order to obtain optimum information for the study. Each of the question helps to indicate events which have occurred in survivor's lives. Additionally, Kleinman's model creates a unique structure and provides room for flexibility when applying different techniques appropriate to the research context to elicit individual and collective perceptions of their condition in an ethnographic manner.

Sort Codes Into Potential Themes Considering How Different Codes May Combine to Form an Overarching Theme: When all the codes were collected and collated into a list, I sorted the codes into potential themes. In order to do this, the codes were cut out and placed on different pieces of paper, which were labelled as potential themes; in this way, I sorted and re-sorted the codes and themes as I went along. Within this process, some codes formed main themes, others sub-themes, and some were disregarded.

Immediately after the interviews, discussions with the female assistant and clarifications of issues that emerged were ratified and detailed notes were taken. I promised to update the participants and eminent persons with the research progress, publication, and provision of the research materials. Six months later, I contacted the co-priest and the female assistant and communicated my study updates to them. Plans for the next interviews were scheduled with the female assistant. There were also opportunities for more informal discussion.

Review and Redefine the Themes: The themes were reviewed as it may have been possible that some themes were not actually themes; other themes may have merged into one theme, and some themes were broken down into a number of themes. During this stage, I was able to ensure that consideration was given to the themes so that they accurately reflected the data. This involved reviewing at the level of the coded theme and ensuring that the themes form a coherent pattern.

Define the Themes and Further Refine Them and Analysing the Data Within Them: This involved identifying what each theme was about and determining what aspect of the data each theme captures. Then, I was able to write the detailed analysis, working out what each theme related to and linking it into the broader research question. It was important to ensure that the themes were also considered in relation to each other, ensuring that there was not too much overlap.

Write the Research Report: Once the themes were fully worked out, I was able to complete the final analysis, and I started to write up the report, providing the information on the data in a concise manner. The stages above were completed independently. With hindsight, it may have been beneficial to have feedback from eminent people and NGOs to provide an independent critical reflection on the themes highlighted and ensure that cultural assumptions were not made.

3.9   Validation of the interview analysis

The validity of the analysis of the interview data was achieved through researcher triangulation and through comparisons with published literature. Furthermore, the preliminary findings were presented at two peer-reviewed conferences, which provided an opportunity for discussion, reflection, and validation.

Throughout the process of research, steps were taken to check the accuracy and credibility of the findings (their validity). Given the methodological rigour, which is described in this chapter, and contribution from the research assistant which include information from both 'insiders' (participants) and 'outsiders' (non-participants), the outcome of the research so far shows that the findings have truth value (credibility), are dependable (reliability), and are applicable to the rest of the local Nigerian women (generalisability).

The quantitative data

Qualitative data collected through the questionnaire provided basic information on a social and cultural context of the community. Simple descriptive analysis was performed and, where possible, relationships and associations were explored. It was found significant in the relevant findings.

Data storage

Tape-recordings or hard copies of information were stored in a locked drawer within a locked room, for which, as a researcher, I had access and a copy of the keys. Electronic information (such as transcripts) was stored in documents that required a password to access them, and only the researcher was aware of the password. Wherever possible, information held during the study period was made anonymous to ensure maximum safety.

In accordance with the fifth principle of the Data Protection Act (1998), personal data processed must not be kept longer than necessary (Brammer, 2007:12). The plans for disposal of information include the following:

1.   Paper will be shredded and placed in confidential bins.
2.   Electronic records will be permanently deleted.
3.   Audio tapes will be destroyed before placing in confidential bins.

3.10 Reflexivity

The next step in the process was reflection of my own position as a male researcher which enabled me to resolve some of the challenges I faced. This would be looking at the whole research setting, which provide women's local stories as context and how women's experiences create patterns and the characteristics of material and social circumstances that connect with inequality and emotional abuse. In the interview, I recognised that women's lack of power is not given enough attention, especially where their own issues are not fully represented. In this situation, many of the women have never even stopped to think about their traumatic experiences. When asking a widow whether her deceased husband's family is maintaining her, she claimed that no member had given them a penny since the husband's death nearly four years ago. It was alleged that as a result of the family's negligence and maltreatment, the widows were exhibiting signs of frustration, and some of them were still a burden on their natural family who were contemplating court action against the deceased husband's family.

A widow's right of inheritance has been a challenge in recent times, which has not received due attention from the magistrate or superior courts in Nigeria. The situation of a Nigerian widow of a customary marriage is still problematic because she has not received adequate provision in the distribution of her deceased husband's intestate estate. The recognition of difference, from a shared experience, provided detailed information on violence related to cultural practices. It enables me as an ethnographic researcher to address pluralistic experiences of a survivor's stressful condition in a comprehensive way.

Additionally, a childless case for a woman, especially in the contemporary Igbo society, is to have less status. My own experience about the condition of these women is that they are being maltreated in so many ways because of a suspicion of being 'witches' who are likely to have been married in the spirit world—water spirit or 'mammy water cult'. Practically, the childless condition of women causes emotional distress to a husband and other members of the extended family. The consequence of stigma particularly affects women, causing low self-esteem and denying couples respect and a stable marriage.

Women's experiences and suffering are something that has become a traditional norm. This stems from the Igbo belief prevalent among the people that a 'childless or sonless' marriage could jeopardise the life of the family and kin group. Traditionally, the fear of childlessness is frustrating to Igbo men. It stands as one of the key factors whereby men cannot withstand the shame by going to the extent of seeking for divorce or a second marriage because of the traditional belief structure that underpins the society.

My challenge as an ethnographer in conducting this study is the way some of the extreme traditionalists show their anxiety over maintaining domination and control over women in the local community. In the course of the interview, some of the traditionalists 'branded' me as brainwashing women with Western ideology. Part of this anxiety showed in their facial expression that women should not be exposed to Western education. When I asked the reason behind this motive, some of them still maintained that Western education is corrupt and cited the role of the early missionaries who conducted ethnographic interviews and misrepresented our culture by using women as a weapon to fight against our tradition and religious practices. Despite this comment, I still maintained my position as a researcher and one with the interest in the plight of women in conducting the interview. In this regard, I found the social and cultural experiences of adult survivors as a way of looking at the layers of what traditional practices look like and why traditional men still use their power to control women. Furthermore, I see the social environment of women in rural areas as a predictor of abuse and risks and that intensifies my curiosity about the reason why patriarchal society has not offered social support and services to improve women's customary rights. With the controversies around women in the traditional society, their experiences became learning tools in understanding the social position of women and the way women can be treated after the death of their husband.

The interview demonstrates also how patriarchal institutions play a strong part in women's productive and reproductive activities and the interpretation given as the cause of women's deprivation of inheritance and implication associated with women health issues. In the interview encounter, I became aware of this suffering experienced in relation to being disadvantaged and some of the discussions centred upon the psychosocial situation of women.

In the interview, I see women's experiences challenging in the conduct of the interview. Part of the social problem is that people who are dominated in one way or another find it difficult to talk about their experiences. In this regard, the awareness of women's situation requires my skilled knowledge and observation of the environment. This explains the reflective way of listening and demonstrating to them, in the interview, that I understood what was being said (e.g. by reflecting back in my own terms). However, the researcher wondered whether participants felt that he could understand the cultural and religious issues associated with the trauma that women experienced. Did this affect the problems of a male researcher dealing with female participants? At the time of the interview, the researcher felt that he did understand, however, on further reflection did the differences in culture and experiences mean that he only felt that he understood.

The researcher also wondered what impact his gender had on the way that he was viewed. Among the rural women, the role many women play in society is to look after the family and maintain the home; many are illiterate. Amidst the study carried out, the researcher felt that he was treated differently than what he expected as a male based upon the stereotypical perspectives of women within the local community. Furthermore, he wondered whether he was seen as a representative of the male dominant group within institutional structures. The researcher did not wish to be cynical of their warm hospitality but wondered if he was being viewed as powerful. During these steps, my role as a priest and researcher requires awareness of boundary and a suspension of judgment.

This study provides an insight into looking at the survival difficulties in relations to their traumatic experiences. For example, if women have their rights they will be empowered. Education has helped some to be resilience to survive. Social and family networks are important tools to this supportive scheme especially from the NGOs who have no need to exploit the property and inheritance rights of the vulnerable people.

As a Nigerian and from the Igbo ethnic group, I could see how patriarchal practices could influence women's status in the way this functioned in local communities and households. There is, therefore, a need for personal self-awareness. Furthermore, I was conscious of my feelings and, at the same time, ensured that it did not adversely affect my role as a researcher. As a researcher, I ensured that my perspective would be objective in the academic tradition. Therefore, the interview remained a pivotal for generating an in-depth knowledge where participants share their emotional experiences. In this way, conducting research on feminine issues becomes significant because it stipulates the notion that women's well-being is of paramount concern.

Access to interview is necessary for the success of the data collection. It looks to see if the goal has been achieved and how the relationship between the interviewer and interviewee is maintained. Cochrane (1998) indicates that without access there can be no research. At the initial stage of the interview, I was preoccupied with fear, doubt, and uncertainty—whether or not the participants would be allowed to turn up or not for the interview. As a male researcher, I became aware that doing feminine research takes into account experience, differences, and gender. All these form the history and social context which Riessman (1993) points out how ethnic and gender difference affects understanding in the interview. This is perhaps particularly true of the dilemma for the male researcher, who is perceived with male superiority and scepticism around his ability to grasp feminine issues. At the time, I did not give much thought to these enquiries but, on reflection, perhaps female domains seemed to be a strange choice for a man. Conversely, my role as a priest has meant that I have had dealings with both males and females, so interviewing females is not a complete departure from my usual role.

The processes set out for the interview helped me to be aware of my position as a priest and researcher and to be careful while conducting research and how I could attempt to handle every outcome from the difficulties in order to overcome any potential problems in the study. How the point of view of a priest as a researcher could affect the outcome of the interview was handled by employing a female assistant who would be part of the interview team (pre-interview and post-interview discussions. See ethical issues). I believe that women feel less threatened and give thorough explanations when there is a female colleague involved in the interview.

In this study I reflected on the differences between being a male and interviewing a female participant. Did the fact that being a male and priest alter how the participants response to the questions? Did I feel that I could not highlight the barriers because of the risk of them complaining of their culturally-specific problems? I related my shocked reactions to those situations and proved them further in an effort to understand participants' experiences. Being brought up in a traditional society, women's subordination (marginalisation) reminds me of several complaints families brought along during the office hours in the rural parish. The intervention of a priest can compound an already problematic situation. Having said that, a priest can also add a positive dimension to the situation in which the aggrieved parties can feel an added sense of reassurance. In this way, I begin to see how patriarchal practice influences women's social status, and I believe that such marginalisation of women could affect their poor living condition as well as their education. The interview procedure demands that my role has been to facilitate a process whereby the participants are enabled to articulate their own beliefs, feelings, emotional expression, and for me to interpret such expression as accurately as I can. In this way, my role should be to be aware of transference issues avoiding involvement in the participant's emotions, which could jeopardise the research and also to avoid willingness to change the situation of the participant's affliction and suffering. Dominelli (2002) talks about how social identity can impact on research, and the potential power that being a male researcher may bring and if he had been, for example, a male and indigenous priest, whether he would have been viewed the same way.

Additionally, to overcome the challenges as a male researcher, I would be more 'diplomatic', using the skill, tact, and awareness of my role in order to maintain detached objective views. I adopted this measure in order to highlight a degree of freedom granted to all participating members for whom the system of interview operates. These approaches enabled me to reflect on what I have learnt in both supervision in counselling, research methods, and other key support facilitation developed during the current research supervision.

As interviews progressed, some of the participants offered me some copies of documents on 'widowhood rites' in Igboland, whilst others made comments that I seemed to 'know my stuff'. As the interviews proceeded, my knowledge and confidence increased. Importantly, the 'barriers' enabled me to be sufficiently reflective in interviews—gathering materials, interpreting data, and being aware of my behaviour. In this way, researcher's reflexivity as an ethnographer becomes important in the processes of the interview.

By using the interviews as a pilot, the researcher ensured that the question he was asking was enabled him to answer the research question. As the data from these interviews provided him with the data he required, the researcher was able to conclude that the interview schedule was satisfactory and could use the initial two interviews carried out to inform the results. However, the researcher did modify the way that some of the questions were asked to ensure that clarity was provided to the participants. As he gained more understanding of what questions worked and which ones required further explanation, the researcher amended the delivery of the questions accordingly.

As the interviews progressed, his confidence and ability as a researcher improved. The researcher felt that the research topic was challenging in that he was engaging a vulnerable group within the local community and discussing a potentially difficult and social stereotype topic. It is acknowledged that as this is the first time the researcher has completed ethnographic research and was learning and refining his skills during this process. At all times, the researcher reflected on both himself and his actions to consistently maintain the integrity of the information.

As a male researcher and a priest, I was brought up in the local community like the women under this study. In this way, I understand the importance of local custom and practice and how it affects women's social status. Furthermore, I understand, on further reflection, the nature of the sensitivity of the culture, but still there is a danger of taken things for granted because of the way we cannot ask question on certain cultural issues as we are not use to it in Igboland. Fear of embarrassment also could be another possible way of raising the issue of challenge as a researcher.

Overcoming this presumption, I wanted to be conscious of the sensitivity of the local custom on women and at the same not to use it against them but to give meaning to their lives by valuing, respecting, and providing them with their dignity as a way of understanding them as they are, even when they do not understand or blame themselves. In this way, I beginning to see that the survivors as not responsible for the condition they are in or the things they have been forced to do. Similarly, I wanted to use this procedure in order to establish a relationship with my participants who will look at me as an 'insider' or 'outsider'. Equally, I discovered that with 'trust', participants are willing to open up and talk to me and share their stories with confidence, which they cannot share with a foreigner (an outsider) because they will feel they will be looked down.

Having access as *emic* (insider), I was conscious of my position and not to overstep the boundaries. Such awareness enables to be in the same level with the participants (sharing power together) and not adopting authoritarian position during the interviews. As *emic*, I was aware of participants' status as well as their situation and will avoid their exploitation based on their vulnerable position. I see these processes as a matter of 'trust'. It shows that being a member of the Igbo community the participant will treat me as one of them. It is important to establish such level of relationship and understand people as they are.

Also participants could see me as 'outsider' because of my living abroad (the UK). They could think that I have money, and therefore they will use the opportunity to participate in the study in order to receive help from me and provide all the necessary information which I needed for the study.

My visits and meetings with key participants and eminent people were achieved through the help of co-pastor and female assistant to whom I have written and explained the aims and outcomes of the study. With this kind of familiarisation, participants were very supportive and willing to share their experiences and potential recommendations to improve future interventions. I have found hospitality amongst the local population, which stimulated a cooperative atmosphere within the three villages. The community has been a very supportive environment in which to conduct interviews for over the period of six weeks that I lived with them. The consultation with the eminent persons provided information regarding their familiarisation with the community and basic information on the sociocultural and political situation of the environment and gaining access into the world view of widows and childless wives experience through the local custom and cultural practice.

As a researcher, at every stages of the interview, I maintained the notes, while the female assistant also helped in recording the place and time of interview and the context within which it happened. For example, if the interview took place in a village hall or consulting room of NGO's office, the female assistant would be asked to describe the physical environment by paying attention to any cultural symbols and other issues relevant to the study such as the presence of the participants, whether there were any interruptions or if an unusual situation occurred, which she noted as well certain other observations which are considered significant. With this procedure, we could gain a better insight into the interview and clarify any points, which may or may have not made full sense on reading the transcripts.

The participants were informed that the main outcome of the research would be a doctoral thesis and that findings would be presented at conferences and publication sought in peer-reviewed journals. There are various strategies in addition to those outlined above that can be employed to protect participants but, at the same time, ensure that the research enters the public domain. For instance, papers can be sent to participants prior to publication, and I have offered to do this. Again, some felt this was unnecessary whilst others requested it before I even had a chance to offer.

Reflexivity is one way in which to claim to the integrity and trustworthiness of the interview. According to Finlay (2002), reflexivity is where researchers engage in explicit, self-aware analysis of their own role. By engaging in reflexivity, the researcher can examine the impact of his position, perspective, and presence and evaluate the research process, methods, and outcomes. Without reflexivity, there is a risk that he may let his unelucidated prejudices dominate the research findings.

Reflexivity can be found in a number of theoretical frameworks, including phenomenology. Phenomenologists focus on the way the subject and object are enmeshed in pre-reflective existence. Phenomenological philosophers such as Heidegger (Finlay, 2002) argued that each researcher will perceive the same phenomenon in a different way, each bringing their experience, specific understandings, and background. This way of being-in-the-world means that researchers cannot help but bring their own involvement and fore understandings into the research.

The intrinsic role played by the researcher as interpreter when formulating findings must be acknowledged, given the way that perceptions are necessarily entangled when accessing experience. While it is important that the researcher attempts to disentangle his perceptions and understandings from the phenomena being studied, he also recognises that his interpretations and the ongoing revelation of the thing under scrutiny are one of the same (Finlay, 2003). After each interview with the female assistant, the researcher ensured that he took the time to reflect on the interview and his role in order to provide clarity and credibility to the research findings.

3.11 A Summary of the participants' demographic information—widows with children and Childless wives is provided below. This data was collected from the fieldwork I carried out in 2006.

Table 3.1: **Shows the number of widows and childless wives**

Participants	Number of People
Widowed with children	31
Married women without children	22
Total	53

Source: Ezeakor, A. (fieldwork 2006)

Marital status

Marriage is considered important and a great achievement within the local community. All the participants were currently married or had previously been married before widowhood. The currently married group were all childless whereas 70 per cent of the widows had children. There is a difference in relation to 'childbearing' in their marital status. However, marital status in Igboland is embedded in kinship systems and depends on those systems for claims to productive and reproductive resources.

Widowed with children

A woman is pronounced a widow at the death of her husband and has an obligation to mourn for her husband. Women are expected to grieve openly and to demonstrate the intensity of their emotional feelings in formalised ways. Far more restrictions are placed on a widow than on a widower. It is widows, not widowers, who must endure the most humiliating rituals.

In Igboland, however, a woman is part of a man's property, and so upon the death of a man, his relatives while inheriting his property also inherit his wife. Even a widow with female children faces very harsh conditions, as female children are not entitled to inherit as their male counterparts. The inheritance status of widows has been the subject of much controversy. Nwankwor (2003:7) have made conflicting claims as to the low status of women accorded by customary marriages to women.

Childless wives

A childless condition is socially perceived as a sign of poor reproductive health. Many factors are likely to be attributed as social consequences, which most of the survivors are stereotyped and stigmatised in the society. Similarly, when a widow is childless, she is in most cases evicted from her marital home based on the fact that she did not have children for her late husband. However, a childless wife worries greatly about the failure of not having a child. As a result of this, most of these women live in fear, which makes them dependent on men.

In the traditional Igbo society, the position of married women without children and a childless widow represent a source of disappointment that faces ejection and disinheritance. Further discussion shows that childlessness is often experienced as a personal tragedy, especially since it is usually the woman who is blamed, even though the problem could be due to male impotency. In many African societies, especially in the Igbo society, 'male barrenness' is a taboo and not to be discussed. This shows how male superiority over women's subordination increases the level of interpersonal violence and emotional abuse towards women.

Table 3.2: **The ages of the participants**

Ages Interviewed (Years)	Number of People
18-25	5
26-35	15
36-45	31
46-55	2
Total	53

Source: Ezeakor, A. (fieldwork 2006)

Age

There is some evidence (Nwankwor, 2004:19) to suggest that younger women in rural areas are expected to be economically viable by male members of the family, but certain sociocultural constraints on economic dispossession and neglect affects their lower status. Age may be a reflection of ideology—younger people (men and women) have shown to adhere to more egalitarian gender role attitudes. It is also the case that, throughout history, men usually attain higher economic status and power (Ozumba, 2005). The young mothers between ages eighteen and fifty represent the majority of the workforce and are the most likely to perform childbearing, agriculture, and domestic labour, which can cause increased 'role conflict' and stress for women as they manage to combine both activities and therefore increase greater domestic involvement.

Occupation

The most common occupations in the rural areas are held by petty traders which involves agricultural activities. Agriculture in the Igbo economy serves as the chief means of livelihood, which cannot be overemphasised. The local people are seen to be primarily subsistence farmers—growing yam, cassava, maize, and other staple crops. The fertility of the land and other natural resources of the local community had provided some economic security which, in part, explains any characteristics of systemic conservatism and the feeling of complacency in this traditional society. However, women use the income generated from these activities to support their families in areas such as children's school fees, clothing, and house maintenance as well as their daily needs. This explains the necessity for many rural dwelling women to travel to the cities to sell their products. These rural women are then influenced by their more sophisticated urban counterparts and bring back some of this increased awareness and education when they return to their local communities.

Education

Educational variables are used to determine the rate of literacy and level of education amongst the female population. According to Abidogu (2007:29-51), education has a positive effect on women's participation in the labour force because it improves employment opportunities for women, and it encourages greater female mobility in search of employment. Acholonu (2001) indicates that education increases the aspirations of women workers, and it minimises the barriers of cultural tradition, which prevents women from becoming independent and autonomous in the labour market. The demographic data describes the level of educational status of women in relation to income wage earnings. Specific indicators look at adult education and attainment to provide a context for literacy and level of opportunities for women. Access to education plays an important role in the development of women, and this is a mechanism to empower the poor. However, there are many barriers across the experiences of women that could not enable them to gain access to education because of poor family background. Ezeilo (2005:18) recounts the effects of colonisation and the Nigerian-Biafrian War as another explanation in some of the reasons of women's lesser participation in education and aspirations to political positions.

Religion

The indigenous religion within the areas of study affirms a pantheon of gods, of which the two most important members are the supreme god (*Chukwu*) and the earth goddess (*Ala*), the patron of morality. Another prominent feature of the religion is witchcraft and veneration of ancestors who protect the members of the family against evil spirits and their human agents. In West Africa, especially in Igboland, it is impossible to discuss the matter of death without taking into consideration the question of witchcraft (Ebigbo, 2005:234). In this kind of atmosphere charged with superstitions, the regime of denials and privations brought on the widow to some extent constituted a means of placing them under oath as a proof that they have not concealed any relevant information on her husband's wealth for the entire duration of the mourning period (Nzewi, 1989).

However, the presence of Christianity within the local community has caused some shrinking of the physical symbols of the traditional religion, such as shrines (Omaliko) and also sacred bushes like (Ogwugwu*).* Nevertheless, almost all the participants in the study come from different religious denominations—Roman Catholic, Anglican, and Pentecostal, and the explanations they offered in relation to their suffering are clearly linked to their belief towards God and that their religion helps keep them happy and healthy.

Importance of language and style

In order to help readers navigate their way through this study, it may be useful to point out a number of philosophical and stylistic issues. In the beginning of this chapter, the methodological approach of this study is firmly located with a participatory philosophy. The usage of 'language' with women in the study is carefully chosen because the study does not stigmatise them by using the word 'victim'; instead, I endeavour to use positive language such as 'survivor' to address the women. The term 'survivor' is used to maintain respect, dignity, and status of women as human beings. In order words, the term 'survivors' implies a woman going through a negative experience and, at the same time, dealing with it in a more positive way that is coming out of her ordeal strongly through social network and support from family, relatives, friends, and other NGOs. It shows that some of the women in the study have come out of their condition through resilience and develop enough positive coping mechanisms which influence changes in their lifestyle. Whereas some women who are elderly become frail and weak in their vulnerable situation and still produce the feelings of sadness, isolation, loneliness, and despair (*Ariri*).

Additionally, it is hoped that the language of this report reflects the term 'participant' which is a preferred term when referring to all those people who provided data for this study. However, readers may find references to 'respondents' (interviewees and informants). These terms are used only when the term 'participant' felt clumsy or confused within the context of the specific sentence or paragraph.

For clarity, the findings will help the reader to understand how the participants' voice is coded through this section. In order words, participants will be referred to by their villages such as V1, V2, and V3. Widows and childless wives from villages will be represented as follows: W—widowed with children and C—childless wives. V1—EM (representing eminent men—clan heads, titled men, and paramount chiefs), V2—EW (representing eminent women—chairs of the womenfolk), M—NGO (representing men from the non-governmental organisation), and W—NGO (representing women from the NGO). It is a way of maintaining their confidentiality and anonymity.

Relevant quantitative findings are mixed with the qualitative findings to provide a complete picture of the theme. Where possible qualitative findings have also been quantified in order to provide a sense of magnitude or measure, these were provided through a theme or sub-theme by the participants. Finally, although the themes are based on findings, which are repeated by a number of participants until they are saturated, individual views, which may contradict or question the consensus or may raise issues not identified by others, are also presented.

CHAPTER 4

Presentation of Data, Analysis, and Interpretation

4.1 Introduction

Having 'set the scene' in Chapter 4, the aim of this chapter is to present and analyse the data and discuss the findings that relate to women's psychosocial condition and correlation of the incidence of psychological oppression and symptoms or difficulties in the context of gender-power inequalities of patrilineal kinship. In this case, I will discuss each of these interviews and having analysed this data, consider the themes that have run through them and how they relate to existing literature.

The narratives, stories, and responses of the adult women survivors form overarching themes through which their vulnerability is contextualised. These themes will shape the interpretation of the findings and results in the context of the participants' social and cultural beliefs and experiences of their violence, abuse, and health issues. Each of the themes will be discussed in turn. Quotes from the participants will be used to evidence the results and inform how each theme is derived.

This chapter is divided into eight major themes, which I have identified below through my research data. These include problems of patriarchal and kinship practices on women, inadequate levels of awareness of cultural rights, women's reasons for *Ariri* (mental health problem), beliefs and experiences of coping with life, exclusion and its implications on women's lives and discussion, psychological effects of abuse and domestic violence, and coping mechanisms to improve life opportunities. These factors will be informed by the results and discussion of the implications of the findings in relation to psychosocial differences—'women with *Ariri*' and those 'prone to *Ariri*'. This is important because the end result of our analysis will clarify the use of terms indicating the significance of *Ariri*—social pathology based on the way individuals perceive their suffering and illnesses. This will help to give significance to *Ariri*, which is a mental health problem embedded in traditional Igbo society; it will also help develop an understanding of women's coping mechanisms. These points indicate the way the contents and structures of the findings are organised. Next, I will look at the final discussion of the findings and conclusions. The recommendations and implications for future research that may be generated in response to this chapter will be considered in the next chapter.

Data analysis

To support my analysis style, I used a focused, semi-structured style of interviewing, which consisted of six open-ended questions. Though I used the same questions within all the interviews, for the sake of consistency, I also wanted to provide space for my participants to explain their opinions and theory base at a deeper level. Davies says that one of the aims of this style of interviewing is 'to keep focus on your topic firmly at the top of your agenda but maximizing the opportunity for your interviewees to express their experiences, feelings and opinions' (Davies, 2007:165). Through in-depth interviews, participant observations, and documentary review data were elicited on the processes and outcome of the participants.

Nigerian land and inheritance custom leaves many single women, especially widows and childless wives, at risk of destitution and poverty (Mezieobi, 2011). Some African customs and much pre-colonial, colonial, and post-colonial influence have alleviated some gender-based violence against women and given widows land rights; yet many Igbo widows suffer unjustly in Nigeria. According to Okoye (2005:97), 'many widows in Nigeria are subjected to health problems and the violations of their rights are condoned by traditional widowhood rites, rituals and practices'. Widowhood practices not only humiliate women, they constitute both visible and invisible barriers to community and human development as well. In the patrilineal system in which property rights are held and transferred through men, women have little or no right of inheritance. Many anthropological studies describe economic systems linked with property in terms of gender inequality and discuss such themes as the relationship between control of economic resources and power relations.

By portraying the domestic abuse and traumatic experiences of women in the patriarchal society, many studies have discovered some of the dehumanising practices that reflect a gender-biased society in dire need of outlawing its inhumane customs that demean women (Ewelukwa, 2002; Ezeilo, 2004; Nwankwor, 2005).

Identified themes

Various strands will form the emerging themes of the data and data analysis, which will illustrate the outcomes of the interviews and their interrelationship. There are eight main themes that I have identified that have run through my research data. These are as follows:

- Problems of patriarchal and kinship practices on women
- Inadequate levels of awareness of cultural rights
- Women's reasons for *Ariri* (mental health problem)
- Beliefs and experiences of coping with life
- Areas of similarities and differences
- Exclusion and its implication on women
- Psychological effects of abuse and domestic violence
- Implications for survivor's care to improve life opportunities

4.2   Problems of patriarchal and kinship practices on women

While the idea of the importance of patriarchal and kinship practice ascribes status of a first principle in anthropology, the internal workings of kinship systems have long been identified as a significant theme within literature reviews as an area of intense controversy. Participants described kinship systems as containing a variety of rules which govern marriage and property relations. Women are not considered as very independent because of the lack of control over the practice of inheritance for widows and childless wives.

> *'Kinship contains all sorts of bewildering rules, which govern whom one may or may not marry . . . I just view kinship rules as controlling . . . Hmm . . . the custom and practice affect inheritance for women. It is very traumatic. Women are subjected to various kinds of violence and domestic abuse'* (V1, W, thirty-five years).

The majority of the widows also spoke about their difficult experiences in relation with customary laws, which discriminate them from family and community services, especially inheritance and property rights. A similar study in South-Eastern Nigeria found that Igbo women express feelings of powerlessness in kinship and patriarchal practices that may hamper adequate care for women (Nwankwor, 2004:17). Many widows in traditional societies have no rights, or very limited rights, to inheritance under customary and religious law, which represents an imbalance of power between the sexes. However the control and subordination of women and the institutionalisation of force comes about by means of the traditional practices.

> 'I think sometimes the community sees it only as a way the customs and traditions brings the social and political activities under control . . . hence, some leaders are reluctant to address the conflict around kinship practices out of respect for culture' (V2, C, forty-seven years).

Given the importance of kinship and family relationships in most women's lives, it is not surprising that 'the family' has occupied a central place in feminist theory and research. According to Ezeilo (2005:9), various aspects of family life have been identified as crucial to an understanding of women's subordination. Additionally, many of the laws, modern as well as religious and customary, administrative policies, actions, and attitudes towards widowhood and widows represent grave breaches of the various international and regional human rights charters and declarations. For example, widowhood practice breaches the 1979 UN's Convention of the Elimination of All Forms of Discrimination Against Women (CEDAW), the Social, Political and Economic Charters, and the 1993 International Declaration on the Elimination of Violence against Women (ICESCR). The Maputo second summit of the African Union (AU) on 11 July 2003 was another declaration which reinforced explicitly and specially the rights of women and established a ban on harmful traditional practices. The recent NGO (2009) report from WACOL states that the leading causes of widowhood practices are death, inheritance, and cultural and religious practices. Consequently, Ezeilo (2005:47) indicates that half a million women in Sub-Saharan Africa suffer psychological oppression and around 1.8 million women suffer from harmful practices every year. These grim statistics constitute a violation of women's rights and reproductive health in Nigeria.

Strict traditional practices represent serious cultural and economic implications associated with subordination of women and relationship to accessing services, which adversely affect women. For example, rigid and long-term traditional practices—mourning and rites of passage—may restrict widows from working in the public sector for a long period of time. Widows' access to land and income-generating opportunities are severely restricted. Some of the participants remarked that

'In many societies, especially in Igbo culture, widowhood—ime ajadu is a process characterised by rituals, forced remarriages, intimidation, rejection, isolation, poverty, loss of status, and fear of the unknown' (V3, W, forty-two years).

Another widow reported her experience of *ime ajadu* as follows:

'At 12 midnight, a group of women came to our compound and took me to Aja-ani *(stream), where I was forced to have sexual intercourse with a traditional chief priests (*eze muo *or* nwa nri*) . . . I was shocked and felt embarrassed. Afterwards, I was taken to the nearby stream for bathing and later clothed in a white gown'* (V1, W, thirty-eight years)

According to Nwankwor (2004:9), ritual cleansing and purification and bathing symbolically represent cutting off any contacts between the widow and the deceased husband. The transitional aspect of change signifies a loss of social status, for example, the shaving of head, defilement, and dispossession. Sossou (2002:106), in another way, remarked that widowhood practices are closely tied to cultural and traditional beliefs about death, suspicion about witchcraft, inheritance, feminine roles, family structure, and family relationships. The degree of expression of the negativities depends on the communities' cultures, religions, and economic systems. One of the eminent women remarked the following:

'I think there is a lot of cultural issues here . . . how can I put this? . . . Hmm . . . stereotypical people have beliefs and attitudes that are maybe stereotypical. Hmm . . . I think that is a cultural practice so you can't interfere. I have heard people say men in society perpetuate the practice, what can you do, people just shrugged it off and thought it is normal and there wasn't really any questioning about' (V3, EW, sixty-two years).

Consequently, cultural taboos and negative stereotyping, as well as the burdens of childcare may impede younger widows from participating in the public domain, thereby increasing their poverty. Widows' poverty is directly related to a lack of access to economic resources, including land ownership and inheritance, access to education and support services, and their marginalisation from the decision-making process. Without land or other collateral, poor widows are unlikely to obtain credit or loans. Without education or training, widows are unable to work their way out of poverty, particularly in traditional societies where restrictions on lifestyle prohibit them from working in the public sphere.

It is also important to emphasise that different treatment meted out to widows and childless wives is due to patriarchal and gender relations which defined males as being in authority over females and also being superior to females. Among the Igbo patrilineal descent, inheritance is passed on to the male relatives of the deceased. The widows could only benefit from these properties if they have grown-up sons or are forced to remarry into their deceased husbands' families again (Nwankwor, 2002:71). Like economic oppression, psychological oppression is institutionalised and systematic, and it serves to make the work of domination easier by breaking the spirit of the dominated and by rendering them incapable of understanding the nature of those agencies responsible for their subjugation.

All participants informed that there was domestic abuse and trauma associated with lack of access to community services, which resulted in feelings of isolation and despair. One of the childless wives reported her ordeal as follows:

> 'Hmm . . . well, there have been a number of things that bothers me actually. My experience at the personal level is that I had problems with my status . . . from when I first realised that I cannot conceive a child, I find it difficult to bear . . . Anyway, I fought, in a way, to get pregnant. I had consultation with a local medicine man. I carried out all prescription and treatments, and those couple of months, I was sad and unhappy and out of touch with reality . . . I stay at home and find the environment a very stressful mess. I live with this stigma and see my situation as awful'
> (V1, C, forty-three years).

In the case of discriminatory practice, the cultural and religious practices reveal categories of groups like widows and childless wives labelled as unclean, profane, and defiled. A widow after suffering all forms of maltreatment from her mother-in-law remarked:

> 'It was difficult for me to cope with the abusive environment, especially where my mother-in-law become a pain in the neck. To start my experience, I didn't know that my mother-in-law would turn against me after the death of my late husband . . . Many women complain about their mothers-in-law. It was now that I began to feel for them. Hmm . . . we have so many unresolved cultural issues. We have reached a point where I was completely out of my mind. We had a terrible argument . . .

with badmouthing and everything. Other people that were there were holding us down so that we do not get into physical violence. After the enquiring about her nasty behaviour towards me, I later found out that her children instigated her to attack me in order to frustrate me. This is all because I claimed the rights of my late husband's access to her property' (V2, W, forty-eight years).

The next participant managed to identify for me other important issues such as humiliation and intimidation that seems to be prevailing. It is a social issue that has created pressure contributing to neglect and rejection of widows and the childless wives for the past four decades. Additionally, the law favours the male's side on certain issues such as landed property that involves inheritance. Moreover, there is also the issue of corruption in inheritance law, which tends to reinforce patriarchal practice to the detriment of women. This puts pressure on women in their effort to achieve gender equality in inheritance law cases. One of the NGOs observed the following:

'Deviance of inheritance law and of their representatives show their incompetence of interpretation of law and social distribution of justice, equity, and fairness . . . we also believe that it is a form of deviance when certain behaviour is unacceptable especially where deprivation of rights of an individual person create a visible difference. There is a great variety of corruption occurring, which facilitates the need to examine customary responsibilities, especially when there is a lack of adequate support and protection of women in their vulnerable state' (M—NGO, forty-nine years).

Kinship and cultural practices have allowed both anthropologists and African feminists to look at women's relationships to marriage and to reconsider the connections between property, inheritance, and marriage. This is highlighted in the study of Sossou (2002:207) on widowhood practices in West Africa. In a similar manner, the study of Mezieobi (2011:78-82) explained that harmful practices towards women are associated with fear and anxiety and not with violating respect for women in general whose behaviour and human dignity and rights are stated in the International declarations of rights (UNCHR). Harmful cultural and religious practices are discussed in Article 5, which indicates, 'no one shall be subjected to torture or to cruel, inhuman or degrading treatment'. The Article 5 as I believe represents vividly the core voices of the participants and is supported by one of the NGOs working with CIRDDOC which noted the following:

'Beliefs about the subordinate position of women are regularly so deep rooted in society that they are regarded as 'natural' or as part of a society's culture and tradition . . . Additionally, women have no guarantee that they will continue to have access to resettlement land if their status changes, for example, if they divorce, become childless, or are widowed. Often women's disinheritance lowers their status in society, which is seen as consequences of their frustration towards the family . . . the concern is to ensure that individuals' most basic needs and rights are protected and delivered regardless of who they are' (F—NGO, forty years).

The findings illustrate the difference in the way disinheritance is reported about the situation of widows and childless wives. The customary law is openly strict and hostile to women. The majority of the stories deal with the problems which participants face. Their key findings include the following: customary marriage strictly limits women's rights, especially if a man dies intestate; however, a widow cannot inherit, own, or dispose off land and property. Whilst statutory law grants legal provision on inheritance and property succession and reinforces the status of women, customary law discriminates against women. As conflict prevails between these systems, and the jurisdiction, which determines the legal status of women, remains problematic. With inheritance and cultural practices, which discriminate against women, violence and abuse tends to increase in the environment and that serves to justify the fear and anxiety affecting women in the patriarchal family. All the participants believe that discriminatory practices are of the highest towards widows and childless wives. The findings look at the impact of patriarchal and kinship on women (i.e, marriage, inheritance, and property relations), which it examines. The socio-economic characteristics theory states that the more power men possess over inheritance and property, the less domestic labour women do. The sex ideology hypothesis maintains that the more traditional the husband's attitudes towards sex roles, the less domestic labour women perform. The demand-response capability hypothesis states that the more productive a task demands from men and the greater the female capacity is to respond to them, there is some female participation, but ultimately there is male domination in inheritance practices.

The findings suggest that traditional agrarian Igbo society demonstrates the social position of women with stereotypes and stigmatisation to awaken economic exploitation related to property. Property relations tend to triumph over human feelings and traditional rights. The problem of poverty defines lack of access to economic resources especially for women. What comes to the fore of marginalisation is the continuing oppression of women under patriarchal practices.

4.3   Inadequate levels of awareness of cultural rights

Throughout my interviews, all the participants commented on the constant and high level of corruption and injustice around customary law. Several barriers were raised by as specifically constraining the poor in seeking and accessing justice and fairness. One of participants remarked the folowing:

> *'If you know people in authority, you can be protected . . . Those who have no voice are all intimidated and silenced. It is all about power relations, which men benefit because of patriarchal institution'* (V1, C, thirty-eight years).

Widows in Igbo society are subjected to destructive rites due to their vulnerability, low literacy, and lack of exposure. Participants who have no source of income find it difficult to resist the customary law and practice for fear of 'excommunication' from their matrimonial homes without any entitlement to the estates of their deceased husbands. All the participants felt that denial of justice, which is concomitantly an expression of the social control within the local community, affects their social status, dignity, and human rights; sometimes all these are connected to illiteracy and ignorance of law. According to Onuoha (2008:7), the fact that female-headed households that are so frequently classified amongst the poorest and vulnerable groups can often be attributed to gender and class relations. In the three villages interviewed, participants admittedly found it increasingly difficult to report cases of domestic abuse to the police because of the fear of being ostracised. Having asked one question about access to legal support in the community, I received three different answers from the participants, all of which were along the lines of what I would have expected them to say. Some of the participants reported the reason why they have not officially complained about cases of domestic abuse and violence. A young widow remarked the following:

> *'The reason why I have never reported cases of domestic abuse is because of illiteracy—not knowing the law. Since I cannot read or write and since I am unable to express myself, I am frightened with the situation to make any complaints of abuse and violence heard in a public'* (V3, W, forty-one years).

My work around my introduction and rationale highlighted for me that that legal representation for the poor and vulnerable was said to be a mockery because of discrepancies between customary law and statutory law over inheritance in relation to intestate customary marriage, given that, on this issue alone, there is corruption and a lack of social distribution of justice amongst the poor. Again, because of the high level of illiteracy, most of the participants were afraid of reporting their abuse cases. For instance, the high professional fees demanded by lawyers and the concentration of lawyers in the urban areas meant that the majority of people and the rural based women, in particular, could not have access to legal advice. It was revealed that although there are legal-aid providers in the country, these are extremely limited. In most cases, people have to incur transport costs to get to those providers, which would not only impoverish them further, but also act as a disincentive to pursue legal redress. A poorly facilitated infrastructure and social amenities and lack of facilitation of the police and courts conspicuously featured in all communities as contributory factors to poor administration of justice. This was said to escalate violence and insecurity in women. For example, guaranteeing women's independent rights in landed property so that widows, childless wives, and the divorced retain their means of socio-economic livelihood is extremely difficult in rural areas. Two female participants recounted their incidents thus:

> 'As a widow, I have never attempted to report any abuse to any of the local authorities because of corruption. In the local custom, it is only men who handle the land disputes, and they use the social status and decide in favour to their male counterparts. My experience so far with people's complaints is that if I come from a wealthy family, justice will be granted in favour of your case' (V1, W, forty-seven years).

The findings in this study have revealed the predicament of Igbo women in relation to domestic abuse where tradition and local custom has kept the oppression and economic exploitation of women in their normal family life. Additionally, financial constraints were described by some of the participants as impinging on social life in less obvious ways than in the family life. Having established women's role in the family and local community, there are constraints or limitations that restrain women from achieving real economic independence from men or gain access to the resources needed for equal participation in community life.

A consideration of culturally specific problems in the study has allowed both anthropologists and African feminists to look at women's relationships to cultural practice and to reconsider the connections between property, inheritance, and marriage and also to address the rights of women within the society. Education provides another opportunity for women to fight for their rights. It would appear to be true to say that women in rural African societies were relegated to a somewhat subordinate position throughout sub-Saharan Africa. This is in sharp contrast to urban Igbo women who are largely enlightened and therefore independent. A childless woman in this way succinctly expressed this aspect of the behaviour expected from a good wage earner:

> '*After our marriage has not been fruitful, I decided to cope with my wage labour in order to increase my responsibility in the household. People respect me because of my financial contribution to the social activities in the village, church organisation, and women's community project scheme. My husband and his family respect me for this and would not even trouble me about our childless problem*' (V2, C, thirty-three years).

Limann (2003) and Ambasa-Shisanya (2007) indicate that most urban women with secondary school education and economic stability ignore the cultural requirement associated with widowhood. By this, they meant that women who are educated or economically independent would be in a better position to seek their basic rights. When I asked to discuss what women's social status could mean for the family, a widow said the following:

> '*Women who are in a better economic status are more respected in the family than those with low income. However, there is an obvious belief that in the villages most of the uneducated women, whether widows and childless wives, command little respect*' (V1, W, forty-four years).

For the majority of women, during the interview, there were viable avenues to enhance their status in society, and these were economic prosperity, on one hand, and, on the other hand, professional training. Sadly, as a result of poverty, many women have failed to use the law to secure the protection to which they were entitled, owing to general lack of awareness of basic legal rights. The paucity of information was voiced in many of the interviews conducted in the villages. This, which many often regarded as 'ignorance', acted against the survivor's ability to enjoy protection of the law. High levels of illiteracy amongst the participants were pointed out as a major cause of this ignorance and indicators of domestic abuse. Illiteracy erodes confidence and breeds powerlessness amongst the vulnerable groups. A childless wife remarked the following:

> '*As a childless wife, I am always ashamed of my illiterate state in the family and feel humiliated by the members of the family . . . especially my mother-in-law, who swore that I would never live at peace with her son. For example, a portion of land, which my father-in-law gave me, was*

*conspired against and removed from me and given to one of the co-wives
with children because I have no child.'* (V3, C, thirty-two years).

On the other hand, the Marriage Ordinance Act, as part of the Nigerian
legal system, should aid the customary law from discriminatory practice and
support women especially the vulnerable groups with legal services, whereas
I believe that the findings from my research would suggest that despite
existing legislation, it is extremely difficult for rural low-income women, the
socio-economic group from which the majority of my participants are drawn,
to access the right to compensation under this legislation.

4.4 Women's reasons for *Ariri* (mental health problem)

The prevalence of harmful cultural and religious practice by participants is
also identified as a significant theme within the literature review. Widowhood
as a bereavement is a natural occurrence associated with grief, humiliation,
and loss of status related to lamentation (*Ikwa Ariri*—mental health problem).
One of the participants narrated her experience as follows:

> *'It is difficult to avoid widow cleansing, particularly with those
> dirty concoction and environment . . . come and see traumatic experience
> such as withdrawal behaviour from survivors and not to talk of shocks
> and fear of HIV infections'* (V2, W, twenty-nine years).

Hitherto, HIV infection associated widowhood practices are common in
a number of problems widows reported as health problem. Sossou (2002:204)
claims that excessive numbers of deaths from HIV/AIDS have begun to be
blamed on widow cleansing in patriarchal and kinship cultures. For instance,
widows are coerced into participatory rituals through their fear of losing status
and protection, of being evicted from the family home, or having their children
taken from them. In this regard, 'cleansing' generally involves a widow having
sexual relations either with a village cleanser (chief priest) or with a relative
of her late husband. According to Ambasa-Shisanya (2007:47-65), in cases
where a husband died of HIV/AIDS, it is likely that the selection of men who
are chosen as 'cleanser' might be HIV victims, since the hygienic and medical
assessment is not provided. In this social context, widowhood practices explain
two fundamental issues: first, the fear and tendencies towards life-threatening
as well as degrading practices, such as ritual cleansing through sex. Second, the
forcing of widows to have sex with designated individuals in order to exorcise
evil spirits and secure widows' inheritance, and this indicates that widows of all
ages, and from different status and cultures, are likely to be subject to multiple

forms of discrimination, neglect, cultural, and psychological oppression and sexual abuse. One of the widows who had suffered from sexual abuse reported the following:

> 'Women are expected to observe a cleansing ritual, which has a sexual component, before reintegrating into the community . . . A widow is confined to her homestead for a whole year since she was considered as culturally impure and dangerous (a witch) to the community. Hence, widowhood taboos were lifted after the post-burial ritual rites' (V3, W, forty-five years).

According to Ezumah (2003:89-99), sex is central to the cleansing rite of widows. It is a prelude to placing a widow under guardianship and is performed by a professional cleanser within the clan. However, this sexual practice can place both the cleanser and the widow in danger of contracting HIV. The enforcement of widowhood ritual has been vested in elderly married women and widows. They have been psyched into believing that the rituals are for the widow's benefit and for those of their children. With fellow women in control of the situation, young widows are silenced into submission (Sossou, 2002), as they are taken through the observation of their rights as willing participants.

At the time of the interview, most of the participants kept repeating how harmful widowhood practice influences the change of status of the adult survivors. It demonstrates the way domestic abuse influences the health of the individual in traditional Igbo society, resulting in frustration, sadness, and despair in marriage. For the vast majority of participants, issues of socio-economic status, specifically the intersection of severe economic and social neglect and gender inequality featured in the inheritance status in the Igboland. The damaging effects lead to an inability to engage and seek help within the community and the subsequent impact of stigmatisation, and individuals with *Ariri* are faced with a constant series of rejections and seclusions from the community. Zack-Williams (2006) argues that it is this agreed need to understand the complex nature of black mental health associated with the disadvantaged in the society. The reason given for this is societal pressure, which is reinforced to various degrees by political economy and inequality as a consequence of women's dependence on men leading to prolonged grief. In addition to Papadopoulos et al.'s (2004) study of the lack of awareness of the local services available and the procedure to access them is always a barrier. Participants recognised the importance of cultural restriction (tradition) but were not in favour of its continuation. Most participants felt that culture is not static but dynamic, and as such, a ritual can be changed overtime. For example, alternative rites of passage which Onadeko's (2002:201-06) study reports as the motivations of harmful cultural and religious practice should be negotiated with alternative rites as have been substituted with varying degrees of success in other African countries like Ghana, Kenya, Uganda, and other places. Two of the participants share the same views as follows:

> 'It is quite interesting—one of the justifications is that it is a rite of passage, that is, a complete distortion of reality. What it does is, it impairs women' (V1, W, thirty-four years).

Some of the participants feel that widowhood practice is a cultural and religious right, which they were brought up in such tradition, and as such, it is not considered as something bad, but now as we are in a civilised society, this is no longer necessary. One of the eminent people supported this statement remarked the following:

> '. . . vulnerable women often suffer from a lack of social recognition and acknowledgement of their dignity from patronising or dismissive treatment and from the subtle impact of social stereotype and stigmatisation. Such an experience can have profoundly negative effects on survivor's loss of self-esteem and their relationship with family and community, leading to an increase in stress-related health problems' (V2, EW, fifty years).

Because survivors tend to reproduce common stereotypes, the patriarchal practices ignores feasibility and diversity of views and holds on a male viewpoint on customary practice which is linked with ancestry ties to local custom and other ambivalent perspectives that sometimes accompany this practice. Although one might imagine that *Ariri* (emotional distress) creates a new urgency for addressing the violation of women's rights leading to psychosocial condition of women. The popular features of the disease, such as lamentation, frustration and despair contributed to the complex web of interpersonal violence and emotional abuse. Although women narrate their traumatic experience in terms of social deprivation and neglect in family, traditional men denied or ignored these risks. The fact that a significant proportion of harmful traditional practices in South-Eastern Nigeria involve cultural stereotype, and stigmatisation of women have shown the social and psychological damage on the social life of survivors in ways that are related to the greatest risk for *Ariri*. Ironically, from the collective experiences of women, it is suggested that the risk of *Ariri* only adds to the violence and abuse. A female informant confirmed the following:

'Women in the traditional Igbo society have suffered from cultural beliefs, practices, and stereotyping which legitimise and exacerbate the persistence and tolerance of violence against women' (F—NGO, forty-eight years).

As in many African societies, people in Igboland commonly attribute men's superiority in sociocultural and political activities, and the fact that this perspective discriminates against woman is well represented in the literature (Anameze, 1996:17). Some eminent people who were interviewed articulated this view. In response to a question about why 'land ownership' and its inheritance are accorded to men, a forty-two-year-old market woman repeated in a Pidgin English phrase:

'Culture favours men than women . . . nwoke bu ide ji ulo (man is the pillar of the house). It is something men need, especially African men. Although it is important to note that many Igbo men and women share a conception of men's superiority, it includes a notion that a man provides shelter and security in the house' (V2, EW, fifty-six years).

Parallel to this, participants held a number of beliefs about *Ariri* which is culturally designated to mean lamentation, sadness, or isolation as an illness, sickness, or disease which may be aggravated by patriarchal control such as marginalisation, discrimination, and stigmatisation. There is some evidence that a higher proportion of Igbo women experienced violence and abuse related to traditional practices, which may likely to lead to *Ariri* (mental health problem). However, saying that, one of the directors of the WON said the following:

'The stigma of a negative self-image and discrimination towards women could result to mental distress which may likely to lead Igbo women to be secretive in expressing their traumatic experience' (F—NGO, forty-five years).

Whilst happiness is the primary 'cause' of health and well-being, unhappiness, sadness, and despair is the primary 'cause' of *Ariri* (mental health problem). The beliefs about the cause of *Ariri* as an illness were presented as follows: poor socio-economic condition, stressful life (neglect, rejection, humiliation, and stereotyping), social isolation or exclusion (loneliness), and supernatural forces (evil or diabolical attack or curse from God). Traditional practices, such as witchcraft were among the indicators of *Ariri*. Witchcraft is a belief system for identifying and categorising diabolical operation, which influence people's destiny—*akaraka*, misfortune, harm, and sickness. Women are the focus of witchcraft belief and accusation. Participants believe that witchcraft could influence stress, excessive worries, family problems, and financial constraints.

Most of the participants described witchcraft as spells, which exacerbate physical, psychological, or spiritual pain. However, religious practices enable some people to wear rosary, medals for protection against the supernatural forces, or burn incense to ward off diabolical attack; such practices are primarily used in Igboland to avoid illness and harm. Like social and psychological elements of *Ariri*, Golightley (2006:36-37) suggested that 'most professionals accept that the most likely cause of mental distress is a complex interaction between a range of factors'.

The comprehensive understanding of women's traumatic experiences shows that participants have been exposed to social isolation and dependence which exacerbates lamentation as a minor effect of mental health problems especially as they are reluctant to admit they have mental difficulties. However, the participants distinguished between 'normal' reactive emotional problems and 'mental illnesses in that the latter would be called madness *Araa* which denotes a psychiatric condition. Most of the participants acknowledged that they had not received any professional support in their abusive condition. More than a quarter of participants felt there were less informal support and care given by family, friends, and relatives. When participants were asked what made them feel ill, two thirds said exclusion, ostracism, humiliation, stigmatisation, or fear of the unknown. Almost half said they felt sad for long periods of time as a result of pre-and post-bereavement episode. From the findings, isolation and loneliness were attributed as major causes of emotional distress, but some believe that the social structures within the rural community prevent loneliness.

4.5   Cultural beliefs and experiences of coping with life

Many of the explanations in relation to beliefs and experiences of coping with life give insight for those who are in a vulnerable position. However, despite the difficulties and stressful life faced in traditional society, some participants retained a positive outlook. For example, a thirty-five-year-old widow with four children who worked as a secretary with the local government explained that she is happy with her employment. 'I had life choices,' she said, 'and I am working towards a goal.'

> *'In general, I am happy with things in my own way because of my*
> *expectation from life. My present career is source of strength . . . I went*

through a path of employment I chose and I like. I am still on the journey, and there is a clear way for the journey, so I am a happy person' (V2, W, thirty-one years).

For some participants, healthiness is achieved by being positive, communicating well with people, and living in harmony with others and one's social environment. It is also shown by enjoying the company of others as one female and one male participant suggested as follows:

'A healthy person . . . enjoys the company of others. He has fun and laughter with them . . . Getting on well with friends is an indicator psychological well-being' (V1, EM, sixty-one years).

For some participants, seeking support is also an aspect of coping with life. A few participants believe that conflict creates anxiety, unhappiness, misery, and sadness and brings division in the family. When asked what makes them feel better in their present condition, nearly all the participants said prayer sessions provided them with courage and hope and a way of improving their social life and opportunities. Participants described that full participation and integration of women as a way of retaining their culture, and this will enable women to achieve and exercise their rights in family and local community. The common thread that runs through many of them is linked to socio-economic activities. Most of the women in the villages manage with little capital to invest in local trade like vegetables, roasting corn along the streets, and hawking to fend for their children and families. It is important to note the difference in their socio-economic deprivation related to property rights and other capacities were to improve access to capital investment for reasonable business. One of the female participants remarked the following:

'As a nurse, I work extra hours to support my family. I work hard to improve my career and gain access to promotion. I know people are suffering because of unemployment, but I'm happy to secure the nursing profession to make a difference in my life' (V3, W, thirty-eight years).

There is some suggestion that the participants understand that there is a need for higher ambition for a good career, good wages, and independence, which are very important for coping in their social condition. Some women believe that struggling hard is a way of providing for the family and protecting their self-worth. This is a likely explanation for some of the survivors who went on to describe what might have been the underlying reason for family support. A young childless wife remarked the following:

'When I noticed my childless problem because of the ill health of my husband, I strived to get admission into polytechnic to read law and better myself. I was also worried for my safety because of the situation of traditional practices in Nigeria, and the fear of being thrown out of my matrimonial home. Even though I felt being childless, I was indirectly preparing myself for the future well-being' (V2, C, thirty-six years).

The traditional perspective put the emphasis on tradition and on patriarchal and kinship practices and suppression of women. The women in the study described tradition as a central reason for health problems. Regarding the social consequences, women described a safe environment lacking non-violence and non-abuse as a new way to boost their self-esteem. This was considered desirable to specific health practice. Participants expressed that the ability to fulfil material needs is perceived as coping behaviour and positive health. However, sociocultural and economic solutions to problems that caused distress were to be handled by some participants through community services and other social network support. Another incident about beliefs and experience of coping is suggested through the implementation of the 'widowhood laws', which, according to the participants, would grant them protection and also help in breaking the cycle of domestic violence and abuse within the local community.

4.6   Areas of similarities and differences

There is no doubt that the documentary sources play a significant role in informing this study about public events, trends, and government policies on the vulnerability of women in the local community. There is also a consensus that the documents from the NGOs throw light into the reality of the widows' traumatic experience(s). According to the report by the Centre for Reproductive Rights (2003), 'Widows in Nigeria often are forced to participate in harmful traditional practices in order to "ensure the continuing support of their husband's family. However, no reference is made to women being considered as part of the property of the late husband's estate"'.

Nwankwor (2005:17) claims that discriminatory practices have been a culturally specific problem, which justifies men's position over women. In addition, with current customary and widowhood practices, there was considerable evidence, which revealed societal abuses and discrimination of women in this arena.

'Women who have refused to participate in widow cleansing have experienced "all sorts of deprivations", with many having to resort to

prostitution in order to support themselves and their family' (*Daily Independent,* 6 March 2007).

Another women reporter from WACOL (24 June 2004) adds the following with regard to the humiliation:

> *'It must however be pointed out that in spite of the changes recorded by women as a result of their advocacy activities, public authorities and institutions still continued practices and enforce cultural practices, which are discriminatory to women. This is because those who are required to implement the recommendations are not in possession of the document and do not feel any concern to follow-up on the commitment of the statutory law.'*

Some of the public documents such as Amnesty International Reports (31 May 2005) demonstrate spousal abuse common in the society, representing the unheard voices and violence against women in the family. A case of a childless wife was reported as follows:

> *'A thirty-nine-year-old childless wife was tortured and eventually forced to leave her matrimonial home after twelve years of marriage in Awka south region. She was accused of bewitching her husband for not begetting a child, a paper reported. The paper looked at women's response to the exposure to humiliation as losing their dignity, status, and rights in rural communities'* (WACOL, 24 June 2004)

A unifying aspect of maltreatment towards women therefore was found to increase stress, frustration, and poor health. Feeling debased and powerless, a widow remarked the following:

> *'Being a widow is like being a disabled person living with other healthy people. One feels as a stranger in the family . . . I was cursed to die by my mother-in-law, which made me to feel homesick and depressed but despite that it is very hard for me to feel that I am part of the family'* (*Vanguard,* 4 February 2011)

The report also states that widows and childless women are the most vulnerable members of the Nigerian society. The individual may desire inclusion or integration but could still be marginalised whereby they are not accepted or supported by either culture. The paper concludes by condemning all those negative portrayals and obnoxious practices that tend to deny women their human rights and perpetuate sexual stereotypes.

According to 15 October 2000 correspondence from Empowering Widows in Development, an international organisation working on widowhood issues in developing countries reports, it is possible, and not uncommon, for an Igbo man to refuse to participate in a levirate marriage. Generally, public documents show the way traditional and cultural practice recreate gender inequality, and inequality is based on unequal distributions of powers. One of the eminent men claimed the following:

> 'Traditional practice is granted to men to maintain and as such women in Igbo society should abide by the local custom and religious practices. This statement indicates that women are always facing persecution consequent to customary law and practice, as the system does not support women' (Field note, 7 June 2006).

Too often, customary law shapes the way women in different social situations in Igboland can be perceived from the mechanisms of the inheritance system and power relations underpinning land tenure affecting and involving women. Two eminent women said the following:

> 'The constraints of widows in customary practice perpetuates violence and abuse towards women . . . For instance, where a widow is being oppressed by her husband's relatives but opts to remain as part of his family, her decision is likely to have been dictated by realisation that if she returns to her natal family or remarries, she could be deprived of her children' (Field note, 10 June 2006).

In her view, another woman remarked the following:

> 'Customary system has always produced a pattern of exclusion, especially with regard to women and their vulnerability. Often widows loosing access to land upon the death of their husband and what is offered as choices have often had the effect of perpetuating the domination of women by further subjecting their interests to the decisions of some male relatives' (Field note, 12 June 2008).

A related argument that might be invoked by those who favour the current state of widows' affairs is that when a male family member dies, his sisters and other kinswomen are usually the ones that take the lead in ensuring the observance of these widowhood rituals. One of the female NGO workers under CIRDDOC (24 March 2002) remarked the following:

> 'It is difficult to avoid damaging of self-esteem, particularly with maltreatment associated with widowhood. Igbo women in their roles as mothers, sisters, and daughters have been the prime agents for the perpetuations and enforcement of widow cleansing in order to satisfy men's desire and these are striking illustration of gendered exclusion.'

In contrast, Jackson (2003:75) claims that the current customary system on acquisition of land in different circumstances through negotiation processes and other diversification opportunities will only contribute a better investment for women. However, the assumption that women owning land and participating for access to property and inheritance would highlight efficiency and ultimately contributing to reducing poverty. Part of the difference is a way of bringing about change of status and position of women in the society. Whitehead and Tsiakata's (2003) study on women and land-tenure system shows that too much emphasis on land rights (inheritance law) and other significant constraints on women and threats to their safety, for instance, can actually reinforce marginalisation. According to Ibhawoh (2002:94-95), families and households should not be seen as centres of repression, exploitation, and marginalisation of women on this interpretation but rather the current customary system should be safeguarding, sustaining, and satisfying in the lives of both women and men. Policies on the current customary law need to be based on a more rounded view of households as being sites of gender inequalities within societies.

4.7   Social exclusion and its implication on women

The issue of exclusion is considered as a personal experience of discrimination amongst the female population. It is linked with the notion of social deprivation or alienation and has much in common with the notion of relative socio-economic differentiation or poverty. Exclusion is one of the extreme reasons why women cannot challenge the traditional practices. Some participants reported that they felt powerless but remain secretive in order not to be ostracised from the community. A majority of participants described exclusion as 'oppressive' and 'undemocratic' patriarchal culture. A middle-aged eminent woman summarised this quite succinctly when she said the following:

> 'I began to sense the reason Igbo custom and cultural practice use taboos to exclude women from certain social and cultural activities.

For past decades exclusion has been perpetuating division on the basis of rights and privileges of women in marriage . . . It's very sad for women to inherit such a generational practice. I was opposed to their policies of ethnicity, and I was forced to leave the community' (V1, EM, seventy-seven years).

Articles 15 and 13, Section C, on 'Women and Health' justify this claim that gender inequalities in the management of resources presents a lack of women's access to participate in local communities and a lack of respect for inadequate promotion and protection of the human rights of women, especially on property. The impact of this approach is a reoccurring theme within the interviews and also the documentary review of NGOs working with disadvantaged women in South-Eastern Nigeria. A female participant recounted her reasons thus:

'Women's status in Igboland, especially in the area of property relation can be seen as a marker of gender inequality and exclusion especially where widows and married women without children act at multiple levels: family, community, and national. Women suffer from low status in comparison to men. A lack of value and respect for the human rights of women in inheritance law and traditional practices are still problematic in the recent decades' (V3, C, thirty-nine years).

One of the eminent people in the community reported the following:

'Lack of vision on the implications of social exclusion had led to the difficulties found in the violation of women's rights in the household and local community. The inference being imbalance in gender which makes the traditional society more oppressive' (V1, EM, seventy years).

Social exclusion between males and females persists even in the most benevolent culture, and tradition is remarkable thing to note in the findings in families and households. A forty-year-old woman, a trader, has been widowed for almost seven years with two female children who are underage. She shared her story as follows:

'After the death of my husband, I suffered nightmares for so many months. After my brother-in-law treated me with scorn and confiscated our land and property, I used to go out to our neighbours and beg for the support of my children and myself. As God would have it, our living condition changed with so much support from friends, which altered my

life. However, the bereavement and grieving process enabled me as a widow to put on an act of confidence' (V2, W, forty years).

Evidence from this study shows that women's role in domestic services are required to help increase the economic power of her late husband and other essential duties of productive action and rearing of the children. For instance, as daughters, mothers, and wives of the family, *umuokpu* are powerful and very influential in policy-making among the female population to a certain extent in the community. However, their role suggests that women serving as a medium of communication in the Igbo society become involved in matters of family conflict. The organisation of *umuokpu* in agricultural and market development in the village enables women to look into the socio-economic and political affairs that concern them. In this regard, women have contributed to the economic development and an overall domestic sustenance of their community.

The awareness of the consequences of constraint among the female population is often incomplete due to numerous barriers as a result of lack of information and education. This implies that women's social roles have generated a poor response in social activities in rural areas. It suggests that the level of socio-economic differences in women associated with sociocultural, economic, and political resources still marginalises women. It shows that despite strong debates on access, equality, and gender disparities, the extent of inequality remains the same.

One of the WACOL participants remarked the following:

'Remember, all these things are done by individuals. They are not really about institutions. Life is not about institutions but individuals within institution or individuals using institutions . . . Institutional structures don't by themselves carry anything, they never actually drive anything, they administer things, yes, but they can take it backwards as well as forwards. It has to do with key individuals that actually make the difference' (M—NGO, fifty-seven years).

Lack of support and neglect has become parallel to two main reasons why women suffer violence. For example a situation may arise where the mother-in-law and daughter-in-law's relationship could end up in verbal abuse and violence as a result of childless situation. My experience with African communities in the UK and other counselling services help to connect the tension of cultural issues which affect women and children in particular. In most African families, a widow is still 'isolated' even overseas.

Childless cases in the Igbo society enable the family to express their feelings of fear and anxiety, which often affect women's ability to share their experiences of abuse with others. In this regard, I view all families as social systems, and I see any change in one part of the system causing changes in all other components of that system. Members of the family can be affected when the issue of 'infertility' becomes a serious threat between partners. At some level, the reactions of the family are important to understand how they express their feelings, unless they are able to work through their difficulties in coping with the situation. I see the inability to adjust emotional pains when considering childless complaints as not a unitary phenomenon, but the latest example of long-term difficulties in the family system, especially in adjusting to life changes. This implies that family pressure or control of reproductive activity is likely to affect marital relationship and intensify distress on women rather than men.

Struggling to cope with social stigma has led to arguments, which participants recounted as too hard in their life. Abuse related to poverty reveal that certain groups of people within a population are associated with a higher risk of being overlooked. Examples of such groups include rural inhabitants and households that are headed by women—widows and the childless.

A common complaint shows that a case of abuse is often demonstrated by women's economic dependency, and most of the time, survivors are afraid to opt for ways to protect themselves for fear that they would be left unsupported. A widow said, 'I was taking all the pains to remain in the family of marriage for the sake of my children'. Parallel to this, a childless wife commented, 'I would not leave my marriage in spite of beatings, threats, and insults I received from the family members, and also people would blame me for the failed marriage'. In this part of the society, failed marriages are blamed on women, and women divorcees are stigmatised.

Of crucial importance, my findings suggest that most women in this study have experienced abuse and violence leading to isolation, threat, and humiliation in their family of origin. A variety of mechanisms are used to define standards of accepting male behaviour and how female violence is treated. In the case of married women without children, the proportion of abuse reported in this study, abuse defined as sexual, psychological, and economic, is as high as 50 per cent compared with 25 per cent of the widows and 2.5 per cent less than others amongst the widower and childless men. In most cases, the traditional practices create 'controversies', demonstrated in my findings, which undermine women's rights.

The role of the family is clear within tradition and is cited as the great influence on people's beliefs. It is clear that tradition remains at the heart of family as a cultural heritage. For instance, a man can never be at fault as he is the abuser or perpetrator. In the worst situation, women are blamed for everything. This is an exceptional case where the family mentality has not yet changed in the Igbo society. Hence, women are forced to conform to the local custom. For example, a childless woman is denied inheritance and property rights because of her condition. In this way, the symbolic rite of passage perpetuates abuse that worsens her social condition.

In addition, the findings take into account all abusive trends occurring within the local community of South-Eastern Nigeria. Abuse is considered as being related to cultural stereotypes that perpetuate mental distress on women, including a variety of verbal and non-verbal behaviours targeted at the emotional level. Participants have been labelled as 'outcast' and are often vulnerable to all forms of abuses. It is as if they are in some way responsible for the death of their husbands through means of witchcraft and must be made to suffer through traditional custom and practice.

Within the traditional society, discriminatory practices exhibit a wide range of fluency with local dialect and having a group in which participants were able to understand each other was obviously important. In this study, 90 per cent of the participants interviewed had difficulties with their in-laws over property and 85 per cent of women were unable to meet their household needs. The local community is where the right to inherit land is linked to cultural practices such as widowhood practice. For example, women have lost their right of property because they refused to have participated in widow cleansing. In most cases, women have difficulty inheriting or owning property, even in instances where they are legally allowed to do so.

Women's social position brings about a 'vacuum' in looking at the level of social interaction and household pressure in the traditional society. The social withdrawal shows how they are traumatised, and this runs parallel to a wide range of views associated with violence. For instance, a widow lives in constant fear as a result of lack of power and voice. This evidence is supported with another language: *ina asi nwayi ajadu mechie onu onye ga ekwuru ya* (if you silence a widow, who will speak for her?). Till today, widows and the childless wives in the Igbo society are less protected by the law because their lives are likely to be determined by local, patriarchal, and kinship interpretations of tradition, custom, and religion. The environment sometimes provokes the usage of offensive language that alienates women. These factors throw light in the way traditional practice becomes culturally patterned and where grief is a common identification in women's vulnerability.

Consequently, the fate of the adult survivors has been closely intertwined with the general course of visible difference in gender. Therefore, conflict and tension are set in motion between the growing, 'modernised' social stratum, which initiated and inspired women to adopt Western ideologies and believe that traditional practices have jeopardised their very existence. The constant exposure of women to the modernised version of 'woman' and the corresponding values of Western culture clashed with traditional practices aggravates violence towards women. The resultant dual-value system, with its constant dilemmas and the alienation it has caused many women, manifested itself in the formation of two distinct groups: one group, made up of highly educated and professional women, modified their traditional attitudes and adapted to the new environment; and the other group, often under pressure from their families, resisted the 'imposed traditional norms' as corrupt and full of abuses. The latter group (those living in the rural areas) felt excluded and isolated. This resulted in resentment and distrust towards certain local custom and cultural practices. It is clear that diversity issues are important in creating this 'awareness' among the female population.

The controversies around 'land' and 'ownership of property' can be drawn from the foregoing discussion that although the level of economic development and the structure of the economy have some influence on women's entry into the production (ownership of land), neither of these factors can adequately explain women's participation rates in inheritance and property rights. Additionally, the effect of marriage and education cannot, of course, be considered in isolation from other factors which affect women's socio-economic status and their position in society. These traditional practices perpetuate struggle and serve as an example why few women in rural areas have migrated to urban cities to gain education and wage earning that could potentially influence their social relations and improve their conditions of everyday life. On the other hand, the very act of leaving behind the old traditions and of participating in social production in the public sphere is a step forward for urban working women regaining their value, dignity, rights, and autonomy. Yet the lack of corresponding supportive social provisions, and effective legal reforms, has made it difficult for the present patriarchal systems to transform women's socio-economic and political roles. Also, the mere participation of women in economic activities and the violation of women's traditional rights have undermined the notion of diversity subject to continual exploitation and violence on women.

Women, in the interviews, said that subordination increases their vulnerability. A majority of the concerns from the eminent women shows that almost 25 per cent of participants recounted the fear of authority as a major reason of not reporting their abusive cases, and challenging traditional practices is reinforced with cultural taboos. What this means is that, in the traditional Igbo society, women's complaints in relation to harmful traditional practices were growing when compared with the same incident in other ethnic groups in Nigeria and, at the same time, less attention is given to address the situation. One of the female informants sought out possible explanations of women status as follows. Traditional beliefs about women being subordinate are perceived as generally selfless service. Therefore, women's customary rights have been overlooked, apparently making their lifestyles unstable. This comment shows that traditional practices according to people's opinion and views are still problematic in dealing with a discriminatory practice that reinforces this impression. One of the female informants notes that of all aspects of traditional family life, the widowed and childless conditions particularly in the rural areas would seem to be one of the most likely casualties of social changes. Ezeilo (2003:17), who wrote of law and family life amongst the Igbos, stipulates that the cultural stereotype of women seems generally true as several harmful traditional practices militate against women in rural areas and have been established. The factors to be taken into account would include, inter alia, the suspicion, discrimination, and marginalisation of women. The degree of lamentation and despair recorded between the Igbos by the WACOL NGOs spotlights a differential of intensity of practice amongst the communities.

From the findings from my study given for rural areas, it may be deduced that the incidence of abuse of property rights of women is higher in the rural areas than urban cities of any ethnic group, but this may not be universally true as the study was carried out only in South-Eastern Nigeria. On the whole, there is a trend of customary law taking the upper hand in women's inheritance status in rural areas. There were a greater number of adult survivors from different levels of households, which demonstrate the incidence of discriminatory practice and customary law. The Igbo sociocultural difference is confirmed. A higher percentage of adult survivors are recorded for the Igbo-speaking people than the other ethnic groups in Nigeria. This could occur due to low education, poor living conditions, and lack of control over the environment (Field notes, 11 June 2006). Womenfolk believe that the native law continues to persist in the villages leading to exclusion of women from inheritance and property rights, which can be validated by their dependency and lack of property rights manifested in their stressful life in the household. This differential provides some evidence of the psychosocial distress found amongst the female population.

Women's property rights, especially in the area of 'intestate' succession, are particularly restricted. In some customary law systems, a married woman has no legal capacity to own or dispose freely of property she has acquired by her own labour. Such property customarily belongs to her husband and is subject to his control. With reference to such succession, in almost all customary laws, a wife cannot inherit her husband's property or any share of it if he dies intestate. In many communities in Igbo land, under customary law, a husband inherits his wife's property, whether or not she leaves children. In addition, a widow's right to remain in the matrimonial home is at best dependent on her 'good behaviour', an imprecise and anomalous term, which underlies a situation in which the widow's position may be liable to violence and abuse.

In contrast, a wife of statutory marriage is in a stronger position with regard to rights to property and rights of inheritance, although certain conflict cases may influence the uncertainty in the laws. The deficiency in women's property rights has been corrected to a minimal extent by legislation, but discriminatory principles, especially in the law of inheritance succession, still remain problematical in several ways. This has been the traditional position, and although there has been a measure of change in certain respects, women's legal status in marriage still falls far below the standard advocated by the Universal Declaration of Human Rights and the Constitution of Nigeria (1999). The higher status occupied by men in African societies has not been altered by the progress of time.

4.7.1 Psychological effects of abuse and domestic violence

Psychological factors for abuse have shown a positive association which manifest themselves in patriarchal institution where individual social status, dignity, and protection of women's rights are undervalued in society. Participants described such maltreatment to refer to the economically disadvantaged as a consequence of their lower status, oppression, marginalisation, and stigmatisation. One of the females recounted the risks as follows:

> '. . . painful. It feels like a disease. It attacks a person not only physically but also emotionally and morally. It eats away one's dignity and drives one into total despair' (F—NGO, sixty years).

The findings examine the link between histories of women's rights as predictors of insecurity, fear, and anxiety associated with unhappiness and despair amongst the vulnerable population. The documentary evidence from Africa Charter on the Rights of Women (1995), Article 5 (d), helps to present the complex problems of abuse and its psychosocial implications. It highlights all necessary legislation that '[a]buse perpetuated on women is harmful to women's social status'. Traditional practices harmful to women's self-actualisation in the local communities have witnessed cases of widowhood practices—*ime ajadu* in Orumba, North of south-eastern region, to justify needs for basic women's rights. Abuse of women's rights in rural areas increases as survivors of patriarchy fall victims of widowhood practices. Despite dialogue and negotiation with the local leaders/authorities on certain cultural practices that dehumanises women, abuse offences, and other crimes on women committed every day become a wider concern. I have identified the most common cases of abuse within the community associated with the adult population. Cases of physical, sexual, emotional abuse and other forms of customary and discriminatory practice recorded are data that comes from a questionnaire survey conducted from this study.

Participants described abuse of women as devaluing their dignity, rights, and respects. Abuse is a major problem, especially when women are labelled as inferior, suffer severe economic hardship, and are dependent on their male counterparts. Such conditions do not allow women to relate well to the rest of society. Unreported violence makes them unassertive, secretive, and living a lonely lifestyle, which is stressful in communities throughout Igboland, as adult survivors are accorded with very few rights. Participants reported that they are regulated by an array of customs, rituals, and practices that involved even sanctions. Most indicators of negative self-image are described by participants as 'damaging' their self-esteem and such common experience sometimes leads to *Ariri*, which sometimes has fatal results. One of the eminent people remarked the following:

> '. . . *majority of the adult survivors often suffer from a lack of social recognition and acknowledgment of their social role of patronising or dismissive treatment and from the subtle impact of social stereotype and stigmatisation. Such an experience can have profoundly negative effects on survivor's loss of self-esteem and her relationships with family and community, leading to an increase in stress-related health problems'* (V1, EW, fifty-six years).

Participants felt that, in general, traditional societies had difficulties in influencing a change in local custom and policies. The tradition had failed to grasp the 'intrinsic value' of human rights, and this is evident in the approach to 'land and property' in the Igbo land. Many participants argued that although there had been a great deal of traditional issues about the value of rights of property, such as promoting social inclusion and reducing abuse and violence against women, controversies around this topic are still problematic.

4.8   Results and discussion

Results from the findings reveal three major areas—patriarchal and kinship practices which affect women status, social deprivation that determine access to and control of property rights, and low status of women and how these factors affect women in their social and psychological areas of life. Fewer than half of the participants said they are aware of their domestic abuse and trauma in their lives, but they have not reported any incidents because of the nature of 'dominant culture'. The centrality of patrilineal and kinship is linked with the control of the ancestors over the customary law and discriminatory practice on access to property. In this respect, harmful traditional practice preoccupies the mind of survivors as most vulnerable groups as well as responses to emotional and psychological dimensions as essential to a more nuanced perspective on *Ariri* (mental health problem). Most Sub-Saharan Africans still perpetuate certain cultural and religious practices that marginalised and distressed women. However, the interview found substantial backing amongst the indigenous traditional society on the ritual, material, and symbols on patriarchal customs and gender relations. It revealed the participants' inability to explain adequately certain gender stereotypes regarding the exercise of male power.

The conflicts which exist between traditional beliefs and practices and new ideas of inheritance and property rights and some degree of independence for both women and men still indicate marginalisation. For instance, lack of access to the claim of land and property belonging to their late husbands can affect survivor's livelihood. This explains that the vulnerable group have fewer rights than the rest of others in the society. When practices such as social deprivation come to light, there is no appropriate action taken to protect the women involved.

The difference in this current study shows that childless wives in the Igbo society have no means towards a better future due to the fact of their stigma associated with their social condition. They are more likely to suffer from *Ariri* (emotional distress), depression, anxiety, sleeplessness, and phobias because of the stigma associated with childlessness. The characteristics of *Ariri* are connected with social, cultural, and psychological factors that have been reported, for example, disinheritance related to unhappiness, fear and anxiety, frustration, and degrading inhuman treatment, which can be deeply distressing. The problems may be immediate or long-term and can be exacerbated by discrimination, poverty, and neglect, leading to women's health issues. These differences exist between and within all ethnic and social groups in Igboland.

Whilst the recognition of cultural diversity is important, the two fieldworks indicate that a predominant patriarchal practice is likely to affect women's social status. Effort has been made to use a culturally competent organisation which can be understood as one that acknowledges and incorporates at all levels the importance of culture, vigilance towards the dynamics that result from differences, expansion of cultural knowledge, and adaptation of services to meet culturally specific needs of adult female survivors.

Harmful practices on women outlined in this study are linked with *Ariri* (mental distress). Historically, contemporary Igbo society has viewed mental distress in a socio-economic context linking the cause to cultural restrictions and patriarchal and kinship practice leading to post stress and traumatic experiences—social neglect and ostracism. For instance, the socio-economic characteristics of women with mental distress demonstrate their lower social status in relation to poor living conditions and stressful life events. A familiar example is the experience of feeling low especially when one looks at the stigma around the situation of widows and childless wives within the community. In this low status, *Ariri* may be translated into mental distress, depending on the factors of symptoms present. What these findings did explain is that *Ariri* is measured as a moral and spiritual force, a state of sadness, frustration, and feeling of despair and loss.

Findings from this study about the relationship between the post-bereavement and the socio-economic characteristics and the risk of mental distress are indicators of *Ariri*. The study by Saxena et al. (2007:878-89) indicates that the incidence of mental distress and the need for care are highest among poor people in rural communities. Similarly, that population with the high rates of socio-economic deprivation have the highest need for mental health care, but the lowest access to it. People with mental health problems are also vulnerable to abuse of their human rights. Scarcity of available resources, gender-power inequalities in their distribution, and inefficiencies in their use pose the three main barriers to better mental health, especially in low-income groups. Zack-William's (2006) study on the mental health of blacks suggested that risks of mental distress are highest amongst the poorest, the least educated, and the unemployed. On the other hand, a study in South-Eastern Nigeria by WACOL and Ezeilo (2004:6) found that age, gender, and education and other indicators of low socio-economic status were significantly associated with *Ariri* (mental health of vulnerable population in developing countries).

My findings indicate that adult survivors have suffered a great deal of injustice about traditional practices, which amount to discrimination and stigmatisation leading to 'women with *Ariri*' (mental health problems). The initial socio-economic deprivation could help examine the level of psychosocial distress amongst the female population. The pattern of risk reveals the varied age group of women. Our findings (based on a more recent cohort) replicate the results of Ewelukwa (2002), Nwankwor and Ezeilo (2005), which showed that the stigma rate is greatly elevated in survivors, specifically, in young, widowed women. It is important to note this pattern among young mothers whose loss of status appears to have a substantial association with stigma rates. At younger ages, being widowed, as compared with being childless, appears to be associated with a higher risk of stigma. The restrictions are imposed on victims who must endure the most humiliating rituals in relation to persecution and accusation of using witchcraft (Sossou, 2002:203).

Within this study, *Ariri* represents a new psychosocial characteristic related to women's vulnerability as constituting a major indicator of lamentation, frustration, and prolonged grief and loss. Additionally, loneliness, reduced income, fear of the future, and despair are some of the common experiences of *Ariri* sufferers. As a result of the post stress and post trauma, participants link their loss of status in the language in which they are addressed, for example, witch, unclean, or profane to describe mental distress. A participant reported the way she was referred to and highlighted the 'stigma', which made it more difficult for her to talk to people in her community about her widowhood practice.

> *'Hmm . . . I know the embarrassment I went through widow cleansing. I still live in pain whenever I came across the perpetrators. Sometimes, it makes me feel tearful. I know people who live with such distress . . . [but] it is difficult to discuss it in our community and say that a widow is abused'* (V2, W, thirty-five years).

The findings from my study show a barrier to seeking help. Within the community, two participants informed that women with *Ariri* (mental distress) are branded with accusations and name-calling related to witchcraft because they are suspected of causing their husbands' deaths. The community, especially the young adults, like to shout and tease the widows and childless wives. Cultural differences in dealing with mental distress and lack of awareness or help-seeking behaviours are still problematic in rural areas. This is due to expectations and emphasis on the family and lack of awareness of available services (limited and different system) such as education regarding mental health symptoms and lack of information on services available within the south-eastern region of Nigeria.

The implication of stigma shows that mental health and cultural issues are significant to examine women's rights and health issues. Mental distress seems to lead to people, especially the victims not being treated as full members of the community. Participants informed that mental distress brings a shame to the family and people with such illnesses receive both physical and verbal abuse. This stigma is widely reported as a problem within the Igbo community and presents itself as a difficulty, especially when people are faced with constant isolation and ostracism (rejections) from the community. The majority of the participants in this study described long-term domestic abuse as a result of traditional practice, which has been deeply rooted in local communities and has existed for more than centuries, despite the legislation put in place to prevent it. In this way, the study clearly draws attention that none of 'women with *Ariri*' has been educated about emotional well-being and implication of long-term abuse and trauma. In other words, lack of access to community services increases cultural awareness of the stigmatisation, which explains the need when trying to encourage people to access new mental health initiatives.

The fifty-three women who participated in the study reported constant abuse, which dehumanised them. That is to say that all had admitted to themselves that they were suffering from abuse and needed help. Although we do not know whether they speak for the vast majority of victims, some of their complaints are so similar that we believe that they represent a pattern common to most women who have endured prolonged abuse at the hands of traditional practices. The comparisons between gender and ethnic groups indicate that both males and females in the south-eastern region of Nigeria were interviewed during the study. Fortunately, the data collection efforts that measure the scale of the situation of cultural stereotype and stigmatisation include the influence of sociocultural, economic, and political norms in determining what constitutes 'women's *Ariri*'.

Okunna (2004:7) writes '[o]ften, society blames the woman for her childless condition, and some women even blame themselves when they are not at fault'. Similarly, Aguwa (1997:20-30) shows the sense of isolation and loneliness, which women experienced, was uniformly painful, and they made repeated, often desperate, efforts to overcome it. Frequently, the result was a pattern of many unresolved emotions. Those relationships, which did become more intense and lasting, were fraught with difficulty. One in every five married women without children complained of marital conflict, either feeling abused by their husbands or being indifferent towards them.

> *A thirty-eight-year-old woman, married for thirteen years without children, complained of how her husband threatened her and never supported the family. She felt she could not leave him because of her family's reputation and myths attached to divorce in Igbo culture as well as her religious values with respect to marriage. His abusive behaviour and 'bullying and beating' in this relationship was all the more striking, since other areas of her life were relatively intact'* (V2, C, thirty-eight years).

Looking at the history of domestic abuse in adult survivors is a plausible explanation for psychological reactions among the vulnerable population studies. Social exclusion, marginalisation, and cultural stereotype throw light in explaining the 'controversies' that is associated with violent trends. The explanation compares abuse trends with socio-cultural and economic factors—women's access to inheritance and other circumstances that undermine women's rights. My findings seek to consider the often, unseen consequences of 'childlessness', including the impact on mental health and general well-being. It shows that there is still lack of knowledge and understanding of 'infertility' and social support for the victims within the Igbo society.

Each of my findings represents a different local story that is unique in women's suffering. As a researcher, the vulnerability in women kept me thinking about the traditional practices, lack of boundaries in local customs, and insecurity associated with women's *Ariri*. In every interview, one out of every four participants in the local community have suffered from related cases of abuse and violent behaviour in their lifetime, survivors often experience anxiety, guilt, nervousness, and fear. They often distrust others and repress their emotions. Women have been working, taken ill, and grieving for the loss of death and state of childlessness. A widow married for twenty-seven years with four children said the following:

> '*I was happy with my marriage and least expected that death would take my husband away soon. What worries me is that I have not learnt to live as a single parent. I couldn't cope with the emotional pains. I keep upsetting myself with guilt* (V1, W, and forty-five years).

4.8.1 Women with *Ariri*

The results from this study show that the consequences of discriminatory practices affect women. It assumes that these practices represent the manifestation of a patriarchal and kinship system and a particular way Igbo people inflict emotional pain on vulnerable women. Sossou's (2002:201) study on 'Widowhood practices in West Africa', the silent victims confirm that '[t]hese practices are by no means systematic, and their frequencies are subject to regional and local variations. The problem is that much of the scanty information within the practice is what may be described as unprocessed information'. Furthermore, Ilika (2005:68) indicates that '[a]lthough widows and childless wives make up a large proportion of the female proportion in all societies, the plurality of African societies shows that such areas of study have not created in-depth research and knowledge in public health'. Violence towards women in Africa occurs because the subordination of women cuts across all socio-economic situations and is deeply embedded in cultures leading some women to assume that it is part of their sexual responsibilities, even to the detriment of their health (Okemgbo, 2002:101-14). Parallel to this, it suggests that social distribution of justice and equity and level of interaction is an important psychosocial predictor of women's health in families and local communities. For instance, evaluations of gender injustice have been associated with unhealthy patterns of emotional responses and certain health problems (Sheppard, 2002:779-97). This study demonstrates the difference in women's perception of inheritance in an Igbo traditional marriage. Therefore, there is evidence that Igbo philosophy solicit ownership of inheritance and property rights via procreation. This statement goes far in shedding light in the Igbo cosmology that 'a child is wealth (*nwakego*), which shows that marriage without a child is fruitless. Igbo society is where procreation has supremacy. However, childless wives are more likely to suffer mental distress (*Ariri*) than widows with children. Another interesting difference is that both types of women experience isolation and despair which exacerbates low self-esteem with varieties of inner disturbances that are likely to produce insecurity, fear and anxiety, excessive worries, paranoia, and withdrawal symptoms (Ewelukwa, 2002).

However, health professionals need to work with these women with *Ariri* to help them understand the factors. If one is to assess 'women with *Ariri*', one must understand the inequality and social deprivation related to traditional practices and how groups gain power and esteem in that society. Understanding of women's social status helps to look at 'gender differences', to demonstrate how abuse-related behaviour, emotional distress, and health-care systems are correlated.

Importantly, women's subordination and marginalisation from my study indicates discrimination against women in patriarchal and kinship system. The researcher then deduces that there is a significant difference in the extent of abuse and violence between men and women. This implies that in Igbo traditional society, women are the most vulnerable because they internalise abuse, which makes them timid.

Figure 4.1: **Shows susceptibility of different age groups to 'Ariri'**

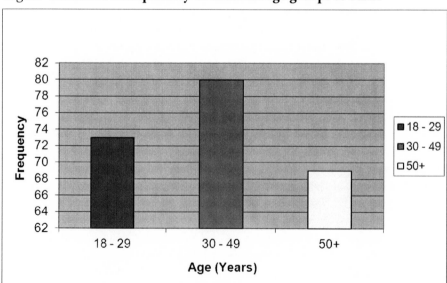

Age

The result confirms that the greatest number of risks in women occurs amongst the age group 30-49. Participants recounted their vulnerability as loss of status, social deprivation and social stereotyping, and unfulfilled psychosocial needs and tensions emanating from unequal power relations in patriarchal family. The local indicators and characteristics provide psychosocial insights into what the concepts of vulnerability meant in local context (*Ikwa Ariri*). Vulnerability is taken to mean people's experience of high risk of events that have adverse impacts on their livelihoods and that their ability to deal with risky events when they occur is impaired. This provides a wider, societal framework of considering different ways in which harmful cultural and religious practices can affect certain age groups, in terms of marginalisation and exhibiting mental distress. Because of its probable effect on women's stressful lives, poor living conditions, and lack of social control over the environment, age is particularly important in considering women's vulnerable position in the light of lack of women's rights, and it is also considered danger to reproductive health reflecting the central hypotheses in the same findings.

According to Figure 4.1, there is a difference in the occurrence of distress in the female population. However, the susceptible age group has had the highest rates of *Ariri* (emotional distress) because they are an active and working age group in the community. From the age of fifty-five, rates decrease gradually because they are less involved in social activities. The age variable suggests that in the south-eastern geopolitical region Nigeria up to 80 per cent of mental health problems in women have occurred in the 30-45 age groups. Information from the WHO Report (2002) shows that violence related to abuse of women in African countries is still problematic. Of crucial importance is the understanding of the age-related health risks amongst women, which stems from a psychosocial viewpoint where physiological and emotional abuse of development are seen to be the most significant factors predicting changes in women's health.

All these factors have to be put in the context of deliberate risks occurring in an area where poverty and inequality is rife. However, the research is dependent upon various bodies of evidence—anthropology, sociology, psychology, law, social policies, and national and international data on how a mental health cases have been established. Apparently, data on violation of women's rights are available as there is a national and international abuse-related network. Cases of abuse recorded on the national level include 8,300 incidents of traditional practice as related to exclusion and marginalisation on inheritance and property rights (report from WACOL, 2004) and more than 1,500 cases of abuses were recorded under marriage tribunal by Onitsha, Nnewi, and Awka dioceses (2000-08) based on childless condition (infertility and impotency) seeking for annulment. According to the WHO (2005), 8.5 million to 115 million girls and women in the world population have been exposed to harmful traditional practices such as disinheritance, forced marriage, and widow cleansing. Similarly to this, Heise (1993) indicates that more than 9 million African women and girls are victims of traditional practice in terms of widowhood. Most of these cases do not even get reported. However, in those instances where they have been reported, there have been very few prosecutions. Why the appropriate authorities have not properly addressed this is not clear.

Ofoegbu (2004) indicates that there is a limited report on the psychological and social harm on the negative health outcome amongst women to determine the rate of morbidity and mortality, as there are no statutory centres or organisations to support the awareness in rural communities. The vast majority of people suffering from emotional distress will find it difficult to make a recovery where there are no therapeutic and counselling facilities and support. Successful and coping mechanisms can involve a variety of different approaches, including self help and social network support and a therapeutic model of treatment and/or medication. The above information provides important practical implications. Most of the Western societies invest much of their resources in increasing the awareness of healthy lifestyles, by encouraging consultation with GPs and counselling. By developing educational programmes and media campaigns, they encourage people to practice healthy-life habits. Many times, these efforts attempt to increase the awareness of potentially negative consequences of unhealthy behaviour. The goal of these appeals is to remind people of their vulnerability due to engagement in unhealthy behaviour and cultural practices, which is still a huge challenge in Nigeria. The present study highlights the fact that sometimes threats and abuse are left unreported, and some cases like inheritance and property rights may even have an adverse effect on women's self-esteem.

Occupation

The modernisation and consequent harsh economic realities indicate how women may be under more serious pressure than their other counterparts. This would imply higher demand of their time and thus more support to the household. The results also examined education and also religion in order to look at the impact of patriarchal and kinship system differently and to encourage the attempts to meet the characteristics and needs of different age and personality groups.

Education

Women's education has a positive role in their social status. This implies that the predicting power of female education in rural area is very weak because of sociocultural expectations, which explain such restrictions. In the opinion of Uzoezie (2007:5), without female education, autonomy, independency, and employment will not have the desired effect because women who are more educated tend to have a good career. This result is significant, and I, therefore, infer that women's dependence on men and cultural practices adversely affects the participation and decision-making power within the household and local community.

4.8.2 Women without *Ariri*

The findings from my study shows that many factors contributed to women's well-being which enable them to be independent without the effects of *Ariri* especially looking at the experience of socio-economic life in the context where the concept of production provide material and economic participation of women in the household. Parallel to the institutional barriers, there are also individuals among women who are important in overcoming everyday problems because of their level of education, family support, and wages. These factors helped to keep them away from emotional distress. This was, in part, due to the efforts of such individuals who managed to keep their economic status and channels of communication open. A woman lawyer who has been a widow for six years narrated how she was supported during her bereavement:

> '*The support from my-in-laws, relatives, and friends gave me confidence and was able to 'smoothen' the way. The support through informal means prevented small problems from escalating into big issues*' (V2, W, forty-three years).

The objective of participation and decision-making draws together the recognition of women's rights and dignity where the women's status demonstrate gender-inclusive environment and addresses the differential impact on women and men at all levels. This reviews the economic struggles and subordination of women in the colonial and postcolonial experience, which represents loss of setbacks in women in relation to politics, economic decision process, and other forms of social opportunities in Nigeria. Today, the growing involvement of women in the democratisation process has been significant. Women participated fully in the struggle and, as a result, achieved greater respect and recognition in society and developed greater confidence as agents of change in the democratisation process. Similarly, most of women who lived in urban and rural areas had undertaken primary, secondary, and university education, and hence negative attitudes towards women are being consistently challenged in recent times.

My findings with regard to women and property relations shows that framework for integrated development brings the experience, knowledge, and the interest of women and men to bear on the development agenda which can transform gender inequality. In this regard, it highlights a form of new awareness on the basis of gender relations and development efforts through NGOs, such as WACOL and other forms of Women's Care Group (WCG), which empower women to address their problems co-corporately and seek solutions to their specific needs.

4.9   Implications for survivor's care to improve life opportunities

This leads me on to my final theme, which is on the implications for survivor's care to improve life opportunities; and identifying sources of network support for coping mechanism. In this study, developing survivor's care lies in the strengths of cultural knowledge and awareness as evidence based practice. However, all my participants recognise the value of emotional, practical, and psychological support when it comes to working towards an evidence-based cognitive therapy (CBT) that can lead to the best outcomes. Cognitive therapy in my finding focuses on the 'survivor-centred approach' as it relates to emotional distress (*Ariri*). However, the cognitive model of therapy improves survivors care by 'empowering' individuals or vulnerable persons to express their traumatic experiences in a therapeutic relationship which the psychoanalytic/psychodynamic therapist explores in depth. The cognitive development in my study improves the way in which individuals construe emotional distress and interpretation of their real-life situations. For example, stressful life events are disruptions in the life story that need to be accommodated into the individual's ongoing storyline. In particular, integrating difficult life experiences into the ongoing life story has been associated with greater physical as well as psychological health and well-being (Pals, 2006). Building an alliance between 'empowerment' and working on people's 'mental activities' provides new insight and understanding through which emotional distress (*Ariri*), which is latent in the psyche, could be unpacked. For example, mental activities motivate a high percentage of human daily activities and real-life situations which can be interpreted or analysed through the help of counselling and psychotherapy.

The cognitive model of therapy is useful to my study as it helps to identify procedural sequences—chains of events, thoughts, emotions, and motivations—that explain how a target problem (for example, long-term abuse related to stigma) is established and maintained. This cognitive model identifies problems which, link with the real-life events focused by PTSD. It also raises the self-awareness and understanding of a specific cultural problem, that is, *Ariri* which survivors face. For example, someone who as a victim of abuse and neglect is perceived as being abandoned would almost certainly be vulnerable to feelings of abandonment. In addition, my findings show that participants are not aware of their cognitive problems, but when probed further, I realised that most of the traumatic event, which has been repressed, gradually affects the cognition. An existential psychotherapist such as Carl Jung, Melanie Klein, and W. D. Winnicott places greater emphasis on the here and now while drawn to awareness in the way individual's current problems are shaped. Cognitive changes in this context show that all human feelings (emotions) and behaviours are important (body-mind-soul or spiritual self) and should be seen and treated as a unified whole person to improve sustainable good practice for healing and restoration. As a result, we foster the positive presence of psychological capacities and resources.

Consistent with my findings, the evidence of 'stigma' raises the question of how patriarchal practices on property inheritance could advance trauma-focused cognitive behaviour in response to PTSD. According to the study of Herman (2003), those women who are abused in their home are more likely to experience a profound somatic effect in their lives. For example, they may have low expectations regarding their rights to autonomy and self-determination, and this is likely to have an impact on their responses to traumatic stressful events. Such effects may include unhappiness, frustration, and despair resulting in social avoidance behaviours or increased compliance with persecution through a sense of learned helplessness (Wethington, 2004) and, when resolved, can lead to lower distress and greater psychological growth (Wethington, 2003).

With the incidence of internalised abuse and low status of adult women survivors, my findings suggest that young women may be at increased risk of developing psychological difficulties due to the various changes that occur in their lives (Pals, 2006). In addition, supportive relationships in cognitive domain have also been enlisted to improve the awareness of potential risk because of internalising traumatic events in the face of life stressors. For example, Papadoplolous and Gebrehiwot (2007) have suggested that it is the cumulative influence of major developmental changes (e.g. discrimination, socio-economic status, poverty, and unemployment), which occur in life events that account for the increased anxiety and other problems often found in adult survivors. According to Dunn et al. (1995), the cognitive model of therapy predicts that both cognitive elements and emotional functioning are involved in the development and maintenance of people experiencing low self-esteem. This is associated with both the emotional and recovered states of traumatic life experiences.

Judith Beck (2005) indicates that individuals who are distressed are encouraged through positive impacts on health care to lessen their frustration and worries, enabling them to behave more functionally, especially in cases of anxiety, as their physiological and emotional arousal abates (Beck, 2005:324). In this study, all my participants recognised the value of improving their traumatic experience through counselling treatment, especially where religion and spiritual care have provided a supporting therapy when it comes to working with vulnerable people towards their traumatic condition that can lead to best outcomes. Several participants said religion was a central part of their cultural identity. For some, it was an important aspect of life that they did not want to lose. A widow remarked the following:

> 'With my own bereavement experience, I come to terms with God through Christian fellowship, and I rediscovered my inner strength in my traumatic condition.' She further adds: 'God's helped a hell of a lot, especially when I'm a bit down, you know? I just pray to him and ask for help and he provides' (V1, W, thirty-two years).

Hodge (2002:109-15) raises the importance of spiritual activities, such as prayer as a positive ritual which rekindles self-esteem and enhances positive visualisation of self as well as benefits achieved from belonging to faith tradition and participating in associated community-based activities. However saying that it does seem that because of different perspective faith leaders see more value in considering and discussing what is the best approach for individual social support, and this means that a truly spiritual model of mental health, consisting of the predisposing, social, psychological, and spiritual elements has a significant role to play. Nevertheless, the importance of religion in relation to belief, faith, and spirituality of those in a vulnerable position cannot be overemphasised.

Head (2004:72-75) also sees religion as proactive to good mental health. The work demonstrating this is drawn together in the *Handbook of Religion and Healthcare* (Koeing et al., 2001). Religion and spiritual care is that care which recognises and responds to the needs of the human spirit (psyche) when faced with trauma, ill health or sadness, and this can include the need for meaning, for self-worth, to express oneself, and for faith support, perhaps for rites or prayer, or sacrament, or simply for a sensitive listener. This cites 1,200 original research studies and 400 reviews with chapters on both spirituality and mental health. In most of these studies, 'religious practice or belief system' was added as psychosocial model incidental to the main study. Looking at various factors relevant to mental health, religious involvement was found through greater self-esteem, life satisfaction, and happiness. National Health Service (NHS) Education for Scotland (2009) further indicates that spiritual care begins with encouraging human contact in compassionate relationship and moves in whatever direction need requires. It increased hope and optimism, adaptation to bereavement (grief/loss), social support (practical and emotional), and less loneliness through connecting or reconnecting with external resources (e.g. within the person's faith community) and decreased levels of anxiety, loneliness, and faster recovery from depression.

The comparison of the findings indicates that spiritual part of a person's life has a significant resource in coping with suffering or illness as well as in the attainment and maintenance of health, well-being, and quality of life. The supplementary interview that forms my Ph.D. data identified religion as a vital role in alleviating emotional pain, suffering, and affliction among the female population. Data findings from religious care provide a complementary component by documenting the experiences of survivors and service providers (spiritual care providers and local faith leaders), including the challenges they face and how best to meet survivors' spiritual needs and what works well and not so well in the provision of spiritual support for 'women with *Ariri*'. My findings inform that spiritual care to the vulnerable Igbo women shows that religion increases their inner strength, prayer life, creates spiritual fulfilment, courage, and hope in their suffering, which not only aid healing effects but also enhances women's vulnerability. Whilst psycho-spiritual care concerns are described as key areas to consider in providing religious needs (e.g. Charismatic Renewal Prayer Ministry and Women Christian Fellowship), such services help in understanding the importance of survivor's strength and their connection with God. In addition, justice and peace groups within the church recognise the significance of psycho-spiritual and practical interaction to bring the women to more assertive level of respect and dignity. One way out of this dilemma would be for strong Igbo women within the group to lead and encourage their contemporaries to raise themselves above this situation and begin to find a stronger voice within the local community. In this regard, women recognise their need to be empowered to move on. Additional data from this study represents a large and innovative body of work on survivor's spiritual needs and resources, and the role of spiritual and religious beliefs in the illness experience as ways survivors cope with their condition. Given these trends, it is essential to understand the spiritual needs of women, the majority of whom identified as Christian and to configure counselling and legal services to meet their psychosocial needs, particularly in rural areas. NGOs also provide essential support to women, such as counselling and legal advice to alleviate the cultural practices associated with women's vulnerable condition.

From this study, almost 70 per cent of women suggested that religion is important to their psychosocial and spiritual life. Additionally, 30 per cent of the participants indicated that at one stage in their life, they have shared about their religious and spiritual matters to someone on different occasions. In more expanded form, participants agreed that religion and spiritual beliefs are very supportive in their *Ariri* (mental health problem).

Results obtained from the participants in my study consider the importance of the spiritual values at each level of professional support to individuals and groups within their specific needs. For instance, some of the activities such as women's programmes and visits to prayer groups contribute to awareness of coping mechanism. Recently, church activities such as fellowship and prayer sessions, talking to friends, positive thinking, and listening to Christian music, including songs, hymns, Psalms, and devotional chants were expressed by participants as ways of coping with mental distress. Religion was seen as a source of hope and courage. Most women pointed to religion as significant to maintaining happiness and well-being. For example, drinking holy water, rubbing blessed oil, and wearing sacramental and prayer symbols were solutions sought to eradicate supernatural forces that could cause misfortune and exacerbate mental distress in Igboland. One participant said the following:

> 'As a widow I joined a charismatic prayer group in the parish, and it was a big relief to my mental anguish . . . I admired the way members treat themselves as a family with respect, and this process helped me to think differently about my ordeal (suffering) and God in a way of coping with my bereavement' (V2, W, forty-nine years).

However, in general, the beneficial effects of religion to mental health considerably outweigh the adverse ones. From the results of the study, practice of one's religious belief is the main way individuals cope with their psychosocial condition. In people's suffering, religion becomes a way of providing a psycho-spiritual support and of many relationships that are interconnected with the sense of divine. It is a two-way connection for the individual, who feels the need of God's presence in his/her suffering.

Participants may experience psychological healing in the way they channel their religious believe towards God in times of difficulty. Another woman who was childless for fifteen years commented the following:

> 'When I was isolated by my husband and mother-in-law because of my childlessness, I found going to the church and staying quietly

before the Blessed Sacrament very soothing and I felt at peace' (V2, C, forty-two years).

With my own experience as a priest and counsellor, working with African families in the UK, I see religion as a powerful means of recovery from mental distress. More importantly, religion stands for people in distress as a psychological well-being. Most of the respondents see religion as a 'symbol' of comfort, relief, refreshment, and repair of the emotional wounds. For example, those that are pushed to the edge or overlooked in the society, see religion as a symbol of comfort that alleviates worries, fears, and anxieties. Apparently, the respondents' belief shows that religion is a source of liberation and breaking the barrier of individual psychosocial conditions. It is about solidarity and 'being with others', which remind people that there is another spiritual dimension to our lives. Psychologically, religion is perceived as interplay, which works on both spiritual and psychological aspects in us and helps to ease people's suffering. Generally, families and communities value religion as sustaining society. A widow remarked the following:

> *'When the news of my late husband was broken, relatives and visitors started coming. I went and collected the younger one from the school, keeping a brave face and a smile, and told the teacher quietly. Took him home and told him. It was like a dream and a difficult experience. I stopped crying all of a sudden when I noticed it was upsetting, especially the young one. Seeing you in distress upsets him and makes him think he is losing you too. With the help of friends, church, and family members, I could recover from the shock'* (V3, W, forty-five years).

Overall, my findings show therapeutically important benefits for trauma-focused cognitive therapy ranging across the female population studied. These include survivors of violence and abuse with traumatic and stressful life events. There is also evidence that trauma-focused mental activities have clinically significant effects on depression and anxiety amongst women with low status. However, the findings show that trauma-focused cognitive, behavioural therapy specifically addresses the long-term abuse and stigmatisation on PTSD. This affects memories of a traumatic event and the personal meanings of that circumstance or event and its consequences.

- The findings attempt to determine what factors are associated with psychosocial, behavioural, and cognitive predictors of *Ariri* and what factors may improve coping mechanism for the population based studies.

- In the process of developmental studies of the risk factors of *Ariri*, evidence through cognitive domain (mental activities) can only show that this risk factor is associated with a higher incidence of specific cultural problems in the population exposed to that risk factor.
- The stronger the relationship of stigmatisation, the more certain the association, but it cannot prove the causation.

Survivor accounts of oppression and stigmatization experiences in my findings reveal striking parallels between inescapable shock responses to unpredictable traumatic events stressors. Psychological responses to marginalization appear to be primarily geared towards maintaining control over oppression stressors through cognitive, behavioural, emotional and psycho-physiological processes.

Additionally, both primary data from my interviews with adult female survivors and empirical evidence from my study strongly suggest that unpredictability and uncontrollability of oppression, marginalization and stigmatization stressors play an important role for major incidence of traumatic events in 'Women's Ariri'—mental health problem.

4.10 Final discussion

From the above presentation of the result, I will now discuss the relative findings according to theory and afterwards answer my research questions.

By investigating the current widowhood and childless practices in the Igbo society, I have discovered deep interpersonal violence and emotional abuse amongst the vulnerable population. Violation of women's rights is widespread not only in families but at the whole range of local communities in Igboland. The problems and restrictions on women are deeply embedded in the patriarchal and kinship structure, producing a climate of isolation, humiliation, and stigmatisation.

The issue of patriarchal and kinship practices and women's status and the relationship between the two are important factors contributing to the above situation of *Ariri* (emotional distress). The nature of patriarchal institution plays a significant part in maintaining the subordination of women and efforts to keep hidden abuse. In effect, interpersonal and informal relationships prevail when looking at the influence of customary laws and discriminatory practices. There, intimidation and even physical violence at some degree can be found. Women do see the state of control as unavoidable, but they will try to influence their cases again by using legal services. Corruptions of public and private activities have been noted many times during the interviews as has corruption of inheritance law. Finally, the main purposes of this system are economic exploitation and avoiding economic strain and standing up to dominate women.

Returning to previous literature and research, it is interesting to note that the situation in South-Eastern Nigeria does contribute to theories, suggesting women's deprivation of property rights. I could note, in this study, that patriarchal practices in Igboland present a cultural way of identifying with the theory of property relations. Since the pre-and postcolonial period, inheritance and property rights of women have been affected by the Nigerian-Biafran war and generational issues of land are viewed from ancestral perspective. One difference noted is that in Igboland, the patriarchal system has a powerful status to influence every rule of law, both customary and statutory, and it is through this operation that exclusion and corruption exists and still persists in Nigeria. Finally, I have to note that in this study exists what Nwankwor (2005:17) has defined as violence towards women, focusing mainly on specific cases of patriarchal practices and patterns of violation of women's inheritance and property rights, which this study examines.

Most participants recounted that the government should have acted to redress women's abuse but the failure to come to an agreement with tradition reflected the nature of the relationships. The relationship between the tradition (customary law) and statutory law is strained; cooperation is limited and both drew criticism from other organisations. The difference is that the number of participants argued that statutory law should make every effort to retain control, tending to work not in isolation but rather in partnership with native law to regulate patriarchal power related to discrimination against women and other forms of abuse. Customary law attracted criticism for its 'rigidity'—the fact that tradition did not make a contribution to addressing women's right of inheritance and negligence on widows and women without children among other women is raised repeatedly in the interviews and also in some of the local printed media. This experience illustrates some of the difficulties of partnership working, especially under pressure of time described by participants as 'overlapping' or even 'complimentary'; it is the differences rather than the similarities that mattered.

It was evident throughout this study, from both documentary sources and the interviews that although local custom was important, so were the people that inhabited them. The study on women's social condition on property seemed to illuminate the micro-political issues in local communities. It was apparent that any analysis of the impact of patriarchy on women had to take into consideration the people's social and cultural beliefs, their emotional expression, and ambitions and actions that had tried to shape this study. These could be taken forward or halted.

Within the policy and political sphere, there appears to be very strongly held opinions about 'participation' and 'social integration'. Within this study, participants argued: 'you can and should attain to participation' such a view had been expressed by the directress of CIRDDOC Nwankwor (CIRDDOC Report, 2003) on women's empowerment and rights.

A majority of the explanations given to the cultural imagery of male dominance lies in the ethnographic evidence that represents 'inequality and stratification' as a social problem. Male dominance as a way of locating men's everyday experiences in a broad framework of patriarchy gives attention to the masculine ideology that stresses domination of women, competition between men, aggressive display, predatory sexuality, and a double standard. The hope of this study considers the complex psychosocial impact of marginalisation and risk factors appeal and bear in mind the full meaning and purpose of health, psychological harm and even sudden death in people's lives.

Some limitations of the study

Importantly, it is believed that the sample size of the participants in this study is small. However, for the purpose of this study, I limit my focus only to the widows and childless wives in the three villages of the study investigation in South-Eastern Nigeria. It is believed that this factor will not distort the findings, and the fifty-three participants used for sampling will give the study reliability and provide an authentic result. This study should have been conducted throughout the whole of the south-eastern region of in Nigeria but due to time factor, to reach to all the local districts in Igboland; this would not have been possible. The time and resources available has become the determining barrier for this 'choice' of the area covered by the study. The study relies on self-reporting measures. Within this study, the aim for reliability is reflected in an open account that remains aware of the partiality and limits of the findings.

Limitations of the research methods

A qualitative method was chosen to enable the exploration of the subjective meaning that NGOs attach to their experiences. However, there are limitations to qualitative methods. These include the difficulty of replicating studies and the researcher's bias. In addition, the fact that this study is heavily dependent on the researcher's skills is another limitation, along with the small size and non-representative samples that are used.

One way in which the trustworthiness of the study was improved was through clear and open discussion of the methods and the underlying assumptions that were central to the research. This helps to ensure that the results can be transferred to other contexts or settings, as the person who wishes to make the transfer is able to make a judgement based on transparency.

Mixed methods research is one way in which rigor, additional perspectives, and insights beyond the scope of qualitative research could have been added to improve the study. Mixed methods refer to those studies that integrate one or more qualitative and quantitative techniques for data collection and analysis (Borkan, 2004). As Cresswell et al. (2004) note, mixed-methods research is more than simply collecting both quantitative and qualitative data; it informs that data will be integrated at some stage of the research process.

Within this study, a quantitative questionnaire could have been used to gain the insights of professionals within mental-health services, along with the qualitative semi-structured interviews. Not only would this study have had the advantages of the deep descriptions to subjects' lived realities explored by qualitative methods, they would also have the potential to contribute to the generalisation and reliability, that is, the strength of the ethnographic study.

Limitations of the research model

The study involved a sample of fifty-three participants. This size of the sample cannot reflect the perspectives of all adult survivors within south-eastern region. However, the findings allow for some consideration of what barriers limit access to social network services.

Most of the fifty-three participants were aged between eighteen and fifty-five years old and had lived in the local community for approximately 15-30 years in the same local government in Anambra State. This study would have benefited from a wider age range of participants and the inclusion of participants who had been outside the town for less time. Future studies should extend the examined age groups to children and adolescents as well as to the elderly population in order to obtain a comprehensive picture of the effects of psychosocial issues in different age groups. Though the participant samples are similar and the experimental procedure is identical, it might be worth replicating within one study.

Another limitation is the willingness of the eminent people—clan heads and *umuokpu* (women heads) of the community to share their views with the researcher. Nwankwor (2003) discusses the rational context of study with the vulnerable population, including the question of trust and openness in data collection. She emphasises the importance of the relationship of trust that the researcher develops with participants. Although the researcher worked to gain trust by ensuring that all potential participants were provided clarity around the aims of the study and the process involved, he feels that more could have been done.

The researcher was aware of the importance of the female role and kept a reflective note to assist him in remaining aware of the theoretical and ethical context within which the research was carried out. He ensured that the research process was described in an open manner to allow readers to draw their own criticisms of the research. However, to further improve results, it would have been beneficial to invite critical feedback from colleagues in the fieldwork during the research process.

Limitations of thematic analysis

It is important to remember that there are limitations to thematic analysis, which should not be overlooked. The researcher felt that thematic analysis was the correct approach for this study as it provided an approach to drawing themes from the study that were not biased by the researcher's own preconceived ideas. In order to work with the limitations of thematic analysis, the researcher ensured that the reader had clarity on the research methods so that they could draw their own conclusion about the reliability of the data

Limitations of the researcher

As the researcher is new to ethnographic research, it is important to be aware of his limitations. I feel that my representation of patriarchal and kinship practices on Igbo women is overemphasised. However, this learning process from my study may have had an important cultural knowledge on the research data.

The benefits of this study are that information is not taken for granted without adequate probing, and as an outsider of the community, the researcher may have been entrusted with more information. However, the benefits for a person from the south-eastern region carrying out the study include the interviews being more culturally specific and because the interview is carried out in the participant's own language, it could be more accurately translated.

Finally, the analysis in the study indicated that only a marginal per cent of domestic abuse is explained. This fact highlights the need to further explore this multifaceted social phenomenon, trying to offer a more coherent picture of variables that might contribute to the decision to keep one's health. Parallel to this, the study promotes access to social justice and equity for all survivors of abuse in cooperation with the United Nations and other NGOs that use international laws as support and protection of the vulnerable in their fundamental human rights. Additionally, funding for the prevention of violence against women is still problematic in Sub-Saharan Africa because only a small amount of pledged funding goes to NGOs even though they provide a large proportion of social support for the less privileged in the society. Because of the motivation and roots in empowerment model of outreach in the local communities, NGOs are not just professionally competent but are interested in the 'whole person', dignity, respect of rights and values, and try to assist the marginalised in different ways to regain their confidence and self-worth. This requires attention to interpersonal, psychological, and social needs for the people. Despite these limitations, this study provides important new evidence regarding the various effects of mental health problems on promoting health-care behaviour.

This study covers a wide range of psychosocial factors related to the way subordination and marginalisation of women are apparent in the kinship system and increase the awareness of women's rights and healthcare. In order to make the most of the opportunities available and to guide communities to shape their health and level of social interaction, the study has used a variety of data sources to confirm the higher risk factors related to isolation, exclusion, humiliation, intimidation, and stigmatisation, which is most marked in the rural areas. Hitherto, the chapter has reported the key findings, drawing upon both the interview data and documentary sources in reflecting upon the decline in customary law and order in the contemporary Igbo traditional society.

Clearly, the social phenomenon, which is connected to the women's status, affects their normal lifestyle. Many people, however, would define this type of social phenomenon as out of the ordinary, assuming that a stressful life event could precipitate women's mental distress. Clearly, any stressful event and poor living conditions are dependent on several levels of cultural norm, and research results are, therefore, need to be interpreted with caution.

Cases of participants from my study revealed far-reaching differences between their relationship with the network society and the power relations. For instance, wife beating and other complaints such as social deprivation and neglect are strongly specified in families and local communities. It is observed that abusive behaviour is a maladaptive pattern and sometimes alcohol related. In this situation, sex discrimination is discovered in the demographic growth of the population, where women are posed with threats. The act of abuse often goes unpunished, reinforcing the climate of hostility and the claims of those who wish to maintain this social discrimination. Abuse is a situation where women may be involved in escalated causes of *Ariri* (mental distress) from my study. Stress related to events supporting discriminatory practices suggests that one in four women in rural areas experience abuse. Approximately, 8 per cent of the fifty-three participants have experienced violence and abuse at any one time. This equates to the series of abusive incidents of the adult survivors occurring in every two minutes, which put women at risks.

The previous literature demonstrates that traditional practices exacerbate emotional pain—'unhappiness' and 'sadness'—that make survivors feel inadequate, unworthy, and vulnerable. Evidence from International Human

Rights bodies such as the International Convention on Civil, Cultural and Political Rights (1996), especially Article 12, defines violence related to harmful traditional practices as marginalisation and discrimination, which most African countries and their governments have not taken serious steps to address among the female population. In a similar way, Okonjo-Iwuala (2010) indicates that the traumatic impact of violence leading to prolonged grief as disinherited widows and childless wives testified their ordeals, following the death of their husbands, becomes a concern as public health issue. Supporting the women's plight, Ilika (2005) claims that violence is likely to lead to women's mental health problems. When considering the scale of the violence and the abusive social environment in families and households as well as local community, Ilika further says that violence puts women at risk and in a vulnerable situation. Okoro (2003:14-29) further indicates that throughout African societies, witchcraft accusations are commonly targeted at women and children in families. In most cases, these accusations have led to ostracisation, persecution, torture, and inhuman and degrading treatment. Similarly, Herman (2003:159-60) argues that the abuse and domestic violence associated with witchcraft in sub Saharan Africa adversely affect women. She further explains that the use of the term 'witch' creates some kind of inferiority complex in women, which continues even in recent times to manifest itself in trauma and stress on women.

Zack-Williams (2006), who studied the relationship of violence and other social factors, described the effect of violence as intensifying mental distress. The social significance of abuse illustrates how violence could cause both physical and emotional pains on the vulnerable groups. It demonstrates also how vulnerable 'women with *Ariri*' could express their abusive experiences that shape the understanding of emotional distress (mental health problems). The prospect of relating to and attempting to examine varieties of psychosocial features around abusive behaviour and threats on women enable the study to explore what it could mean to the female population to associate violence with mental health problems. For instance, social conditions inherent in women's deprivation and economic exploitation on land and property of women illustrate people's beliefs and assumption that women's anxiety and fear could be interpreted as a result of socio-economic differentiation in inheritance law. This demonstrates that most of the legal systems should see that the 'economic rights' of the marginalised should be protected.

As indicated in this study, inheritance status has been a more common problem among the female population and is thought to increase women's vulnerability slightly every year but underreported cases in rural areas suggest ineffectiveness of oppressive systems where women's cases are overlooked. The agrarian society in Igboland suggests that property rights could widen the economic disadvantages of the survivors with the age in the prevalence of mental health problems amongst widows and childless wives. It should be noted that this study was looking at the impact of patriarchy on women as a test of hypothesis to look at 'women's *Ariri*', which was prevalent amongst the vulnerable groups. The data shows a high and growing proportion of alienation with multiple needs. Concern remains that those left under strict tradition on customary rights of inheritance are the most vulnerable. They are people with the most entrenched and difficult problems. Social deprivation has become a normalised experience for many young women amongst adult survivors. Violence and abuse has become a huge problem in the family unit. Osiora and Okoye (2002) from Ministry of Women Affairs Social and Economic Development, Anambra State, Nigeria, indicate that cases of married women without children in proportion to the abuse are as high as 50 per cent, compared with 25 per cent of the widows.

One of the central arguments for the customary rights of inheritance has been that the integration of women as a disadvantaged group makes it impossible to protect the vulnerable without stigmatisation. For instance, report from the office of the Federal Ministry of Women's Affairs Awka, Nigeria (2006) shows that women in the poorest socio-economic conditions are almost seven times as likely to be abused or psychologically harmed as those in the top income group. The social status of women in this case also makes a difference, where cultural differences, social stereotypes demonstrate men's superiority over female subordination. The stigma relates to women's dependency on culture, allowing men to dominate and control women. The problem of stigma shows people whose status is already low, for example, people on low incomes or people living in poor areas. People who are likely to be overlooked will probably be doubly stigmatised. The problem the survivors are experiencing is the social rejection of their condition. There is argument to support the position, which described as stigmatising. The problem of social stigma related to survivors' experience of loss of status has been an important element in the cause of lamentation (*Ariri*).

This view, which emphasises the harmful traditional practice, seeks to interpret social problems in terms of women's subordination and marginalisation. The understanding of gender divisions has become increasingly important for the discussion of property relations and issues affecting women, which legislation and social policy must tackle. Hence, women on customary rights of inheritance can be used to distinguish Weberian characteristics of underclass that are marginal to property relations-labour market (Weber, 2002). This argument is important to define the groups to which a concern is necessary. Spicker (2008) shows that there are strong objections to the term from some who see the argument as a way of grouping together people in very different circumstances and stigmatising them for their circumstances. I used Weber's economic status in the discussion of the data because his idea of property relations is important for policy purposes, although it still shapes the way in which many people think about economic society. The possibility has been demonstrated as an alternative approach starting from the concept of person, and viewing social relations in terms of a network of rights and social justice. From this standpoint, social change can only occur when statutory law can take precedence over traditional practices as reinforcement to the rights and obligations of a relationship.

The Kleinman's Exploratory (EM) model is used to better understand any phenomenon about which little is known on the scanty study of widows and childless wives in the South-Eastern region of Nigeria. In this regard, the method of data collection becomes useful. With this in mind, it is impossible for any other person to relate their 'experience/story' in the same manner as the participants. The findings enabled the researcher to break down the sample of participants' stages of life according to relevant features—sex, age, occupation, marital status, education, religion, and place of residence—to include in each category to reflect the sub-groups targeted. The link between women's social status plays an important role in analysing and interpreting the effect of patriarchal and kinship on women. It investigated an in-depth understanding of women's collective experiences in their family of origin, which illustrate some of the harmful traditional practices that are relevant to know in Igbo society. Anthropologically, the data demonstrated the impact of cultural diversity when considering women's rights in patriarchal institution which differed from matrilineal culture and secular market-based and state-controlled societies in the Western culture especially where marriage, inheritance, and property gives women status. This led to a focus on religion and myth and on the kinship systems that are generally thought to provide the structure of traditional societies. Both of these enquiries are rich sources of information in terms of the relationship and implication about the dominant behaviour in women's social roles in production and reproductive activities. Although some of these culturally sensitive elements may be important to various degrees in groups with non-Igbo population, I emphasised them based on interpersonal relationship (connections) and life experiences to sociocultural issues. In addition, I selected these specific elements seriously and consider it necessary in analysing women's social condition in the local community. The analysis and interpretation of reports accumulating in a cultural setting where abuse on women is debated by feminism, psychoanalysis, and the sex role theory explain power relations, which underpin women's inferiority and subordination.

What the findings from my study have convincingly shown is the need for a holistic gender-based approach, which must be understood in the light of a large-scale social structures and psychological outcomes. Women's problems with the customary rights in contemporary Igboland have made 'huge difference' in women's lives.

Although there was much evidence to support this claim, what was also interesting within this study was that the family appeared to be almost strong to their individuals in their suffering. Previous literature such as Nwankwor and Ezeilo (2005) indicate that individuals with high profiles of socio-economic status stand a better chance of coping with *Ariri* (emotional distress).

As an ethnographer in this study, the data provided an opportunity to reflect upon and draw difference from the local stories related to 'women's *Ariri*' and the way women respond to their coping style of life. I began to look at the social position of women in Igbo society as a resource that is culturally patterned with power relations. Of crucial importance, domestic abuse related to traditional practice still holds women back in Nigeria. This pattern links with some of the negative comments:

'Ariri egbuonam' (I'm emotionally distressed or stressed out).

'Ike uwa agwugom' (I'm tired of this life).

'Kama nga adi ndu n'eri afufu nile okaram mma ikwu udo' (I prefer to commit suicide than see myself in this suffering).

The findings identify painful utterances (verbalisation) as externalisation of abusive complaint and what they signify in local experience. It shows that most of the violent behaviour, which is not dealt with, could manifest through women's distress. In this way, I became aware that unresolved emotions could be a trigger to psychosocial condition of women. In attempt to prioritise women's rights and health care, I began to think about what could happen to young mothers when they are not legally protected as well as supported in their state of grieving and loss. In the cause of thinking, I became aware of the risks that could be associated with women's psychosocial differences. Thus, empowering people to gain access to social network services, such as a system of reporting abuse, is an additional useful skill, which this study has successfully achieved, that is, advancing a different experience in effective reduction of harmful practices towards women.

I have worked with the mental health organisation such as Afro-Caribbean 'Minority Ethnic Groups' (MEG) and the Nigerian Community in South-East London, and I use the empowerment model to assist the disadvantaged groups in rediscovering what held them back in their past. African communities represent a wider range of ethnic minorities in the inner city of Borough of Southwark, Lambeth, and Haringey. This includes a multicultural population and a high socio-economic prevalence of mental distress, providing counselling services for combating cultural stereotypes and stigmatisation of Nigeria communities in the UK, and people with mental health histories. In my experience with a vulnerable population, I look at the missing link between violence and social deprivation and draw on notions of community and sustainable human development as ability to learn different experiences in dealing with vulnerable people and their illnesses.

I have illustrated the background controversies, cultural differences, legal, social, and psychological interpretations that influence inequality around women, which affect their affliction and suffering. Cultural examples are also offered which have implications on the decline of customary law and order. It enables me, as a researcher, to look at the existential conflicts on how cultural rites can increase the risk of domestic violence and abuse towards women. The narratives on women's traumatic experiences have provoked a chain of thinking in relating to these questions: How does the Human Rights Act (1998) impact upon women in Nigeria? And what meaning and purpose does social deprivation create for women? However, it is important that this study looks upon long-term abuse and trauma and provide health-care messages to families and local communities and improve the legal and economic positions of women, which is needed in the modern society.

Women's participation in the study is something positive and it is a means of learning about the psychology of the community and how the marginal groups could understand and handle their vulnerability. Participatory approaches provide a mechanism for the researcher to understand the impact of patriarchy on women, oversight on women's subordination, and rigidity on decisions and policy formulation in traditional levels. It is suggested that with cultural knowledge, capacities, and priorities as the basis for learning, action and policy formulation, and participation enhances diversity and empowerment in gender. Despite women living in poverty, most of the participants, especially the widows, believed that Women's Care Group (WCG) such as NGOs and Christian Women's Organization (CWO), family members and their children were the social network sources of support in coping with *Ariri* (mental health problems).

Importantly, I hope that my study will provide the impetus for health professionals, social workers, psychologists, human rights activists, and policymakers to strengthen their commitment towards risk awareness in women's rights and health care. The idea here is to use women's empowerment model to promote political will, energy, and resources in concert with aid agencies and civil society to bridge dominance and inequalities in women's status. Many people in Nigeria think that lamentation and despair are a result of patterns of abuse; therefore, it does not represent a psychosocial problem. This study has provided evidence differently alongside with strict tradition and how the marginal groups can be seriously affected. This study has also emphasised the need to understand some of these constraints from the perspective of the local custom and traditional practices in which escalation of violence and domestic abuse is obtained. We need one clear, consistent message to communicate that discriminatory practice under the inheritance law could exacerbate mental distress. This needs to be reassessed in the light of evidence about links between infertility, widowhood, mental distress, and interpersonal difficulties of life. Okunna (2004) indicates that knowing the degree to which and how property relations in kinship system are related to the various aspects of human life is deemed to be critical beginning points of understanding women's mental distress. Therefore, understanding women's perception of disinheritance and symbolic devices (rites of passage) leading to psychological abuse will, in turn, provide information about the quality and social support provided to women and their ability to identify mental health problems in Nigeria. This result is designed to use the flow of information and educational awareness to produce cultural sensitivity on inheritance law and other traditional practices that could reinforce women's access to their inheritance and property rights. By identifying and quantifying gender-based violence and abuse in this study, it is hoped that the outcome provides policymakers with a tool, offering direction and focus for the work of significantly improving the target base for Igbo women in Nigeria. It is of significance that the federal institution and local state should liaise together to develop social policies suitable for vulnerable people with psychosocial and legal support to make sure that adequate supervision, training, monitoring, protection, and a safe environment is granted in families and local communities in the south-eastern region of Nigeria.

4.11 Conclusion

This study has clearly shown that there exists a complex interrelationship between women's inheritance and property relations in patriarchal and kinship practice, which could influence the domestic abuse and trauma on women. In this study, the multiple factors such as gendered dimensions of risk, insecurity, and poverty for understanding women's vulnerability remain essential. Cultural restrictions could account for this, considering its adverse consequences on women's access to productive resources and level of participation in the decision-making process. The result from the findings showed that stigma, in relation to traditional practices, promotes inadequate emotional resources or strength to offer women support and a fear of authority within the patriarchal society and may also contribute to Igbo women's reluctance to seek help from their abusive environment. The results indicate that vulnerable Igbo women in the study participate in a uniquely stigmatising condition from the rest of others because of insensitive reactions from the public, such as hostile behaviour, which intensifies insecurity, fear, and anxiety, which has been specifically ignored and remain invisible to health and other social-network services. Furthermore, women with low-income status from rural areas are more likely to see themselves as being overlooked and stigmatised. Although 'stigma' has been a mental health issue and an issue of concern amongst the deprived groups, the increase in public awareness of the disease and the efficiency in the local community still remain poorly understood in rural areas. These factors have a tendency to indicate a lack of legal protection and security for women as well as understanding the implication of social stigma amongst the female population. In this regard, the vulnerability of women has helped me to establish, in this study, the causative factors that have encouraged and maintained the relationship between traditional practice and psychosocial consequences of harmful practice on the Igbo women.

Key messages of the research findings

Two aims for this study were highlighted at the outset in Chapter 1. The first aim was to understand the barriers for survivors seeking social network services and support within the local community. Participants felt that there are barriers, which stop them from seeking and accessing customary rights of inheritance. A summary of their key messages are highlighted as follows:

- There is a stigma attached to widowhood and childlessness, and this may stop people from discussing *Ariri* (mental health problems) and accessing services.
- The belief that mental distress is a moral or spiritual issue remains important to some within the family and community and impacts their help-seeking behaviour.
- The expectation of the family play an important role in both caring for the person and advising whether they should access services.
- The mental health service in South-Eastern Nigeria is limited, and thus the communities are not accustomed to the range of services available in the society.
- Participants felt that the community had a lack of knowledge of the impact of traditional practice in relation to widowhood.
- There are few words for mental health problems in Igbo local dialect, meaning that people cannot always express what they want to say to professionals.
- There is a general lack of knowledge about mental-health symptoms within the local community.
- There are concerns that translators do not keep information confidential, and people are afraid that the community will be told about their problems.

- There is a mixed opinion about the work of GPs and local medicine personnel (*juju* or traditional men) in providing support for the vulnerable population.
- Feelings about professionals are linked to trust or mistrust rather than fear.

The second aim of this study was to make recommendations for improving access to services to adult survivors within the local community. Participants' key messages were as follows:

- Social network services and NGOs should work together to educate the community about services available for the vulnerable groups.
- Further education about the indicators and symptoms of *Ariri* (mental health problems), both for young women and adults within the community should be carried out.
- Psychosocial support would be beneficial to support those in the community who remain isolated and marginalised.
- Culturally-specific mental-health services would provide a more appropriate service to the community.

CHAPTER 5

Conclusions and recommendations

5.1 Outline of the key topics

The key topic of this study includes contribution to knowledge of gender and power, limitations of the research and action, recommendations for further research, implications for future research, and a conclusion. The ethnographic features of the research account for the use of linguistic, sociocultural, and political resources in relation to the case study participants (widows and childless wives) to glimpse the social environment and community in question through the eyes of the participants, enabling a clearer view of what is more or less important for them to achieve. It sheds light on how participants develop and shape their identities, their realities, their social relations, and what opportunities and difficulties they encounter. In this context, the ideal stance of a researcher is to be an intelligent, sympathetic, and non-judgemental listener to all his members. It provides participants' accounts from their perspective and enables effective data sources to be achieved with reference to the dissemination of research findings to research participants. Making research known to research participants is not a straightforward task, particularly in ethnographic studies when researchers are often engaged in the study of marginalised groups or unequal power relations.

5.2 Contribution to knowledge of gender and power

The study demonstrates the predicament of women in relation to inheritance and property relations based on their gender, in support of Onuoha (2008:41-43) who claims that 'the patterns of inheritance and succession, particularly under intestate estate under customary law in Nigeria, have almost as many variations as there are ethnic groups in the country, and many of the variations are discriminatory in practice'. This study highlights the impact of patriarchal tendencies that limit women's rights in property relations and the contribution of cultural rituals and taboos (ostracism) or exclusion to illnesses, which need more attention by future research. The study demonstrated that one of the factors responsible for disinheritance of Nigerian women is the relations of gender and power leading to the legally incorrect interpretation of inheritance and property laws. This is linked to the culture and exaltation of the male sex as superior at the expense of female gender. However, the long-held traditional practice has led to wider inequality that affects women's fundamental rights in contravention of Article 23 of the protocol to Africa Magna Charter, which explains women's rights.

The deprivation of women of property rights indicated in the study show how patriarchal practices exert power over women in contemporary societies. The investigation into this research has provided a valuable contribution to the study of women's marginalisation and vulnerability to account for the psychosocial condition of Igbo women. The study demonstrates the interaction between patriarchal domination and women's deprivation as indicators of social inequality and reasons for women's economic dispossession and poverty during past decades. Nwankwor (2004) and Afigbo (2005) claim that these phenomena have been under-researched in South-Eastern Nigeria, and this study has attempted to fill a gap in this book.

Additionally, this study advocates a movement towards gender relations within which the equal social status of women as equal to men should be encouraged and recognised. These include the challenges of inequality women face and how best to meet their human rights needs in the local community. Razavi (2003:1479-500) tries to explain that in this way women should also be in the forefront of the awareness especially where their negative self-image is sustained by marginalisation. In contrast, Weber (2002:272-303) claims that the relationships between inequalities in possessions and control of material resources and social position of women in property relations illustrate the way in which gender relations shape the 'class status' and 'subordination' of women. Weber used property relations and women's social status to justify economic exploitation which various theorists use as a ground of social injustice and imbalance of power. The significance of these relationships enables this study to argue that women in patriarchal societies are more oppressed, which suggests that dominant trends of control are the common factors in traditional society.

One of the contributions to research on the psychosocial condition of women in the study is the cultural stereotyping and stigmatisation of widows and childless women. This helps to explain both the enormous observable variation in cultural understandings of what the categories of 'man' and 'woman' mean and the fact that certain notions about gender reinforce the inequality in a wider range of traditional society (Ilika, 2005:65). It is clear that women's status can be interpreted in the broader context of social inequality based on a shared theoretical framework to explain the marginalisation of women. Many of the cultural issues are derived from the fact of male heir inheritance status. These point to the universal fact and the cultural variation constitute the understanding of social problems in the study.

It is important to say that a focus on property relations has contributed to the new ways of conceptualising and theorising the way Igbo women could be stereotyped and stigmatised. The feminist anthropologists alongside Weber and other theorists have offered a new perspective in this study by using gendered property relations to identify patriarchal societies and consider exclusion of women as key factors of psychological 'exploitation', 'oppression', and 'stigmatisation'. The awareness of oppression reveals the exploitative strategies through which patriarchal practice is maintained and also the reason that dominant behaviour remains unchallenged in the society (Zack-Williams, 2006:35). The findings presented in this study show a specific cultural variation of such practices and relate it to the incidence of *Ariri* (mental health problems).

Our discussions have shown that women have limited rights in Igbo society. The issue of women's property rights in intestate marriage is important not only for Nigerian women, for the specific areas of their status as a spouse and a widow and a childless wife, but also for women who face the eventual death of their husbands and the women who suffer when their status as a wives is at stake. They are currently not sufficiently protected by the law, and they remain vulnerable. In this investigation, women's low status is reflected in discriminatory practice and lack of participation in decision-making and access to other forms of social-network support evidence to their psychosocial distress. It is well noted that women's social condition can only improve if their sense of autonomy is improved.

This study has contributed to a better way of providing cultural competence, for example, expansion of social and cultural knowledge in creating awareness of the potential and actual cultural and social factors that explain women's psychosocial condition. The studies of Nwankwor and Ezeilo (2005) noted that not only has the methodological and ideological question of male perspective plagued the studies of Igbo women but so has prejudice. In effect, African women have become a centre of research upon which the Western world has played out some of its concerns about women in general. For example, colonialism in their view would foster the emancipation of non-Western women by raising living and educational standards. At the same time, women would be freed from oppression of social customs that were said to include deprivation of inheritance and property rights, lack of choice in marriage partners, and few or no divorce rights. Whitehead and Tsiakata (2003) dealt with the problems of women's inheritance and property status and supported reforms designed to improve women's inheritance rights. Such analysis reflects the conception of African women as subjugated and oppressed members of a largely patriarchal society.

It also highlighted the extent to which patriarchal and kinship practices affect women's status. The relationship between women and kinship-based practice, such as gender relations, is central to understanding rural and urban migration since each has an impact on women's lives and is mobilised within specific social contexts and historical periods. Evidence has shown that women were sometimes active in the labour force and social process. Hitherto, we recognised that there are social structures and mechanisms, such as land and control of valuable products that prevent women from enjoying full equality with men in the discussion of Igbo women's roles.

In Chapter 2, we examined the psychosocial aspects of the concepts behind social inequalities and property relations. Given the centrality of gender, marriage and property claims, which encourage inequalities in kinship system, this study provides how gender divisions and women's disinheritance shed lights in the vulnerable position of women. It suggests that the effects of property is only one form of social closure by which kinship groups try to maintain exclusive control over resources especially where women, as the largest group, have had little to gain from the trend towards property relations. With the breakdown of the security of a lineage system, many women are discriminated against and lose the protection of the conjugal bond. I have also raised the practical issues of how discriminatory practices have operated. For example, one major basis of inheritance rights is to be found in inequalities associated with widowhood practices, where property inheritance and feminine roles, family structure, and relationships form the basis of the cosmology of the people. This involves much wider issues ranging from the family, the kin group, and the community as a whole. But this point notwithstanding, there is no doubt that women's inheritance and property relations are burdensome to women.

I have attempted to take up the question of how patriarchal and kinship practices have affected the widow and childless wives within conjugal arrangement in Igboland. In order to understand the mechanism by which this functions, I discussed the various forms of marriage and their impact on the Igbo social system. I emphasised the importance of kinship relations among the Igbo in order to understand how it can affect the women as well as how it is related to gender issues in society. Other features of family issues, such as widowhood practice, evidence to property rights, and socio-economic status were examined. I have reviewed those activities which women undertook as well as the constraints they face in terms of inheritance of land in particular. Attempts were made to show how important land as a resource is in Igbo society and why women could not inherit it. I offered three explanations for this. First women had no customary right over land; they could not inherit it and the traditional value attached to land made it a male prerogative. Second, traditional religious values have been a source of power for men but subsequently a source of subordination for women. In this regard, religious beliefs reflect and reinforce the subordination of women.

Finally, the importance of land in Igbo economy and its social and cosmological factors increases its value. It also increases interest in its inheritance as well as strengthening patrilineal descent. It would appear that as land has become more individualised under the influence of the colonial requirement for agricultural products, women's access to land for subsistence farming, especially for economic value, was circumscribed as a result of the discriminatory role in the subsistence economy. I have argued in this study that men used these reasons to rationalise their continued control of land or land alienation.

The colonial and postcolonial legal system also barred women from owning land. The system reinforced the patriarchal power in land ownership. In this regard, while the modern legal system offers the formal possibility for the inheritance of land by widows and childless wives, actual legal judgments commonly defer to the traditional customs which routinely deny a woman's right to land. In other words, ignorance (lack of information and education), poverty, tradition, and outright male opposition represent formidable barriers to women's ability to obtain the legal rights. Importantly, not only do women receive land of declining size and quality, their use and exercise of rights are becoming increasingly insecure.

On the other hand, there has been a considerable decline in communal and kin group assistance to the widow and childless wives. The lack of communal support may be attributed to a breakdown of kinship institutions resulting from a tendency towards individualism and capital expansion, although this was not demonstrated in the villages of this study. Certainly these developments have transformed most societies, including the Igbo, by modifying social structures.

Chapters 3 and 4 relate to research findings demonstrating available evidence relevant to the psychosocial condition of Igbo women, reinforced by the findings of fieldwork conducted for the purpose of this study in a selected Igbo rural area in Nigeria. The findings shows the collective experience of the participants, the local informants, NGOs methodology, and previous literature suggest that rural based women suffer from emotional abuse in relation to disinheritance, which leads to *Ariri*. Several studies have suggested that harmful traditional practices increase women's mental health problems. Holland (1990) remarked how African women in patriarchal society suffer from 3Ds—domination, discrimination, and deprivation in marriage. She further maintained that these factors are predictors for women's mental distress. Thus, *Ariri* from the findings amongst the poor and vulnerable shows how patterns of feelings in the culture become mirrored in multiple ways of expression of discrimination, exclusion, and stigmatisation related to severe economic differentiation, which is fundamentally influenced by cultural conditions based on seeing *Ariri* as located in the personal pathology of individuals. The findings demonstrate the negative impact on Igbo women and virilocal residence, which include the arranged and forced marriage embedded in kinship systems. It highlights dowry (marriage consideration) as a legal essential of a traditional valid marriage and its refund as an essential of a valid divorce—exclusion of unwanted women. It shows the extent to which divorce laws discriminate against women especially the childless wives. It explains that gendered divisions of labour and inequalities within domestic institutions (families and relations) reinforce rights of succession to property relations specific to widowhood as a result of pervasiveness of patriarchal gender relations.

The findings, for example, suggest that economic dispossession of widows and childless condition of women in the societies is a route to social exclusion of women under inheritance law. Women's property rights, especially in the area of intestate succession, are particularly restricted. It is argued that violence and abuse mark gender inequality and are key factors that contribute to 'women's *Ariri*' (mental health problems).

5.3 Limitations of the research and action

The study is limited to some extent by the lack of data on the proportion of widows and childless wives who do not succumb to *Ariri*. Nevertheless, it shows that in rural contexts, the patriarchal views of women expressed in rituals and customary practice together with patrilineal kinship and the monopoly of male property ownership are key elements in the social conditions, which exacerbate *Ariri*.

Another limitation relates to the gender, status, and insider/outsider position of the researcher. My male gender made the use of female assistants in interviewing the village women a necessity, and this mediated form of data collection raises issues. More collaboration with women's associations may have been a means to benefit from their experience. The failure to do so may relate to issues regarding my own cultural background, which merits some reflection at this point.

The issue of my own community standing and cultural background and its impact on the collection and analysis of data needs to be reviewed at this stage of the study process. However, the 'insider' dimension of my position as the researcher raises a number of issues, both methodological and ethical. The ethical issues discussed in Section 3.5 relate to the composition of the sample and, in the initial phase, issues around the non-coercive achievement of informed consent. Methodological issues related to my position in the community are also addressed in the same section in so far as they related to the composition of the sample and the possible constraints on the participants' responses to questions if they were attempting to provide data which they thought the researcher wanted to hear. This may have impacted on the collection of data.

Other aspects of my cultural background may have influenced the analysis of the data as frequently occurs in research despite the most strenuous attempts at objectivity. In my case, the selection of a large proportion of African sources for the ethnographic literature seems to indicate an initial preference for the 'insider' assumptions about gender relations and kinship rather than the fundamental questions raised about the power dimension of gender by 'outsider' ethnographers and theorists, such as Moore and Hirschon, discussed in Chapter 2 which proved central to my analysis. My own cultural tradition, of the beliefs and rituals of a patriarchal society, may have left traces which influenced the research methods, such as not taking advantage of the knowledge base of the women's associations, and the analysis of the data. The critical distance of the 'outsider' status of a researcher, together with the experiences of living in Europe and the UK for many years have contributed to the identification of these limitations and to my own development as a researcher.

In relation to status, my position as a priest and the contributions of a fellow priest in identifying the sample may have contributed to an overrepresentation of Christians. Finally, my insider/outsider position combining 'insider' knowledge with 'outsider' standpoint inevitably influences the identification of samples, data collection, and research questions and also the selection of 'eminent people'. However, this situation arguably benefits the linguistic and symbolic ritual related to widows and childless women.

The second, supplementary fieldwork trip included some widows and some women without children who did not suffer from the condition. This provided evidence that lapsing into a condition of *Ariri* is an established local custom for women in this category, but has not yet demonstrated in any simple or direct way, factors which were significant in tipping some women into *Ariri* where others of that same category did not succumb. This remains to be investigated.

5.4   Recommendations for further research

This study demonstrates that many local communities are unaware of the implications of harmful traditional practice and do not have specific procedures to serve affected survivors. It recommends that custodians of culture in communities should be cautious of gender-based violence and help to abrogate all the harmful cultural practices that encourage the violations of the rights of women, especially widows and childless wives. There should be increased awareness and sensitisation at the grassroots level to ensure that the existence of law is well publicised and women made aware that they have rights. More coordinated inter-agency training is recommended for all professionals working with affected communities, enabling them to provide effective and culturally sensitive support to those affected and to protect vulnerable women by being sensitised to warning signs. Other activities aimed at curbing widowhood practices, include training (awareness) and support to help understanding the symptoms of mental distress (*Ariri*) and recommend appropriate care pathways. Public health services should work closely with NGOs to promote mental health awareness within the local community and to provide information on accessing services. NGOs need to be more involved in service planning with Human Rights advocacy and mental health teams in relation to empowering women. Also NGOs and community leaders and representatives need more understanding of barriers for women in the Igbo community to access inheritance and property rights. Women with *Ariri* have specific needs; it cannot be assumed that their needs will be met by generic services already in place. Further employing other organisations and research needs to be carried out to explore the benefits of providing culturally specific services, for example, training bicultural experts or professionals who understand the subtleties of culture and religious services.

Most of the women interviewed for the purpose of the study responded to beliefs and practices identified in this academic work as patriarchy which negatively affected their psychosocial condition. The reasons given by survivors are varied and interesting, giving a useful picture of marginalisation, isolation, humiliation, and blame, but the sum total of the reasons given was the women's view of the strict tradition on inheritance law and superiority of men in Nigerian society. However, much violence and abuse occurs among women in traditional cultures, where women's status and self-worth may depend almost entirely on customary marriage and childbearing. In this respect, most of the young married women who are childless are exposed to pressure and life-threatening conditions when it becomes clear that the condition will not go away. This study shows that a 'childless marriage' has negative consequences for men and women. In most cases, women are blamed for this childless condition and divorced. Sending a wife home to her family of origin without support is viewed as an act of divorce by the Igbo culture and is likely to occur only if the woman has no male heir or is childless. It frees the woman and her kin group from any future obligation to the husband's people but frequently leaves the divorced woman without social or economic status.

All the women interviewed reveal that they are aware of the better legal and social status of Nigerian men, which if given the opportunity, they would wish to enjoy. Nigerian society has changed to some extent from its traditional patterns, but in many cases, Nigerian customary law has remain unchanged so that there is a disparity between native law, statutory law, and actual practice. This study shows that women are sometimes active in the economic and social process with the assertion of some degree of independence.

The study examines kinship Igbo marriage, the birth of male heirs, and the importance of inheritance and practice. Marriage is identified as essential for the completeness of the individual in Igbo society. Various forms of marriage and its impact on the property status of women are discussed with an emphasis on the close connection of the social and cultural ties related to different varieties of the institution of marriage; drawing from the domestic units of patrilineal succession, the relationships that are socially constructed. Ezeilo (2005:28) indicates that kinship provides a key source of social and economic power and influences most of the cultural practices both in the precolonial and post-independence development policies, which have focused on providing greater economic opportunities to men than to women. According to Sossou (2002:206), such policies have left African women of Sub-Saharan Africa even more dependent upon male kin, particularly fathers and husbands, and have contributed to marital conflicts. The patriarchal conflict and crisis under customary rights of inheritance revealed by this study enable a greater understanding of how widows and childless women can be marginalised and fall ill.

The emphasis on patriarchy helps to explain the system of power relations in land ownership. The barriers to these factors demonstrate that women and customary rights of inheritance suggest ignorance, poverty, and inadequacy to tradition and outright male opposition to women's rights to obtain the legal or civil support. For instance, not only do women receive land of declining size and quality, their rights to land use are becoming increasingly insecure. This not withstanding the women who have access to money could buy land. To understand the nature of the women's position, this work reviews those activities undertaken by women as well as the constraints which they face in terms of inheritance and property rights. Women have no customary rights over land; they cannot inherit it and the spiritual value attached to land makes land a male prerogative. In this regard, power relations over property rights are a source of power for men.

The main result of this study supports the promotion of women's rights in terms of what is really needed for a consistent, comprehensive, and systematic challenge to patriarchal power and domination in a way that will enable full integration, participation, and bargaining power of women in socio-economic and political activities in all aspects of life. As far as this study is concerned, power, economy, and politics in traditional practices exacerbates interpersonal violence and psychological abuse on women as a response to *Ariri* (mental health problem). Importantly, we must note that discrimination, exclusion, and stigmatisation of women need to be overcome through educational awareness as a new emerging trend in this study and should serve as anti-discriminatory practice in order to consolidate the legal and social support to Igbo women. Their significant emotional and social relations are ties to human rights. In this regard, we assume that the statutory law may be regarded as a permanent status of some independence for women in civil and public sector in the future as a means of alleviating psychosocial distress on the basis of the rules of the discriminatory practice on inheritance and customary law in Igboland.

5.5   Implications for future research

In future, this book will help in developing a critical awareness of the specific social relations of post-colonial domination in gendered property rights in South-Eastern Nigeria. There has already been an examination of the effect of the Biafran war on gender roles. The outcome of this study is to use gender awareness in contemporary Igbo society as a method of promoting women's rights and their health issues. Reform needs to occur at both national and regional levels. Women's groups at local level should promote the increasing female literacy awareness. Furthermore, these women's groups should actively encourage female participation in the political process. This would help to promote links between urban and rural populations so that women in rural areas can learn about their human rights and how to enforce them. The church also has a role to play in the promotion of women's rights by organisation of seminars for women, which will reinforce the work of the NGOs. Further study should attempt to identify other forms of cultural practices that could result in psychosocial distress in elderly women in Igbo society.

Previous study from Nwankwor (2005:8) has highlighted the number of widows suffering from domestic abuse and trauma within communities. However, it is very difficult for the government to eradicate a practice that has been deeply rooted in some communities and existed for centuries despite the legislation put in place. Most professionals in Nigeria feel powerless and ill equipped to deal with cases of widowhood. According to Sossou (2002:204), professionals with survivors of traditional practice face multiple challenges, including linguistic differences, pressures of finite time, inadequate cultural awareness, and deficient expertise. This is the reason up to this point study had not been carried out specifically within the local community in the south-eastern region of Nigeria. This study clearly demonstrates that from the perspectives of traditional practice, there are barriers for women with *Ariri* to gain access to the social-network services. With evidence that there is a greater need within communities for support of the vulnerable groups, it is important that these communities can access services. This study does provide an important starting point to understand the specific problems and needs of the contemporary Igbo society. What this study provides for the future is widowhood education and childless condition especially those practising communities, such as clan heads, church leaders and various subgroup leaders, men and women, about the danger of psychological effects for abuse associated with harmful traditional practice, since this will help to break the cycle of violence against women. However, in the recent times, professionals working in collaboration with NGOs to protect women from the abuse and trauma (psychological risks/harms) should help to identify their specific needs. This can be only achieved if professionals demonstrate adequate awareness of the origins, cultural and psychosocial implications of harmful practice with cultural sensitivity.

There is also a case for 'empowerment' and greater 'participation' in formal religious activities (e.g. Christian fellowship and prayer) as a coping mechanism and to counter some aspects of local cosmology and custom. Future studies may wish to consider other types of religious participation (e.g. spiritual counselling) in gaining a positive outcome. Furthermore, using both ethnographic and qualitative research methodologies, future researchers should explore the roles of specific religion, spiritual, and African and cultural coping mechanisms in buffering *Ariri* and mental health symptoms among the Igbo women. Such investigations may illuminate important information about the associations among religion, spirituality, coping, and *Ariri* (mental health problems). This study develops anti-discriminatory practice primarily through a concern for the improvement of women's rights over their inheritance and property in Nigeria.

5.6 Conclusion

The trigger for this study came from a desire to gain further understanding of how different groups of women within the traditional Igbo society can be excluded or denied access to community services. As this study has been about the impact of patriarchal practice and psychosocial condition of Igbo women, it has meant that the vulnerable condition of Nigerian women is a concern in recent times. Altogether, such an ethnographic study shows that for the past four decades in the south-eastern region of Nigeria, traditional practice has deprived women of inheritance and rights to property in the interpretation of customary law and practice. It has argued that the economic dispossession of women not only reinforces difference in gender but also leads today's young mothers into severe economic hardship, poverty, and stress as indicator of *Ariri* (mental health problem). The refusal of a woman to subject herself to the rituals of customary law leads to violence and/or intimidation in achieving traditional male interests which are perceived as the interests of the whole kinship group.

It is clear that opposition to women's rights is sustained by gender inequality, and this merits close attention in South-Eastern Nigeria. It is argued that the focus on inheritance and property relations in this study has opened up a new field of research into more meaningful and continuous ways of looking at the processes and explanations of patriarchal and kinship practices on women in relation to *Ariri*.

These are bound up with the beliefs and practices of Igbo kinship, the centrality of kinship as a form of social and economic organisation, the perception of women as men's property, and hence their situation as not full political subjects. Virilocal marriage and bride price, which effectively cuts off women from their families of origin and the integration of women as wives only after the birth of a child, all contribute to maintaining patriarchy.

To come to terms with discriminatory property inheritance laws, Igbo women must therefore be helped with gender advocates associated with the statutory law to redress the gaps, the inadequacies, and the harsh consequences of some customary law applications on women in a way that integrates their experiences into their personalities and thereby gain control over their destinies. It is on this note that the Igbo people will begin to respond to the unique nature in 'gender' and its complementary approach that respect individual rights as effective mechanism for women's inclusion.

However, it is considered important that the rule of law respects the aspirations of all and consequently maximises their human rights. Statutory law with the highest ethical standards should seek this line of action in order to preserve people's freedom and choice against every corruption and practice. The observation so far shows that problems arising from patriarchal practices have widened the violation of women's human rights in Nigeria. However, Section 42 (para 2) of the 1999 Constitution of the Federal Republic of Nigeria warns that 'no citizen of Nigeria shall be subjected to any disability or deprivation merely by reason of the circumstances of social status or condition'. This is reaffirmed by the Universal Declaration of Human Rights (1948), especially in Article 17, Section 1, strengthening the role of women in general and ensuring their equal rights that 'everyone has the right to own property alone as well as in association with others'. In a similar way, Section 2 states that 'no one shall be arbitrarily deprived of his/her property'. The international and regional normative policy from these instruments draws together the implementation and development of women's social status central to the fundamental rights of women that prevent them from integration and participation in sociocultural and political activities. Parallel to this, women's rights thus require new meaning and dimension at different points in history as marginalised groups demand recognition of their rights, status, identity, and new conditions, giving rise to the need for new protection. It is on this basis that policy recommendation in this current study raises educational awareness and to encourage actions designed to eliminate unequal power relations between men and women, which have led to the domination, subordination, and inferior position of women.

My findings have been echoed by other research, especially that of Nwankwor (2005) on stigmatisation of widows in the south-eastern region. It seems, however, that some agreed for clarity on the impact of patriarchal practice on women by NGOs and other professionals may be a useful way to enable women's rights and reproductive health to receive specific attention and provide psychological support intervention at an earlier stage of a young person's distress. It seems to me that the essential thing as regard to this research is to discuss views and opinions around harmful practices towards women across professions, which will influences a positive change and access support that will have lasting outcomes for the vulnerable population. An ongoing and open debate will also enable further understanding and cultural knowledge from other theoretical views and perspectives, supporting partnership and collaborative working practices.

Women's disinheritance in the study increases the awareness and recognition of Human Rights issues. The African Commission on Human and People's Rights (ACHPR) is a tool for the promotion and protection of human rights of women in spite of the weaknesses highlighted above.

The study carried out represents an important step in understanding what empowering women and men can do to ensure equality of access, whether this is through culturally specific services or by improving access to mainstream provision. Culturally specific services have the advantages of better understanding of the community and human development; however, they can also further marginalise the community. Careful consideration backed up by evidence needs to inform this decision.

This study has been, for me, a rich experience and has shed light on areas of *Ariri* (mental health problem). Such light has given greater understanding of specific social problems experienced by disadvantaged Nigerian women. I hope it contributes to a greater awareness of the predicament of these disinherited women. And that in a small way, it will help towards a greater awareness of women's abuse and trauma and subsequently to a satisfactory future remedy.

I do not claim that this piece of academic work supplies all the answers to the research problems created by patriarchal impact on the psychosocial condition of the Igbo women. Rather, I wish to share a thought, thereby helping to bring about a better formulation of this concept and theoretical framework that underpin the study. While I accept that this study is not exhaustive, it shows to what extent specific issues relating to women on inheritance and property relations have sometimes been underestimated. Based on the sociocultural experiences of women in our study, I recommend that further research be done in this area, which can be understood as the result of cultural ideologies, in order to contribute to psychosocial practice on the ground of gender and studies of women in general.

BIBLIOGRAPHY

Abidogu, J. (2007). Western education's impact on northern Igbo gender roles in Nsukka. *Africa Today*, 54 (1): 29-51.

Achebe, C. (1994). *Things Fall Apart* (revised edition). New York: Doubleday.

Acholonu, R. (2001). Gender and development in Nigeria: Issues and challenges. WOREC, *Journal of Gender Studies*, 1 (1): 138.

Adichie, C. N. (2006). *Half of a Yellow Sun*. New York: Random House.

Afigbo, A.E. (2002). Ropes of sand: Igbo history and culture. Cambridge: University press.

_____(2005). *Igbo History and Society*. Trenton, NJ: African World Press.

_____(2006). History of Nigeria, *Journal of African History*, Vol. 33:155-178.

Agarwal, B. (2003). Gender and command over property: A critical gap in economic analysis and policy in South Asia. *World Development*, 22 (10): 1455-77.

Agbajajobi, D. T. (2009). Women's participation and the political process in Nigeria: Problems and prospects. *African Journal of Political Science and International Relations*, 4 (2): 25-82.

Agbasiere, J. T. (2000). *Women in Igbo Life and Thought*. London: Routledge.

Aguwa, J. C. U. (1997). Widowhood practices in Uturu: Traditional values in changing religious milieu. *Anthropological Quarterly*, 70 (1): 20-30.

Akaolisa, U. (2005). *Gender Issues in Nigeria*. Enugu: Fourth Dimension Publishers.

Akoma, C. (2009). Verbal miscues or cultural agency? Icheoku. *Research in African Literatures*, 40 (1): 83-96.

Alumona, I. M. (2010). The February 6, 2010 Gubernatorial election in Anambra State Nigeria: A study in political behaviour. *Pakistan Journal of Social Science*, 17 (3): 279-86.

Amadi, S. (2003). Sentenced to death by stoning for adultery—Safiya's case. *This Day* (online). Available at http://www.state.gov> . . . >Africa (Accessed 31/3/2003).

Ambasa-Shisanya, C. R. (2007). Widowhood in the era of HIV/AIDS: A case study of Sisaya District, Kenya. *Journal of Social Aspects of HIV/AIDS*, 4 (2): 47-65.

Amnesty International (AI) (31 May 2005). *Nigeria—Unheard Voices: Violence Against Women in the Family*. Available at http://web.amensty. org/en/Library/assest/AFR44/004/2005/en/dom-AFR440042005en.pdf (Accessed 4/4/2005).

Anambra State Ministry of Domestic Affairs (2008). Map of Anambra State. Available at http://www.anambrastate.gov.ng.

Anameze, L. (1996). *Marriage Among Igbos: An Analytical Study of Past and Present Practices*. Enugu: CPA & GOLD Productions.

Aniagolu, C. (1975). The elements of status. *Science of Jurisprudence International and Comparative Law Quarterly*, 4 (2): 76-120.

Anifowose, R. (2004). Women political participation in Nigeria: Problems and prospects, in S. O. Akinboye (Ed.). *Paradox of Gender Equality in Nigerian Politics*. Lagos: Concept Publication Ltd.

Anyabolu, O. I. (2003). *Nigeria, Past to the Present: 500 BC to the Present*. Enugu: Classic Publishing.

Arbor, A. (2001). *Qualitative Research in Anthropology* (3rd edn.). London: Unwin Hyman.

Ardener, E. (1972). Belief and the problem of women, in J. Lafontaine (Ed.). *The Interpretation of Ritual*. London: Tavistock.

Atani, C., Igbuzor, O., and Moru, J. (2005). *Federal Republic of Nigeria, Nigeria Millennium Development Goals Report, Abuja*. The National Planning Commission. Available at http://www.whiteband.org/ . . . / . . . /development . . . national . . . /REVIEW%20OF%20Nigeria%20 MELLENIUM%DEVELOPMENT (Accessed 27/12/2010).

Atkinson, P. and Hammersley, M. (2007). *Ethnography: Principles in Practice*. (3rd edn.). London: Routledge.

Ayittey, G. (2001). The dynamics of witchcraft and indigenous shrines among the Akan. *Ghana Review International*, 2 (77): 17-19.

Babalola, E. (2011). The world of widows: Agony is thy name. *Vanguard* [online]. Available at http://www.vanguardngr.com/2011/02/the-world-of-widows. agony-is-thy-name/ (Accessed 4/2/2011).

Bamgbose, O. (2002). *Customary Law Practices and Violence Against Women: The Position Under the Nigerian Legal System*. Paper presented at Eighth International Interdisciplinary Congress on Women hosted by Department of Women and Gender Studies. Kampala: University of Makerere.

Barber, K. (1995) Going too far in Okuku: Some ideas about gender, access and political power, in M. Reh and G. Ludwar-Ene (Eds.). *Gender and Identity in Africa.* Hamburg: Lit Verlag.

Basden, G. T. (1966). *Niger Ibos.* London: Frank Cass.

Bassett, C. (2004). Phenomenology, in C. Bassett (Ed.). *Qualitative Research in Health Care.* London: Whurr Publishers.

Beck, A. T. (1999). *Prisoners of Hate: The Cognitive Basis of Anger, Hostility and Violence.* New York: HarperCollins.

Beck, J. S. (2005). *Cognitive Therapy for Challenging Problems: What to Do When the Basics Don't Work.* New York: Guildford.

Becker, H.S. (1998). *Method of research . . . While You're Doing It.* Chicago: University of Chicago press.

Beechey, V. C. (1978). Women and production: A critical analysis of some sociological theories of women's work, in A. Kuhu and A. M. Wolpe (Eds.). *Feminism and Materialism.* London: Routledge and Kegan Paul.

Bell, J. (1999). *Doing your research project: A guide for first-time researchers in education and social science* (3rd ed.). Buckingham; Philadelphia: Open University press.

Borkan, J. M. (2004). Mixed methods studies: A foundation for primary care research. *Annal of Family Medicine,* 1 (2): 4-6.

Boyatzis, R. E. (1998). *Transforming Qualitative Information: Thematic Analysis and Code Development.* London: Sage.

Brammer, A. (2007). Human Rights Act 1988: Implications for adult protection. *Journal of Adult Protection,* 3 (1): 43-52.

Braun, V. and Clarke, V. (2006). Using thematic analysis in psychology. *Journal of Qualitative Research in Psychology,* 1 (3): 77-101.

British Sociological Association (2002). Ethical practice. Available at http:// www.bristsol.co.uk/equality/statement+Ethical+Practice.htm (Accessed 18/5/2004).

Brown, B. (2004). *Sex Crimes on Trial: The Use of Sexual Evidence in Scottish Courts.* Edinburgh: Edinburgh University Press.

Bryman, A. (2004). *Social Research Methods* (2nd edn.). London: Oxford University Press.

Champman, C. (1995). The feminist approach, in D. Marsh and G. Stoker (Eds.). *Theories and Methods in Political Science.* London: Macmillan.

Chiegboka, A. (1997). *Women Status and Dignity.* Enugu: Pearl Functions Limited.

Chukwuezi, B. (2001). Through thick and thin: Igbo rural-urban circularity, identity and investment. *Journal of Contemporary African Studies,* 19 (1): 55-66.

Cochrane, A. (1998). Illusions of power: Interviewing local elites. *Journal of Environment and Planning A,* 30 (12): 2121-32.

Coltraine, S. (2000). *The Gendered Society Reader.* New York: Oxford University Press.

Constitution of the Federal Republic of Nigeria (1999). Available at http://www.nigeria-law.org/ConstitutionOfTheFederalRepublicOfNigeria.htm (Accessed 9/8/2004).

Convention on Economic, Social and Cultural Rights (1966). Entry into force: 3 January 1976, in accordance with Article 27. Available at http://www.right-t-education.org/node/218.

Convention on the Elimination of All Forms of Discrimination Against Women (CEDAW) (2001). Widowhood: Invisible women, secluded or excluded. Available at http://www.un.org/womenwatch/daw/cedaw/index.html.

Cornwall, A. (2002). *Making Spaces, Changing Places: Situating Participation in Development,* IDS Working Paper No. 170. Available at http://www.openlibrary.org/works/OL9046096w/making_spaces_changing_places_situating_participation_in_Development.

Cresswell, J. W., Fetters, M. D., and Ivankova, N. V. (2004). Designing a mixed methods study in primary care. *Annals of Family Medicine,* (2): 7-12.

Davies, D. and Dodd, J. (2002). Qualitative research and the question of rigor. *Qualitative Health Research,* 12 (2): 279-89.

Davies, M. B. (2007). *Doing a Successful Research Project: Using Qualitative or Quantitative Methods.* London: Palgrave Macmillan.

Dehen, N. (2005). Igbo marriage customs. *African Journal of Marriage and Family,* 75 (1): 30-45.

Denscombe, M. (2003). *The Good Research Guide: For Small-Scale Social Research Projects.* Buckingham: Open University Press.

Dokobor-Asari, A. (2005). The unfinished business of compensating victims of the January 1988, Idoho 24, *Pipeline in the Niger Delta, Region of Nigeria: Protest Against Unfair Intimidation, Oppression and Deprivation of Legitimate Dues Through Judicial Manipulation.* Available at http://www.akumafiete.org/ (Accessed 23/1/2006).

Dolphyne, F. A. (1991). *The Emancipation of Women: An African Perspective.* Accra: Ghana University Press.

Dominelli, L. (2002). *Anti-Oppressive Social Work: Theory and Practice.* Hampshire: Palgrave Macmillan.

Douglas, M. (2003). *Purity and Danger: An Analysis of Concepts of Pollution and Taboo* (2nd edn.). London: Routledge.

Dreher, M. (1994). Qualitative research methods from the reviewer's perspective, in J. M. Morse (Ed.). *Critical Issues in Qualitative Research Methods.* Thousand Oaks, CA: Sage.

Duke, K. (2002). Getting beyond the 'official line': Reflections on dilemmas of access, knowledge and power in researching policy networks. *Journal of Social Policy*, (31): 39-59.

Dunn, R. C. and Schwebel, A. I. (1995). Meta-analytic review of marital therapy outcome research. *Journal of Family Psychology*, 9 (1): 58-68.

Durojaiye, R. (2007). Societal abuses and discrimination against women. *Daily Independent* [online]. Available at http://www.state.gov> . . . Africa (Accessed 6/3/2007).

Eberegbulam, N. J. E. (1990). *The Igbos of Nigeria: Ancient Rites, Changes, and Survival*. Lewiston: Edwin Mellen Press.

Ebigbo, P. O. (1981). Depression and learned helplessness: A case study. *Journal of Psychology*, (8): 84-91.

Ebigbo, P. O. and Ohaeri, C. (1990). Anxiety in Nigerian female. *African Journal of Mental Health and Society*, 5 (1): 127-36.

Eboh, L. O. and Boye, T. E. (2005). Widowhood in African society and its effects on women's health. *Journal of African Health Sciences*, 5 (4): 348.

Edholm, F. (1982). *The Unnatural Family, from Whitelegg: The Changing Experience of Women*. London: Open University Press, pp. 167-77.

Ekechi, F. K. (2002). *African Market Women and Economic Power: The Role of Women in African Economic Development*. New York: Green Wood Press.

Eliade, M. (1993). *The Sacred and the Profane: The Nature of Religion*. New York: Harcourt Brace Jovanovich.

Ember, C. R. and Ember, M. (2006). *Cultural Anthropology*. Upper Saddle River, NJ: Pearson Prentice-Hall.

Enemo, I. (2003). Domestic, regional and international protection of Nigerian women against discrimination: Constraints and possibilities. *African Studies Quarterly*, 6 (3): 44-47.

Enwereji, E. (2008). Indigenous marriage institutions and divorce in Nigeria: The case of Abia State of Nigeria. *European Journal of General Medicine*, 5 (3): 165-69.

Enwerem, I. (1995). *African Systems of Kinship and Marriage*. London: Oxford University Press.

Ewelukwa, U. C. (1988). Widows in Africa: Caught between tradition, The courts and survival. Paper presented at the *Second International Conference on Women in Africa and the African Diaspora, Health and Human Rights*, October 23-27. Indianapolis: Indiana University Press.

_____(2002). Post-colonialism, gender, customary injustice: Widows in African societies. *Human Rights Quarterly*, 24 (2): 424-86.

Ezeagbor, P. (2004). *Negotiating Power and Privilege: Igbo Career Women in Contemporary Nigeria*. Ohio: Ohio University Press.

Ezeilo, J. (2001). *The Prohibition of Infringement of a Widow's Fundamental Rights Law.* Enugu, Nigeria. Available at http://www.wacolnigeria.org/enugu_widowbill.doc (accessed 23/2/2006).

_____(2003). *The Rights of Widows and the Wrongs of Widowhood in Nigerian Women.* Enugu: A publication of Women Aid Collective, Nigeria.

_____(2004). *Experiences on Marginalization of Women from Nigeria Politics.* Enugu: A publication of Women Aid Collective, Nigeria.

_____(2005). Laws and practices relating to women's inheritance rights in Nigeria: An overview, *Nigerian Juridical Review.* Available at http://www.wacolnigeria.org/lawandpractices.doc (Accessed 24/2/2006).

Ezumah, N. N. (2003). Gender issues in the prevention and control of STIs and HIV/AIDS: Lessons from Awka and Agulu, Anambra State, Nigeria. *African Journal of Reproductive Health,* 7 (2): 89-99.

Fielding, N. and Thomas, H. (2001). Qualitative interviewing, in N. Gilbert (Ed.) *Researching Social Life.* London: Sage.

Filmer, R. (1680). *Patriarcha or the natural power of kings,* London: Sage

Finlay, L. (2002). 'Outing' the researcher: The provenance, process, and practice of reflexivity. *Qualitative Health Research,* 12 (4): 531-45.

_____(2003). Through the looking glass: Intersubjectivity and hermeneutic reflection, in L. Finlay and B. Gough (Eds.). *Reflexivity: A Practical Guide for Researchers in Health and Social Sciences.* Oxford: Blackwell Sciences.

Flick, U. (2006). *An Introduction to Qualitative Research* (3rd edn.). London: Sage.

Fortes, M. (1970). *Kinship and the Social Order.* London: Routledge and Kegan Paul.

Fourth Beijing World Conference on Women (1995). *Asserted Women's Rights as Human Rights* (September 4-15). Beijing. Available at http://www.un.org/womenwatch/un/who/htm.

Fox, D. J. (2005). Women's human rights in Africa: Beyond the debate over the universality or relativity of human rights. *African Studies Quarterly,* 9 (1): 14.

Francis, E. (2002). Rural livelihoods, institutions and vulnerability in North West province, South Africa. *Journal of Southern African Studies,* 28 (3): 531-50.

Gardner, P. (2006). *Feminism and Culture.* Manchester: Sage.

Garg, S. (2001). Socio-cultural aspects of menstruation in an urban slum in Delhi, India. *Journal of Reproductive Health,* 9 (7): 16-25.

George, A. (1994). It happens to us: Menstruation as perceived by poor women in Bombay, in J. Gittelsohn, M. E. Bently, J. P. Pertti, M. Nag, S. Pachauri, A. D. Harrison, and L. T. Landman (Eds.). *Listening to Women Talk About*

Their Health: Issues and Evidence from India. New Delhi: Har-Anand Publications.

Gerth, H. and Wright Mills C. (1958). *Max Weber: Essays in Sociology.* New York: Oxford University Press.

Giddens, A. (1995). *A Contemporary Critique of Historical Materialism* (2nd edn.). London: Macmillan.

Golightley, M. (2006). *Social Work and Mental Health* (2nd edn.). Exeter: Learning Matters, pp. 36-37.

Gomm, R. (2004). *Social Research Methodology: A Critical Introduction.* London: Palgrave Macmillan.

Goody, J. (1961). Religion and ritual: The definitional problem. *The British Journal of Sociology,* 12 (2): 142-64.

Hafkin, N. J. (2000). *Convergence of Concepts: Gender and ICTs in Africa.* Canada: International Development Research Centre Canada.

Harnischfeger, J. (2008). Magic, ritual and witchcraft in South-Eastern Nigeria. *International African Journal,* 1 (1): 56-78.

Hartmann, H. (1978). *The Unhappy Marriage of Marxism and Feminism: Towards a More Progressive Union, Capital and Class.* London: Macmillan.

Head, J. (2004). Please pray for me: The significance of prayer for mental and emotional well-being. Spirituality and psychiatry special interest group. *Newsletter,* 21 June (21): 72-75.

Heger, E. H. (2001). Female genital cutting: Cultural conflict in the global community. *International Journal of Reproductive Health,* 48 (4): 524-44.

Heider, K. (2001). *Seeing Anthropology.* Upper Saddle River, NJ: Prentice-Hall.

Heise, L. (1993). *Violence, Health and Development Programme, Centre for Women's Global Leadership.* New Brunswick, NJ: Rutgers University.

Herman, J. L. (2003). The mental health of crime victims: Impact of legal intervention. *Journal of Traumatic Stress,* 16 (2): 159-60.

Hirschon, R. (1984). *Women and Property—Women as Property.* London: Palgrave Macmillan Press.

Hodge, S. (2002). Mental health, depression, and dimensions of spirituality and religion. *Journal of Adult Development,* 9 (2): 109-15.

Holland, S. (1990). Oppression and social action: Gender, race and class in black woman's depression, in R. Perelberg and A. Miller (Eds.). *Gender and Power in Families.* London: Routledge, pp. 15-27.

Holloway, I. (2005). *Qualitative Research in Health Care.* Berkshire: Open University Press.

Ibhawoh, B. (2002). *Between Culture and Constitution: The Cultural Legitimacy of Human Rights in Nigeria.* Lagos: Southern University of Law Press.

Igbuzor, O. (2003). ActionAid: global education review. *International Education Unit, ActionAid*. Available at http://www.ActionAid-nigeria.org/.

Ilika, A. L. (2005). Women's perception of partner violence in a rural Igbo community. *African Journal of Reproductive Health*, 9 (3): 77-88.

Iroegbu, P. (2005). Healing insanity: Skills and expert knowledge of Igbo healers in African development. CODESRIA (Council for Social Science Development Research in Africa), 30 (3): 78-92.

Isichei, E. (1997). *A History of African Societies*. Cambridge: Cambridge University Press.

Iwobi, A. U. (2008). No cause for merriment: The position of widows under Nigerian law. *Canadian Journal of Women and the Law*, 20 (1): 37-86.

Jackson, C. (2003). Gender analysis of land: Beyond land rights for women. *Journal of Agrarian Change*, 3 (4): 453-80.

Kleinman, A. (2006). *The Illness Narratives: Suffering, Healing, and the Human Condition*. New York: Basic Books.

Koeing, H. G., Mc Cullough, M. E., and Lavson, D. B. (2001). *Handbook of Religion and Health*. London: Oxford University Press.

Korieh, C. J. (1996). *Widowhood Among the Igbo of Eastern Nigeria*. Norway: University of Bergen. Available at http://www.ub.uib.no/elpub/1996/h/506001/korieh/chima.html (Accessed 24/2/2006).

_____(2001). The invisible farmer? Women, gender, and colonial agricultural policy in the Igbo region of Nigeria. *African Journal of Economic History* (29): 117-162.

Kuenyehia, A. (2006). Women, marriage and intestate succession in the context of legal pluralism in Africa. *Journal of Law Review*, 40 (2): 385-387.

Lee, R. M. (1993). *Doing Research on Sensitive Topics*. Newbury Park, CA: Sage.

Leedy, P. and Ormond, J. (2005). *Practical Research, Planning and Design*. Upper Saddle River, NJ: Pearson Menhill/Prentice-Hall.

Levi-Strauss, C. (1971). *Elementary Structures of Kinship*. Boston: Beacon Press.

Limann, L. H. (2003). *Widowhood Rites and the Rights of Women in Africa: The Uganda Experience*. Faculty of Law, Kampala: Makerere University Press.

Loutan (1999). Impact of trauma and torture on aslylum-seekers. *European Journal of Public Health*, 9 (2): 93-96.

Luke, N. (2001). *The Cultural Significance of Widowhood: Widow Inheritance and the Position of Luo Widows in the Kenya Census*. Paper prepared for the *Virtual Conference on African Households*. Population Studies Centre, November 21-24, University of Pennsylvania.

Lyons, E. and Coyle, A. (2007). *Analysing Qualitative Data in Psychology*. London: Sage.

Mann, K. (1985). *Marrying Well: Marriage Status and Social Change Among the Educated Elite in Colonial Lagos.* Cambridge: Cambridge University Press.

Maritikainen, P. (2002). Psychosocial determinants of health in social epidemiology. *International Journal of Epidemiology*, 4 (2): 313.

Mesaki, S. (2009). Witchcraft and the law in Tanzania. *International Journal of Sociology and Anthropology*, 1 (8): 132-38.

Metuh, E. I. (1985). *African Religions in Western Conceptual Schemes.* Jos-Nigeria: Imico Press, p. 109.

Mezieobi, D.I. (2011). Widowhood Practices among Igbos of South-Eastern Nigeria as a Betrayal of the Fundamental Human Rights of Women. LWATI: *Journal of Contemporary Research*, 8(2):72-83.

Mezue, U. R. (2006). *Africa and Diaspora: The Black Scholar and Society.* Baltimore, MD: Black Academy Press.

Mikell, G. (1995). African feminism toward new politics of representation. *Journal of Feminist Studies*, 21 (2): 405-24.

Moore, H. (1988). *Feminism and Anthropology.* London: Polity Press.

_____(1995). *Feminism and Anthropology.* London: Polity Press.

Murray, S. (2007). *Reopening Nigerian's Civil War Wounds.* Available at http://www.unhcr.org/ (Accessed 31/7/2007).

Ndiokwere, N. (1998). *Search for Greener Pastures: Igbo and African Experience.* Nebraska: Morris Publications.

Njoku, O.N. (2003). *Troubled journey: Nigeria since the civil war.* New York: University press of America

Nnadozie, U. (2007). History of elections in Nigeria, in J. Attahiru and O. Ibeanu (Eds.). *Election and the Future of Democracy in Nigeria.* Lagos: A publication of the Nigeria Political Science Association.

Nwachukwu, L. A. (2004). *Troubled Journey: Nigeria Since Civil War.* Lagos: University Press America.

Nwadinobi, E.A. (2008). *Widowhood: facts, feelings & the law.* Enugu-Nigeria: Widows Development Organization.

Nwagbara, E. N. (2007). The Igbo of Southeast Nigeria: The same yesterday, today and tomorrow? *Dialectical Anthropology*, 31 (3): 99-110.

Nwankwor, J.O. (2007). *The Traditional Religion Custom of 'Ichu Iyi Iri' in Amaokpala in the light of Christian Theology.* Onitsha: Blessed Iwene Tansi Majory Seminary.

Nwankwor, O. (2001). *Women and Customary Right of Inheritance: Muojekwu Vs. Muojekwu and Other Landmark.* Civil Resource Development and Documentation Centre, Public Education Series No. 1. Enugu: Fourth Dimension Publishers.

_____(2002). *Tribunal on Violations of Human Rights in Nigeria*. Civil Resource Development and Documentation Centre, Public Education Series No. 12. Enugu: Fourth Dimension Publishers.

_____(2003). *Women's Human Right Advocacy*. Civil Resource Development and Documentation Centre, Public Education Series No. 15. Enugu: Fourth Dimension Publishers.

_____(2004). *Reproductive Rights Are Human Rights: The Proceedings of a National Tribunal on the Violation of Reproductive Health and Rights of Women in Nigeria*. Civil Resource Development and Documentation Centre, Public Education Series No. 23. Enugu: Fourth Dimension Publishers.

_____(2005). *Gender Inequality and Political Rights*. Civil Resource Development and Documentation Centre, Public Education Series No. 24. Enugu: Fourth Dimension Publishers.

Nwankwor, O. N. and Ezeilo, J. N. (2001). *Engendering Human Rights: Cultural and Socioeconomic Realities in Africa*. New York: Palgrave Macmillan.

Nyiam, T. (2002). *Nigerian National Question and Answer*. Lagos: Pumark Nigerian Publications.

Nzewi, D. (1989). *Widowhood Practices: A Female Perspective*. A paper presented at a *Workshop on Widowhood Practices in Imo State*, June 6-7, Owerri: Owerri Government Publications, Nigeria.

Nzomiwu, J. P. C. (1999). *The Concept of Justice Among the Traditional Igbo: An Ethical Inquiry*. Awka: Fides Publishers, p. 41.

Obiora, I. F. and Edozien, N. (2001). *Understanding Africa: Traditional Legal Reasoning Jurisprudence and Justice in Igboland as a Basis for Culturally Rooted and Sustainable Development*. Enugu: CIDJAP Publications.

Ofoegbu, E. (2004). *Violence Against Women*. Enugu: Fourth Dimension Publishers.

Ogbaa, K. (1995). *Igbo: Heritage Library of Africa Peoples*. New York: Rosen Publishing Group.

Okagbue, I. (1995). *Igbo customary law and the rights of women in the family*. Lagos: Nigerian Institute of Advanced Legal Studies, 4 (2): 201-10.

Okaro, M. (2008). *Integration of the Customary and the General (English) Laws of Succession in South-Eastern Nigeria*. Ibadan: Institute of African Studies, Africana Publishing Corporation.

Okemgbo, C. N. (2002). Prevalence, patterns and correlates of domestic violence in selected Igbo communities of Imo State Nigeria. *African Journal of Reproductive Health*, 6 (2): 101-14.

Okezie, U. (1995). *Gender Equality: Striving for Justice in Igboland*. Awka: Artworld Publications.

Okonjo-Iwuala, N. (2010). *The Impact of Urbanization on the Igbo Family Structure.* Goffinger Philosophischa Dissertation. http://content.usatoday.com/communities/kindness/post/2010/06/world-banks-dr-ngozi-okonjo-iweala-share-her-thoughts-on-women-deliver/1 (Accessed 21/6/2010).

Okonkwor, B. C. (2003). Law and the status of women's rights in Nigeria. *Journal of African Law,* 41 (2): 28-29.

Okoro, C. B. (2003). On causality and science towards a deconstruction of African theory of forces, in M. Falaiye (Ed.). *African Spirit and Black Nationalism: A Discourse in Africa and Afro-American Studies.* Lagos: Foresight Press.

Okoye, A. (2005). *Widowhood: A Natural or Cultural Tragedy.* Enugu: Nucik Publishers.

Okunna, U. (2004). Empowering women: The call for women's rights. *Action Woman Quarterly,* 5 (2): 15-18.

Ola, T. M. (2009). The socio-cultural perception and implications of childlessness in Nigeria. *International Journal of Epidemiology,* 29 (2): 285-91.

Omiyi, S. (1980). A critical appraisal of the legal status of the widow under the Nigerian law, in Awa U. Kalu and Yemi Osinbajo (Eds.). *Women and Children under Nigerian Law.* Lagos: Federal Ministry of Justice.

Onadeko, M. O. (2002). Problems of widowhood: A study of widows in a tertiary institution in Ibadan, Southwest Nigeria. *African Journal of Medical Science,* 31 (3): 201-06.

Onokah, M. C. (2003). *Family Law.* Ibadan: Spectrum.

Onuoha, R. A. (2008). Discriminatory property inheritance under customary law in Nigeria: NGOs to the rescue. *Journal of Nigeria Law,* 10 (2): 41-43.

Osiora, E. and Okoye, C. (2002). *Report of Rapid Assessment in Selected LGAs in Anambra State.* Lagos: Family Health International.

Oyakanmi, T. (2001). Benin Chief Condemns Assembly over Widow's Bill. *Punch,* [online]. Available at 130.102.44.246/journals/Canadian_journal_of_women_and-t . . . (Accessed 29/11/2001).

Ozumba, G. (2005). Gender sensitivity in Igbo culture: A philosophical re-appraisal. *Quodibet Journal,* 7 (2): 77-83.

Palmer, D. (2007a). An exploration into the impact of the resettlement experiences, traditional health beliefs and customs on mental health and suicide rates in the Ethiopian community in London. *International Journal of Migration, Health and Social Care,* 3 (1): 44-55.

_____(2007b). Caught between inequality and stigma: The impact of psychosocial factors and stigma on the mental health of Somali forced migrants in the London Borough of Camden. *Diversity in Health and Social Care*, 4 (3): 177-91.

Pals, J. L. (2006). Narrative identity processing of difficult life experiences: Pathways of personality development and positive self-transformation in adulthood. *Journal of Personality*, (74): 1079-110.

Papadopoulos, I., Lees, S., Lay, M., and Gebrehiwot, A. (2004). Ethiopian refugees in the UK: Migration, adaptation and settlement experiences and their relevance to health. *Ethnicity and Health*, 9 (1): 55-73.

Papadopoulos, I. and Gebrehiwot, A. (2007). *Safer UK: Preventing Sexual Maltreatment of Unaccompanied Asylum Seeking Minors and Improving Services for Them*. London: Middlesex University Publisher.

Parkin, R. and Stone, L. (2004). *Kinship and Family: An Anthropological Reader*. Oxford: Blackwell Publishing.

Patterson, M. E. and Williams, D. R. (1980). Paradigms and problems: The practice of social science in natural resource management. *Journal of Society and Natural Resources*, 4 (2): 78-79.

Patton, A. (1990). *Qualitative Evaluation and Research Methods*. London: Sage.

Patton, M. Q. (2002). *Qualitative Evaluation and Research Methods* (3rd edn.). Thousand Oaks, CA: Sage.

Pauline, D. (1971). *Women of Tropical Africa*. Berkeley: University of California Press.

Potash, C. (1985). *Widows in African Societies: Choices and Constraints*. California: Stanford University Press.

Radcliff-Brown, A. R. (1950). *African Systems of Kinship and Marriage*. London: Oxford University Press.

Radcliff-Brown, A. R. and Forde, D. (1979). *African Systems of Kinship and Marriage*. London: Oxford University Press.

Razavi, S. (2003). Introduction: Agrarian change, gender and land rights, in Shahra Razavi (Ed.) *Agrarian Change, Gender and Land Rights*. London: Blackwell Publishing, pp. 2-32.

Rich, A. (1977). *Of Woman Born*. Maryland: Bantan Books.

Richardson, L. (2000). Evaluating ethnography. *Qualitative Inquiry*, 6 (2): 253-55.

Riche, B. C. (2003). Gender entrapment and African-American women: An analysis of race, ethnicity, gender and intimate violence, in D. F. Hawkins (Ed.). *Violent Crime: Accessing Race and Ethnic Differences*. New York: Cambridge University Press.

Riessman, C. K. (1993). *Narrative Analysis*. Thousand Oaks, CA: Sage.

Ritchie, J. and Lewis, J. (2003). *Qualitative Research Practice: A Guide for Social Science Students and Researchers*. London: Sage.

Robson, C. (2004). *Real World Research. A Research for Social Scientists and Practitioner-Researchers* (2nd edn.). Oxford: Blackwell Publishers.

Rollo, M. (1972). *Power and Innocence.* New York: Dell.

Rothman, R. (2005). *Inequality and Stratification: Race, Class, and Gender* (5th edn.). Upper Saddle River, NJ: Pearson Education.

Rudduck, S. (1982). Maternal thinking, in Barrie Thorne and Marilyn Yalom (Eds.). *Rethinking the Family.* New York: Longman, pp. 76-94.

Saxena, S., Thornicroft, G., Knapp, M. and Whiteford, H. (2007). Resources for mental health: Scarcity, inequity and inefficiency. *Lancet,* 370 (9590): 878-89.

Schineider, D. M. (1984). *The Nature of Kinship.* Michigan: Michigan University Press.

Sen, G. (1999). *Development, Crises and Alternative Visions: Third World Women's Perspectives.* New York: Sage.

Sheppard, M. (2002). Mental health and social justice: Gender, race and psychological consequences of unfairness. *The British Journal of Social Work,* 32 (6): 779-97.

Smith, D. J. (2000). *Policy Responses to Social Exclusion: Towards Inclusion?* Buckingham: Open University Press.

Smith, D. J. (2004a). Premarital sex, procreation and HIV risk in Nigeria. *Journal of family planning,* 35 (4):223-235.

_____(2005). Legacies of Biafra: Marriage, 'home people' and reproduction among the Igbo of Nigeria. *International African Journal,* 75 (1): 54-67.

Smith, M. & Glass, G. (1987). *Research and evaluation in education and the social sciences.* EngelwoodCliffs, NJ: Prentice-Hall.

Sossou, M. A. (2002). Widowhood practices in West Africa: The silent victims. *International Journal of Social Welfare,* 11 (3): 201-09.

Spicker (2008). *Social Policy.* London: Hobbs Printing Press.

Stanworth, M. and Siltanen, J. (1984). Women and class analysis. *Journal of Sociology,* 18 (2): 159-70.

Stiles, W. B. (1993). Quality control in qualitative research. *Clinical Psychology Review,* 13 (60): 593-618.

Stitcher, S. B. and Parpart, J. L. (1988). *Patriarchy and Class.* London: West View Press.

Stones, R. (1998). *Key Sociological Thinkers.* London: Macmillan.

Strathern, M. (1981). *Kinship at the Core.* London: Cambridge University Press.

Strauss, A. and Corbin, J. (1990). *Basics of Qualitative Research: Grounded Theory Procedures and Techniques.* London: Sage.

Tew, J. (2005). *Social Perspectives in Mental Health: Developing Social Methods to Understanding and Work with Mental Distress.* London: Jessica Kingsley Publishers.

The Protocol to the African Charter (1995). *On the Rights of Women in Africa*. Available at http://www.equalitynow.org/ . . . /africa-protocol/africa-protocol_en.html.

The United Nations (1948). Universal Declaration of Human Rights adopted 10 December. G. A. Res. 217A (111), United Nations Document A/810 at 71. New York. Available at http://www.un.org/en/documents/udhr/index-shtml.

The United Nations Commission for Refugees (UNHCR). Available at http://www.unhcr.ch/.

Tong, R. (1989). *Feminist Thought: A Comprehensive Introduction*. Boulder: West View Press.

Truman, C., Mertens, D. M., and Humphries, B. (2000). *Research and Inequality*. London: UCL Press.

Turner, V. (1969). *The Forest of Symbols: Aspects of Ndembu Ritual*. Ithaca, NY: Cornell University Press.

Uchendu, V. C. (1965). *The Igbo of Southern Nigeria*. New York: Harcourt Brace Jovanovich College Publishers, Rinehart and Winston.

Udemezue, C. C. (2010). Widows and violations of their rights in Southeastern Nigeria. Available at http://www.brighthub.com/society/cultures-custom/articles/73317.aspx (Accessed 18/8/2010).

Ugorji, C. U. C. (2009). Reflections on address politeness in Igbo family. *The International Journal of Language Society and Culture*, 27: 67-68.

Ukachukwu, C. M. (2007). The sacred festival of Iri Ji Ohuru in Igboland, Nigeria. *Nordic Journal of African Studies*, 16 (2): 244-60.

Ukpokolo, C. (2007). Gender, symbol and peace building among the Nanka Igbo of South-Eastern Nigeria. *Journal of Environment and Culture*, 4 (2): 41-68.

Umar, B. and Adoba, I. (2002). The state of education in Nigeria and the health of the nation. ThisDay. Available at *http://www.nigerdeltacongress.com/* . . . / state_of_education_in_nigeria_an.ht (Accessed 12/6/2001).

Umeora, O. U. J. (2009). Menstruation: Attitudes, beliefs and practices. *Journal of Reproductive Health*, 12 (2): 109-15.

Umeora, O.E.V. (2008). Age at menarche and the menstrual pattern of Igbo women of Southeast Nigeria. *African Journal of Reproductive Health*, 12 (1):90-5.

Uzodike, E. N. and Onokah, M. C. (2003). New legislative approach towards widowhood and other family law developments in Nigeria. *Journal of African Law*, 43 (1): 71-78.

Uzoezie, C. E. (2007). *Women in Leadership: Development and Democracy*. Awka: Nuel Publishers.

Uzoigwe, G.N. (2004). *Conflict over control of natural resources in Nigeria:* The case of the oil-producing Niger Delta communities of the South-South region, Lagos Historical Review, 4

Valerie, M. B., Shapiro, J. J. (1998). *Mindful Inquiry in Social Research.* Thousands Oaks, CA: Sage.

Walby, S. (1989). Theorizing patriarchy. *Journal of Sociology*, 23 (2): 213-34.

Wallace, A. (1990). *Culture and Personality.* New York: Random House.

Weber, M. (1994). *Socialism in Peter Lassman and Ronaldo Speirs* (reprinted). *Political Writings.* Cambridge: Cambridge University Press, pp. 272-303.

_____(2002). *The Protestant Ethic and the Spirit of Capitalism* (reprinted). Translated by Stephen Kalberg Pearsons. Los Angeles, CA: Roxbury Publishing.

_____(2004). In D. Owen and T. B. Strong (Eds.). *The Vocational Lectures.* Indianapolis, IN: Hackett Publishing Company.

_____(2005). Theory, culture and society. *Journal on Max Weber Theories on Property Relations*, 22 (4): 23-38.

Wethington, E. (2004, 2003). Turning points as opportunities for psychological growth, in L. L. Keyes and J. Haidt (Eds.). Flouring: *Positive Psychology and the Life Well-Lived.* Washington, DC: American Psychological Association, pp. 37-53.

Whitehead, A. (1984). *Women and Men: Kinship and Property.* London: St. Martin's Press.

_____(2002). Tracking livelihood change: Theoretical, methodological and empirical perspectives from North-East Ghana. *Journal of Southern Africa Studies*, 28 (3): 575-98.

Whitehead, A. and Kabeer, N. (2001). *Living with Uncertainty: Gender, Livelihoods and Pro-poor Growth in Rural Sub-Saharan Africa*, IDS Working Paper No. 134, Brighton.

Whitehead, A. and Tsiakata, D. (2003). Policy discourses on women's land rights in sub-Saharan Africa, in S. Razavi (Ed.). *Agrarian Change, Gender and Land Rights.* London: Blackwell Publishing, pp. 67-112.

Whitehorn, J. (2002). Female genital mutilation: Cultural and psychological implications. *Journal of Sexual and Relationship Therapy*, 17 (2): 161-70.

WHO (World Health Organization Report) (2002). Reducing risks, promoting healthy life. Geneva. Available at http//:www.who.int/whr/2002/en.

WHO (World Health Organization Report) (2005). Make every mother and child count. Geneva. Available at http://www.who.int/whr/2005/en/index.html.

WHO (World Health Organization Report) (2008). Female genital mutilation. Available at http://www.who.int/mediacentre/factsheets/fs241/en/.

Wilkinson, R. G. (1996). *Unhealthy Societies: The Affiliations of Inequality.* London: Routledge.

Worell, J. and Etaugh, C. (1994). Transforming theory and research with women. *Psychology of Women Quarterly*, 18 (4): 443-50.

Worell, J. and Remer, P. (1996). *Feminist Perspectives in Therapy: An Empowerment Model for Women.* New York: Wiley.

Zack-Williams, T. (2006). Impact of political economy of inequality and outcomes of exploitation and oppression for the marginalized families in West Africa. *Journal of Community Mental Health*, 34 (5): 430-39.

WOMEN AID COLLECTIVE
(WACOL)
"Women for Women"

RC. 388132

Enugu Office
No 9 Upuana Street
Uwani Opp. New Haven,
P.O.Box 2718 Enugu State.
Tel: 042-256515
Fax: 042-256491
E-mail:
wacol@gmail.com,
wacolenugu@wacolnigeria.org

Port Harcout Office
35 Mogu Street, D/Line,
P.O.Box 9030, Port Harcourt,
Rivers State
Tel: 084-872993, 084-893190
E-mail:
wacolph@yahoo.com,
wacolph@wacolnigeria.org

Abuja Office
No 9 Kampala Street
Off Les Street Area 11,
P.O.Box 521 Garki Abuja.
Tel/Fax:
09-2342541, 09-6711534
E-mail:
wacol@cpa.org,
wacol_abuja@yahoo.com

Anambra Office
6th Floor Esther, Near Oerama
Police Office, Kwata-Ugidi
Ogidi Anambra State
E-mail:
wacolanambra@wacolnigeria.org

Ebonyi Office
Amazu,
Near Magu Junction
E-mail:
wacolebonyi@wacolnigeria.org

Free Legal Aid Hotline
Tel 042-2020369

June 2008

Rev. Fr. Ezeakor A.
2 Knatchbull Road
Camberwell
London SE5 9QS

Dear Rev. Fr. Ezeakor

Thank you for your letter of 18th May 2008 concerning your PhD research. It is interesting to note that the area of your investigation has been under researched. We hope a lot of states in Nigeria will benefit from this piece of academic work.

We could provide information on most of the areas raised in your questions but a good deal of work would be involved. Perhaps the best course would be for you to visit Nigeria and discuss it with the various NGO's dealing with Human Rights and health related issues

With regard to your outstanding questions, you will be supported the much information that is available within our capacity.

Yours sincerely,

Joy Ezeilo (OON)
UN Special Rapporteur on Trafficking in Persons especially Women and Children
Also Founding Executive Director (WACOL)

Website: www.wacolnigeria.org

CIRDDOC Nigeria
(Civil Resource Development and Documentation Centre)

HEADQUARTERS: Fourth Dimension Complex, 16 Fifth Avenue, City Layout, New Haven, P. O. Box 1686, Enugu, Nigeria
Tel: +234-42-314892, 303315, 08033132493, Fax: +234-42-456964, e-mails: cirddoc@aol.com, cirddoc96@yahoo.com, cirddoc@gmail.com, info@cirddoc.org Website:http//www.cirddoc.org

May 1, 2006

Rev. Fr. Adolphus Ezeakor
2 Katchbull Road
Camberwell
London SE% 9QS

Dear Fr. Adolphus

I'm glad to know that your research is on patriarchal practice and its psychosocial effect on women in Eastern-Nigeria.

Our CIRDDOC Legal Department is willing to provide the materials requested to enable your investigation and fieldwork.

I am happy that this research is moving forward and I shall be available to discuss in more details my experience with disinheritance cases of women in Nigeria.

Best compliments
CIRDDOC Nigeria

Oby Nwankwo (Mrs.)
Executive Director

GOVERNMENT OF ANAMBRA STATE OF NIGERIA

MINISTRY OF WOMEN AFFAIRS AND SOCIAL DEVELOPMENT

OFFICE OF THE HONOURABLE COMMISSIONER

Phone:

E-mail:

Our Ref.:..

Your Ref.:...

Women Dev. Centre
Near Unizik Main Gate
P. M. B. 5016
Awka

4th May,   09
..........................,20......

Revd. A.I.Ezeakor
2 Knatchbull Road Comberwell
London SE 5 9QS

Dear Fr. Ezeakor

Thanks for your letter indicating to make use of our data on inheritance and property rights of women focused on your Ph.D research. As far as I am aware there has been no published research in this area despite the obvious public interest.

Although the local State and Federal Government is continually seeking ways of improving relationships with minority ethnic groups our public attitude surveys show a considerable level of mistrust of the whole legal and public complaints procedure amongs disinherited women. Research in this area would therefore be a particular benefit to the community leaders, clan heads and womenfolk in addition to meeting a much wider public need.
Perhaps the best course would be for you to visit the NGO's which deals with cases of the vulnerable women and discuss how the project of this nature can be progressed.

As for myself, I will provide you with some of other detail contacts and materials from our library which should enable you to facilitate your research.

Yours sincerely,

Dr. Ego Uzoezie
Commissioner, MWASD,Awka

All replies to be addressed to the Honourable Commissioner.

APPENDICES

Appendix 1

Semi-structured interview by Kleinman Explanatory Model (EM) and participant's method for data collection

The main method for data collection is semi-structured interview, organised by Kleinman's Explanatory Framework (2006) and informed by ethno-history and ethnographic sources. The Explanatory Model (EM) in Sub-Saharan Africa is the stories that people construct to make sense of an illness within the context of their culture. It stimulates researchers with interaction dynamics in being effective in gathering information from the study. Its flexibility makes it possible for researchers to invent new tools or techniques, which are appropriate to the research context. The explanatory model is an attempt to help individuals from different cultural backgrounds to have an insight into thoughts, behaviour, feelings, and general attitude to their own problem. The ethnographic research method is multi-method in focus as it enables the researcher the use of multiple or mixed methods and reflects an attempt to secure an in-depth understanding of the group in question (Flick, 2006).

Interview questions for the participants to identify the cause of their cultural specific illness or problems (Ariri) as follows:

1. How would you describe your social situation?
2. In your situation as a widow how much domestic abuse and violence have you experienced?
3. In your condition as a childless woman how much domestic abuse and violence have you experienced?
4. What is your illness or problem called?
5. What do you think your problem does to you?
6. What do you fear most in your problem?

7. Why do you think this illness or problem has occurred?
8. Do you consider *Ikwa Ariri* to be a form of a cultural specific mental health problem?
9. Have you sought any help for your problem and whom did you consult?
10. Given this opinion, in your situation, which treatment would you recommend for a woman suffering from *Ariri*?
11. Given your view, in your situation, what support would you recommend for a woman suffering from *Ariri*?

Thanks for your participation in this research.
All confidentiality about this research will be maintained.

Appendix 2

Terminologies

Within this study, the following terminologies were used:

Traditional Practice

Patriarchal and kinship practice is central in cultural, socio-economic and political life of every community, especially when such practices are perceived to be determined by the productive and reproductive activities of women. The practices are closely tied to cultural and traditional beliefs about death, supernatural forces, inheritance and property relations, feminine roles, and family and kinship structure on various dominant views. Ethno-historic evidence shows that harmful traditional practice has influenced cultures, behaviour, beliefs, and attitudes of people. For example, attempts to understand widowhood practice in relation to patriarchal control and property relations constitute the fear and anxiety survivors developed in African societies.

Access

Within this research, facilitating access is concerned with assisting people to utilise social-network support and services within the local community. If services are available, then people may 'have access', but the extent to which access is gained can depend on administrative, political, social, and cultural factors.

Cultural Barriers

Within this research, a barrier is anything which hinders or restricts survivors from accessing inheritance and property rights as well as reporting an incident of abuse. Barriers may be physical, psychological, or cultural and can originate from patriarchal control and dominance.

APPENDIX 3

Transcript (W—V1)

Socio-Demographic Data

The participant comes from V1. She is a widow. She is twenty-eight years of age and is a primary school teacher. She is a Pentecostal. She had been married for six years with two female children.

The interview centres around three key questions regarding the following:

- Women with *Ariri*
- Women without *Ariri*
- Coping mechanism(s) available for women

The questions were asked to explore women's *Ariri*. This is to find out the cultural beliefs and social activities that perpetuate violation of women's rights and whether that could exclude certain groups of women not fully integrated into their social organisation.

Interviewer: 'What would you call your present condition?'
Participant: 'Widowhood situation.'
Interviewer: 'Tell me more about the circumstances that affect you as a widow?'
Participant: 'OK. Hmm . . . I am a widow with two children and the second wife of my husband. My husband died of cancer and had told members of his family before his death that I should be spared from the ordeals of customs and tradition, his reasons being that I have suffered from looking after him in the hospital and also my religious beliefs.

'I think after the burial of my late husband, my stepson began to threaten me. The stepson took over the husband's property entirely from me and demanded the piece of land given to me by my husband for farming. I was beaten for refusing to relinquish the farmland. I took the matter to the traditional ruler of the community. This made the matter worse as the young man drove me out of the family house.

'Out of sympathy, I was offered accommodation with some in-laws who gave me a piece of land for my farming. The traditional ruler once summoned the stepson, and he promised to settle the matter but has done nothing. I have two children whom I find difficult to cater for.'

Interviewer: 'How would you describe the widowhood condition in the Igbo language?'

Participant: 'In the traditional setting, the mention of widowhood has different connotations in families and communities. Some perceive widowhood as problematic. Whilst some feel that widows are a burden to the family. The social condition of widows in the Igbo society is a complex one. It involves a lot of issues such as sexual intercourse with a traditional cleanser as a process of cleansing. You know . . . women are exposed to sexual harassment and some of them end up with contracting HIV/AIDS. It is often observed that the problems created for women are by women. The attitude towards women during widowhood by men and their fellow women suggests maltreatment, social deprivation, and oppression. Some women are instruments of oppression and injustice at the hands of their fellow women in the family. A woman may have a problem with her husband when he was alive and the case is reported to *umuada* after his death. The *umuada* will use that case against the widow during her bereavement. Amidst controversy, the sympathisers leave the widow and her household to handle their funeral and desert the compound of the deceased. Sometimes the *umuada* may force the widow to do some odd things against her wishes. If she resists, such a person is disgraced and humiliated. This often constitutes a great embarrassment and prolonged grief for a widow.

'On the other hand, there is a belief that a widow without a male child has no right to inheritance. This is to affirm the male position in continuity of the patrilineage. It accounts the reason that sex discrimination over inheritance and property rights are still problematic. It is meant to understand that a widow has no compensation on economic benefits for sustenance of children left behind.

'The widowhood condition is a traumatic experience and other forms of practices include forcing a widow to marry an in-law, forcing her to sleep with the corpse, and forbidding her from eating certain food items. I was forced to remain without bathing for days or weeks, including shaving my hair. Also, I was forced to perform certain rituals during which I had carnal knowledge with the traditional chief priest of the shrine. The cultural belief and social activities are humiliating and degrading. It doesn't recognise human value and dignity.'

Interviewer: 'What incident do you think usually provokes this situation?'

Participant: 'The incident of humiliation in the family triggers the repeated violence and abuse which I faced after the death of my husband. Before the funeral, I was instructed what to do and what not to do. Amongst the warnings, one was not to drop sand in his grave. I felt embarrassed and shocked because I believed that sand symbolises farewell. I was worried about these restrictions and family decisions. One of the awful experiences was the beating I received from my brother-in-law when I had a quarrel with his wife. The pressure from the brother-in-law was an attempt to keep me miserable and unhappy so that I will be frustrated to leave the family. All these set-up are an attempt to make me feel that I have no strong base in the family because I have no male child.

'Each time I remember the injustice surrounding our land case, I feel distressed. Once in a while, I meet the village traditional ruler, reminding him about our land case, and he would say that the council of the elders would look into my case, yet nothing has been done. As a widow, I'm always disturbed. Partly because I was married to a polygamous family who still believe that culture and traditional practices are the only way of controlling women.

'Insecurity and loneliness provoke my widowhood situation. I always see myself in dilemma and struggling to do things alone. Violence and power imbalance favour men and is disadvantageous to women.'

Interviewer: 'How does your condition affect the level of interaction with other members of the family?'

Participant: 'The experience after the funeral of my late husband proves that a widow can be neglected in the family. I had a disagreement with my brothers-in-law over the property of my late husband, which affected our relationship. I was not allowed to touch the fruits in the compound, and my children are banned also to visit the sisters-in-laws.

'One day, I went to pluck oranges in the compound for my visitors, which belonged to my late husband, and one of my brothers-in-law saw me, came out, confronted me, and asked who authorised me to do so. Before I knew it, he pushed me away and warned me that I should not touch the oranges again, and if I like, I should report him to the grave of his late brother. All these create stress and anxiety and, at times, make me not to be at peace with the family.'

Interviewer: 'Are you still part of the family?'

Participant: 'I'm still part of the family. My children and I have our own apartment in the family. I see my children as a source of joy and my womanhood. I work hard to care for my children. I believe the investment on my children is rewarding.'

Interviewer: 'What are you looking forward to in your current situation?'

Participant: 'I'm concerned about family support. As my children are still growing and their dad is dead, I need my brothers-in-law to assist us. My children are scared of being alone . . . I cannot ignore this. Now they are growing . . . I know my children miss their dad, and each time they keep asking me about their uncles and their children . . . I would like good relations in the family in order to restore the family strength.

'Instability is represented everywhere in the family . . . I have been misunderstood in various ways. This always raises anger on my own part. I believe it has caused a lot of damage to me. In this regard, I need cooperation and would like my brothers-in-law not to push my children and me away. We should come together, rather than live apart. I'm worried about the effects of family conflicts on me and my children.'

Interviewer: 'What sort of help will enable you to cope with your condition?'

Participant: 'I received help through some of Christian friends who enrolled me into their prayer group. In the prayer group, I spend some quiet time with the Lord and feel his presence. In this way, I was taught how to discuss my negative feelings and concerns. I always allow God to take care of me and grant me healing. My immediate sisters have supported me. So far, I have learnt to manage and cope with the little salary I earn to support my family. It is a big relief to me and my children.'

Transcript (W—V2)

Socio-Demographic Data

The participant comes from V2. She is a widow. She is thirty-nine years of age and is a petty trader. She had been married for eight years with four children who are still dependent. She is an Anglican

The interview centres around three key questions regarding the following:

- Women with *Ariri*
- Women without *Ariri*
- Coping mechanism(s) available for women

The key guide to the interview questions are focused on women with *Ariri*. This is to find out the cultural beliefs and social structures that perpetuate violation of women's rights and could exclude certain groups of women not fully integrated into their local community and social organisations in the Igbo land. The questions were asked as follows:

Interviewer: 'Tell me what would you call your present condition?'
Participant: 'A widow . . . you can see the way I'm dressed.'
Interviewer: 'What are the social circumstances that affect your condition as a widow?'
Participant: 'The death of my husband affected my social life. I am a petty trader, and I have been married for sixteen years. My husband died in a ghastly motor accident. We had a good marital relationship and were blessed with four children. The fact is that I lived peacefully with my husband, and I took good care of him. A fact that was common in our family and community and my in-laws would be sympathetic and loving in their actions towards me.

'Furthermore, it was the shocking and traumatic the effect of my husband's death had on my children and me. Contrary to my expectation, immediately after the remains of my husband were lowered in the grave, I was cautious not to put sand in his grave as a sign of a final farewell. Later, I was invited for hair shaving by the *umuada*. I could not believe that under those circumstances, people would be thinking of shaving my hair. So I refused to comply. I was told that the *umuada* had left the compound with anger because of my refusal to comply with cultural and traditional practices. My mother in-law accused me of being unfaithful. It was heart breaking for me.

'I stood my ground and insisted that the custom was just meant towards humiliating and intimidating me. I told the women that it is against the scripture that widows should not be maltreated, and there is nowhere in the Bible where a widow should shave their hair in honour of their dead husband. Rather, Deuteronomy 14: 1 says that the shaving of hair for dead husbands is a heathen practice, which should be against my Christian belief and practice.

'The kindred arranged to use masquerader (customary law enforcement agent) to have my hair shaved. The masquerader arrived and chased people away. I was overpowered and physically my hair was scrapped, leaving razor cuts and bruises on my scalp. I was deprived with my children of all condolence gifts and donations by friends and relations for the upkeep of my children and towards the funeral.'

Interviewer: 'How would you describe your widowhood condition in the Igbo land?'

Participant: 'Widowhood in the traditional Igbo society is still problematic. Women generally are overlooked and marginalised (*ileghara nwanyi mkpe anya*) . . . and lack legal protection. Under customary law, *Omenala* (discrimination against women) begins at the death of their husband and determines their life course. A woman can neither inherit property from her father nor her husband nor be head of the family. These continue to be issues in the family, especially where inheritance and wife possession (*nkuchi nwanyi* or widow inheritance) exists. (A brother-in-law acquires marital rights over the wife of his deceased brother, which sometimes constitute a major problem.)

'Conversely, a widower does not experience these cultural and social beliefs. The *umunna* unit—extended family favours male control and monopoly over women, irrespective of the widow's productive and reproductive rights. While there is insistence on marital fidelity for the female population, there are indications that men in the Igbo society do not have to conform to these expectations.

'Hitherto, some local communities believe that a widow has evil intentions and can cause destruction and harm in the community through "witchcraft". Others remarked that a widow uses "witchcraft" as a means of inflicting suffering and sickness on people. Importantly, there is a belief that widows usually bring bad luck to the members of the family.'

Interviewer: 'What incident do you think usually provokes this situation?'

Participant: 'Whenever I think of my husband's death, I'm overwhelmed with sadness and grief. An incident occurred after the wedding of my last daughter. 'Judith' asked me why Uncle John doesn't visit us? Her question reminded me of their late father. I feel the pain inside me when answering her question. Each time I keep promising to tell her but never did because the incident that surrounds my late husband and funeral and what their uncle planned against me.

'The most difficult experience I will never forget is during the family meeting and arrangements of the funeral of my late husband. The first question my-brother-in-law asked for was my late husband's bank account. I told him that he has no bank account based on the nature of his job as a carpenter, and that we had a hand-to-mouth existence, but he wouldn't believe me. All he could say is that we can sell one portion of his land to prepare for his funeral. I could not believe myself. With tears, I knelt down and begged every one of them to help me with any amount of financial support, but surprisingly, I was left alone. It was my brothers and sisters with their friends who rescued me from my situation.

'Another incident was the "birthday" of my late husband, which we celebrated after Christmas. It was well organised and our family and friends visited us. Since I lost my husband, the Christmas period was filled with moments of distress and sadness. I felt disappointed and angry because my husband left us to suffer without his presence. On the day of his birthday, it was a nightmare. The family pictures with friends around us intensify our post-stress and post-traumatic experience. As children begin to feel the absence of their dad, they worry about our loneliness.'

Interviewer: 'How does your condition affect the level of interaction with other members of the family?'

Participant: 'We relate in a different ways. I still believe that the family members betrayed me in those occasions relating to my husband's death. All the traditional practices to justify some of the widowhood rites that I experienced were encouraged by the family members. As a widow, I have not yet recovered from the shock. Sometimes I worried a lot about myself and my four children.

'I respect my brothers-in-law and the sisters and their parents. My children sometimes visit them whenever they wish. I don't stop them. It is only my first daughter who feels unhappy whenever she remembers the incidents of her dad's death'

Interviewer: 'What do you worry or fear most about your social condition?'

Participant: 'As a widow, I was subjected into ritualistic activities of widowhood. I was forced to visit the *Aja ani* shrine as well as hold a small knife (*mma ekwu*) as a symbol of widowhood, but other Christians around me would rather prefer a crucifix. Generally, I felt humiliated . . . hmm . . . I felt incapacitated. The experience left me with unhappiness and shame. I worried about my children almost every day. Shouldering every responsibility in the house is very stressful. As a lone parent, I see myself struggling with financial constraints, shouldering household and domestic activities alone—children's school fees, feeding, house maintenance, and clothing for the children. Sometimes, I find it difficult to make ends meet.

'I encountered sexual harassment and fear about contacting HIV/AIDS by some of the village men since my husband died. Some of these men visit me with sympathy but have different motives at the end. I feel embarrassed when I see myself in this condition. I mean I felt insecure and lonely within me. There could be more said about my condition. I'm always careful with people because of the nature of my husband's family, village, and community, especially where gossip is the order of the day.

'Another incident of worry is that my bother-in-law sold one of our family lands. He uses the money for his own family and makes the land inaccessible again for cultivation. I cried to the kindred (*umunna*) and reported the case, but nothing was done or said about it.

'Interestingly, my brothers-in-law were visiting us when my husband was alive and bringing gifts for the children. Sadly, much has changed since the death of my husband. There is so much isolation now than before. My mother-in-law never asks us how we are getting on. She often gangs up her children and even other co-wives against me. All is intimidation stresses me not to have peace of mind in the family.'

Interviewer: 'What have you done about this condition?'

Participant: 'I'm struggling with a small amount of money in my business to keep the family together. Instead of doing one business, I combined two things—supplying meat pie and soft drinks to the factory canteen. My children sometimes will join in hawking orange and banana during holidays as a way of supporting me. I was meant to understand that the immediate family members will take care of my children's school fees.'

Interviewer: 'Are you still part of the family?'

Participant: 'My position as a widow in the family is important to me. I cannot leave my children for another family. My children and I live under one roof. So I am still part of my family no matter our differences. We have enough land that belongs to my husband which my sons and daughters cultivate yam, cassava, and vegetables. According to the Igbo tradition, as long as the widow is alive with her male children, she will be cultivating the land of her late husband.'

Interviewer: 'What are you looking forward to in your current situation?'

Participant: 'I need the family to understand my situation as a widow. I am not quarrelling or competing with any person, but I want a safe environment where I should have a peace of mind in my bereavement. My mother-in-law is always violent with me. As a mother, she should respect me and take me as I am with my children rather than looking down on us.'

Interviewer: 'What sort of help will enable you to cope with your condition?'

Participant: 'I see my children as a source of coping with widowhood. I thank God that I have children who have lifted me up in the family. I always count on their presence and help, especially in supporting me with my small-scale business.

'We have some piece of landed property, which is an economic strength to the family. With this, I am coping with the grieving situation I found myself in and which can be changed. My immediate family supports me, and this is a big relief to alleviate the burden of managing the house. Also I received emotional and moral support from the charismatic prayer group, which helped me through prayers and constant visits to cope with grieving and the bereavement process.'

Transcript (W—V3)

Socio-Demographic Data

The participant comes from V3. She is a widow. She is thirty-one years of age and a primary school teacher. She is a Catholic. She had been married for nine years with three children.

The interview centres around three key questions regarding the following:

- Women with *Ariri*
- Women without *Ariri*
- Coping mechanism(s) available for women

The questions were asked to explore on women with *Ariri*. This is to find out the cultural beliefs and social activities that perpetuate violation of women's rights and whether that could exclude certain groups of women not fully integrated into their social organisation.

Interviewer: 'What would you call your present condition?'
Participant: 'Widowed.'
Interviewer: 'Tell me more about the circumstances that affect you as a widow?'
Participant: 'I had a happy married life, and the circumstances related to my husband's illness affected my condition of life. His illness took us to many hospitals within our localities, and eventually I was told that he would not survive. My husband died of AIDS.

'The whole burden was on me alone, although his brothers and sisters occasionally visited us. Frankly, they were involved in the arrangement of his funeral. I was invited to the both pre and post meeting about the burial with the family members and kindred (*umunna*). I picked an offence with my brothers-in-law because of certain discussions, which weren't in my opinion, and my late husband would not be happy about it. I was instructed not to see the corpse of my husband and to follow the local tradition of widowhood. The cultural restrictions imposed enable me to feel isolated.

'After the burial of my late husband, I was terribly tortured. I found myself with physical confrontation. I couldn't sleep. I was anxious and scared about everything and even people around me. I see my life always in danger as abuse running all over me. My brother-in-law demanded to take back the piece of land given to me before my husband died. Once I was beaten for refusing to relinquish the farmland. Out of sympathy I was offered accommodation by one of our in-laws who gave me a piece of land to cultivate crops and vegetables. I have two children whom I find difficult to either feed or pay their school fees. I find it very difficult to explain.

Interviewer: 'How would you describe your widowhood condition in the Igbo language?'

Participant: 'Widowhood is quite upsetting. Some communities perceive widowhood as problematic, whilst others may associate the state of widowhood with suffering, poverty and stigmatization. Sometimes the *umuada* may force the widow to do some odd things against her wish such as *ime ajadu* or *Aja ani* taking a widow to the shrine to have sexual intercourse with the traditional priest to lift her widowhood. It could take another form as drinking the water washed from the corpse of her late husband as evidence of her innocence over her death. Such maltreatment is witnessed especially during the ritual practice. In this regard, a widow becomes a murderer and a suspect who deserved to be isolated.

Interviewer: 'What incident do you think usually provokes this situation?'

Participant: 'The incident of humiliation, isolation, and deprivation of property expected to take care of the children and settle the outstanding debts incurred before and after burial. Inability to carry out certain duties or responsibilities, which would have been undertaken by the husband, provokes the fear and anxiety of being a widow. Of course, the women know the effect humiliation has on their health and emotions. I think it is a good idea to let people know what is happening. For instance, when my children start misbehaving without being controlled, such incidents, reminds me of being a lone parent which is difficult and frustrating.

'Other co-wives in the family isolate me for no just reason. We used to have a good time outside, but since my husband died, they look at me with suspicion. In this regard, I related the context of my late husbands suffering and death, and as a widow I feel humiliated. The neglect from the brothers-in-law is an attempt to keep a widow unhappy and miserable. Each time I remember the injustice surrounding my life as a widow I feel distressed. I always see myself in a dilemma and struggling in doing things alone.'

Interviewer: 'How does your condition affect the level of interaction with other members of the family?'

Participant: 'As a result of suspicion, the relationship with the family members is always difficult to maintain, and in the midst of other activities in the family, I feel like a stranger. I see myself living like a stranger because of the way I have been treated. A stranger is unaccepted, unloved, and that is what I experience with my children.

'The experience after the funeral of my late husband proves a lot to me. I had a disagreement with my brothers-in-law over the property of my late husband, which affected our relationship. In this sense, I felt overlooked and not supported. Once I was disturbed about these conflicts going on, and it affected my health, which resulted in experiencing bad dreams, sleepless nights, and a general weakness.'

Interviewer: 'Are you still part of the family?'

Participant: 'Having been blessed with four children, I decided to stay with the family. Since my husband is no longer alive, I stand for them as a mother. I see my children as a source of joy. I work hard to care for them. I believe the investment on my children is rewarding. As my children are growing up, my brothers-in-law started changing their minds positively towards me. They begin to understand my plight as a widow and that makes me feel integrated into the family.'

Interviewer: 'What are you looking forward to in your current situation?'

Participant: 'I am concerned about the future of my children. As my children are still growing and their dad is dead, I need my brothers-in-law to assist us. I know my children miss their dad, and each time, they keep asking me about their uncles and their children. In this case I would like to maintain good relations with everybody in the family. Supporting the welfare of my family with my salary and little investment left from my late husband is my strength.'

Interviewer: 'What sort of help will enable you cope with your condition?'

Participant: 'When I see my children well behaved and progressing, it gives me hope. All my effort is to invest in them so that in return they will take care of me, especially in my old age. I see them as a huge resource and special gift from God. I have started experiencing some benefits from my first daughter who is an accountant with the Zenith Bank. The little money she provides helps in supporting the household activities. So far, we have started putting up a four-bedroom bungalow house for the rest of the children. In this way, I have learnt to manage and cope with the little salary and other support from my children.

'I joined women Christian fellowship in the parish and it is a source of encouragement. We developed a social network of activities like 'palm oil mill' and production of local soap in the village and marketing this local stuff has helped us in small scale investments.'

Transcript (C—V1)

Socio-Demographic Data

The participant comes from V1. She is a childless woman. She is thirty years of age and a civil servant. She had been married for seven years and is a Catholic.

The interview started with the questions that are based on the following:-

- Women with *Ariri*
- Women without *Ariri*
- Coping mechanism(s) available for women

The first set from the interview focuses on women with *Ariri*. The aims of these questions are to find out the social circumstances that could exclude certain women not fully integrated in their social structure in the Igboland. The questions were asked as follows:

Interviewer: 'Tell me what you would call your present condition?'
Participant: 'A childless woman—*onye amutaghi nwa.*'
Interviewer: 'What are the social circumstances that affect your condition as a childless woman?'
Participant: 'I married at the age of twenty-three. According to the social standard, our wedding was admired by people. I was full of happiness and felt fulfilled like other women. Our parents, brothers, and sisters as well as relatives made a big impact in our reception. Of crucial importance, my ex-boyfriend bought me gold-plated jewellery as a present. I see the day like my second birth.

'We lived for almost seven years without a child, and I was disturbed emotionally throughout. I least anticipated myself living such a long period as childless. The circumstances kept everybody in suspense. Previously, I had strong feelings, which I kept to myself. My husband had a sexual problem. I was afraid to discuss this with him, but I allowed my observation to be proved by him at one stage.

'Later, I reported the incident to my friend to seek advice or a second opinion. She came up with lots of family experiences related to sexual problems linked with HIV infection and other related venereal diseases that had contributed to my fertility problem. Other childless women who discussed their situation opened up with tears. It has been a dreadful and painful experience. I was advised to discuss my feelings with him . . . part of me accepted to do so, while another part of me left me in perpetual fear because of a false allegation. The more I repressed my emotion, the more unhappy I become. My uncertainty invariably affected our relationship.

'One day, we had a misunderstanding. I lost my temper and told my husband off, and he reacted violently towards me. I was terribly beaten and bruised. I didn't expect that he would behave to such an extent. I blamed myself for such a careless remark against him. Although we had this row, I didn't report the incident to anybody. I kept struggling with our childless condition. I started loosing weight as a result of excessive worries. It was a nightmare and very hard as a young wife to start experiencing such a difficulties in the relationship.'

Interviewer: 'How would you describe this condition in the Igbo language?'

Participant: 'Being childless in the traditional Igbo society is still problematic. The kin group doesn't take it lightly. A couple live under pressure, which is depressive (*Ikwa Ariri*). Generally, people believe that being childless is a sign of ill luck to the family. It is perceived as an end of a lineage. This is why an Igbo man intensifies fear about a childless condition and would rather seek a second marriage for childbearing.

'Several factors account for childless marriages. The elders consult diviners through a ritualistic performance to ward off the cause of infertility and impotency amongst the couples. A ritual ceremony is performed for cleansing of the womb by using *Ojirisi* tree planted in a compound to signify *omumu* (fertility). The *Ojirisi* tree is powerful and medicinal and can be used for all sorts of things in Igboland. A ritual is where a spirit of ancestors are proclaimed and implored for protection. This ritual is invoked to drive away fear and evil spirit from families. The people's attitude to it is controlled by their needs and aspirations as well as the social structure of the village group with a view of discovering their impact on marriage.

'This practice stresses the profound authority, which the father exercises in his family. Each parent would like their married child to beget children. In this regard, parents pray with kola nut (*ojii*), calling upon the ancestors for approval and support. The man offers to the earth goddess or deity a cock, some yams, palm wine, and an amount of money specified by the diviner.'

Interviewer: 'What incident do you think usually provokes this situation?'

Participant: 'Several factors contribute to guilt of childlessness. Sometimes, I longed to have a child when I hear babies crying. In most cases, I usually dream, either I am with a new baby or in a labour room. Whenever I get up thinking about the dream, I end up with tears, feeling unwell, sad, and depressed. Situations like this affect my mood and make me miserable throughout the day.

'Another occasion is when family celebrations take place. Christenings may provoke my childless situation. In this situation, I see families and children around events living better than me and that intensifies my worries and feelings of jealousy and anxiety (*obi erughi ala*). The atmosphere in the social gatherings makes me suspicious of people talking about my childlessness.

'One experience when I went to the main market was that I saw a couple shopping for the pregnant wife, and I started crying, thinking about all sorts of things—especially my husband who had not done enough to make me feel like a woman. I always compare him with other married men, and in this way, I thought about neglect and rejection in our marriage. Working alone in most cases in the village is difficult for me.'

Interviewer: 'How does your condition affect the level of interaction with members of the family?'

Participant: 'It is difficult to explain the level of social interaction. Reasons being that a woman without a child is already condemned. I see myself in the family as a stranger because of our poor relationship. I bear the blame of our childlessness, and I am always ready to give an explanation to people regarding such a situation.

'Because of my little experience, my mother-in-law calls me all sorts of names. We live under one roof, but she doesn't relate well with me. She succeeded in poisoning the mind of her son, who turns against me in everything I do or say. My mother-in-law interferes in our privacy. Whenever I am eating or sleeping, she will try to draw the attention of my husband. I wash her clothes and cook meals for the family, but she finds it difficult to appreciate my efforts.

'My husband comes late in the evening . . . Most of the time, he refuses to give out money for food and other domestic maintenance. He started drinking and would refuse to eat in the house. Sometimes, he comes back from work and prefers keeping to himself. He has no time for me, even for family planning. He denies me information and would confide in his mother and sisters.'

Interviewer: 'What do you worry or fear most about your social condition?'

Participant: 'I think with the recent changes in our marital relationship, I am afraid that my husband will one day abandon me for a second marriage. My fear is that I cannot trust him anymore. I'm worried about the breaking off our marriage. I'm worried also about my family and their feeling of disappointment. In this way, I pray that my husband will not break my heart or bring shame by divorcing me. As a woman, I believe that lots of married men have betrayed their wives in so many ways.

'The Igbo traditional society regards divorce as a challenge. It's a sign of humiliation. I feel uncomfortable and worried as a woman being kicked out of my matrimonial home. Women use divorce as a powerful weapon against their fellow women. I'm apprehensive about this situation.'

Interviewer: 'Are you still part of the family?'

Participant: 'I believe I am still part of the family because I have not yet been summoned by the kindred, regarding our childless marriage. It suggests that the *umunna* in a social way tried to maintain my marital status as their wife, if not for the help from the kindred, things would have been very difficult for me.'

Interviewer: 'What are you looking forward to in your current situation?'

Participant: 'I am looking forward for any improvement that will lift our childless situation. I am looking for a child that will console me. I still feel like the rest of the other married women with children. If my husband will listen to advice, we would have started medical treatment. I believe my husband will learn from our difficulties and think better for our family planning and fertility programme. I love children, and I still believe in a divine providence for us.'

Interviewer: 'What sort of help will enable you to cope with your condition?'

Participant: 'I have not been supported enough by my husband. Sometimes, I find it difficult with my poor health. But my brothers and sisters are the source of my financial support, which alleviate some of my burden. I joined a charismatic prayer group, which has brought relief in the way I reason before. The prayer group offers counselling through a healing service. As a matter of fact, everybody in this fellowship has the feeling of living as a family. In this way, people feel for one another and support each other through corporate prayer. Evidence shows that some people cope better in groups than alone.'

Transcript (C—V2)

Socio-Demographic Data

The participant comes from V2. She is a childless woman. She is thirty-nine years of age and is a petty trader. She has been married for twelve years. She is a Methodist.

The interview centres around three key questions regarding the following:

- Women with *Ariri*
- Women without *Ariri*
- Coping strategies available for women

The key guides to the first interview questions are centred on 'women with *Ariri*'. This shall decide whether patriarchy can negatively affect or result in women's *Ariri*. These questions were asked as follows:

Interviewer: 'What would you call your condition?'

Participant: 'A childless condition.'

Interviewer: 'Tell me about the social circumstances that can affect this condition?'

Participant: 'I am a thirty-nine-year-old woman, and I have been married for twelve years, and I am without a child. Before getting married, I worked in the same bakery with my husband. We used to go for lunch together and exchange gifts on our birthdays. Our friendship continued to grow stronger until he proposed to me. It was like a dream come true after our wedding. My husband was such a lovely man who stood by me in everything.

'After our wedding, my husband planned that we leave the village and start a hotel business in a city, but because of his father's health condition, we decided to stay and help him. Both of us have lost our mothers. As a newly married person in the family, my husband always advises me to watch myself, especially with other married women in the extended family. One of his weaknesses is that he keeps friends. People visit us, and we share food and drink together in our house.

'We lived like eight years without a child, but we continued to love each other. Some of the family members had started gossiping already that I am responsible, since I am older than my husband. He understands the childless condition more than I do. He tells me not to let such situations worry me that if it is the will of God, we shall have a child. He is a strong believer, and I admire him for his faith. We always pray together whenever we go to church. One day, I started feeling heavy in my womb and told my husband that I had pregnancy symptoms. When we visited the village health centre for a check-up, nothing of such was found. I felt unhappy and miserable throughout that day.

'I always think about my age and possibility of conception. In this regard, I become apprehensive about my childless condition. Excessive worries and pressure from people sets me into a state of panic and restlessness. Our godparent used to visit us with some medical advice. Both of us went together. After the test, I discovered that my husband had a venereal infection that affects his low sperm count. He was placed under medical treatment. Since then, nothing has changed, but I strongly believe that things will take a turn for the good.'

Interviewer: 'How would you describe the childless condition in the Igbo language?'

Participant: 'Igbo people believe that being "childless" is a void. It's worrying and a concern for the family and an entire community at large. A childless marriage goes with the myth that a childless couple are *akalogoli* (less important or useless people in the community). A woman is regarded an "outcast" or someone who has misused her fertility through abortion during her adolescence. Powerful language such as "profane" is associated with such victims.

'There is a strong ritual connection with fertility in the Igbo society. It links both the living and the ancestors. Ceremonies are performed with kola nut and libation as blessings for marriage with children. Parents pray for it with thanksgiving. It demonstrates a woman's fecundity. Conversely, a childless marriage is believed to cause misery in a family and such conditions are likely to attract ancestral calamities in a family.

'Igbo people believe that a childless marriage is a disgrace to our ancestors. A cultural myth is outstanding here. Couples are a failure if they cannot produce a child. It shows an end of the lineage, which can never be remembered, just like the Igbo's name reveals *Obiechina* or *Afamefuna*—meaning family will never cut-off. My mother-in-law ridicules me so that I should remember that there is no difference between me and a man. In this sense, I have no position of any claim of rights of inheritance in this family.'

Interviewer: 'What have you done about this condition?'

Participant: 'As I mentioned earlier, we have been for medical treatment, and my husband is still on treatment at the moment. Some people have advised alternative medications, for example, herbal treatment and spiritual deliverance. We have attended a Pentecostal service—mountain of fire and the pastor prophesised that my husband's uncle is responsible for his fertility problem. He suggested intensive prayers such as fasting and anointing for liberation.

'After the prayer session, my husband invited my uncle and narrated the story, which he denied. We followed things up by contacting another group of charismatic prayer ministry from the city that visited our compound and conducted night vigil prayers to ward-off any diabolical spirit in the family. So far we are still in constant prayer.'

Interviewer: 'How does this condition affect the social interaction with other members of the family?'

Participant: 'The childless problem has helped us to intensify our relationship with my husband. All we have decided to do is to curtail visiting friends in order to find time for ourselves.

'Sometimes, as a woman, I think differently about our childlessness, and in this way, I distance from my husband emotionally. Whenever I see my women of my age with children, I became upset and angry that my husband has ruined my future. This makes me feel like leaving the marriage. I always see myself withdrawn from others.'

Interviewer: 'What do you worry or fear most about you childless experience?'

Participant: 'I worry that if my husband is not better, I cannot have a child. I see my husband being very important to me. I believe in him, and we love each other very much. As I see things happening now, I cannot cope when I have no child, and such a condition creates long suffering and this fear intensifies distress.'

Interviewer: 'What incident do you think usually provokes this childless situation?'

Participant: 'Threat and intimidation makes me feel insecure in our marriage. Sometimes, I begin to ask myself: Is this really happening to me? This can be followed by numbness. When a woman feels threatened, it is likely that she remembers her painful or worst side of her life. In most cases, such a situation keeps me miserable. Apart from this, women's meetings can provoke the thinking of my childless condition. A case of an appeal for a childless woman in our village during the women's annual meeting left me with mixed feelings and distress. Immediately as the announcement was made, some women who knew me started looking at me as if I am the one. Such eye contact was an embarrassment that put me off in the midst of the crowd.'

Interviewer: 'Are you still part of the family?'

Participant: 'Yes! I believe that marriage is a bond that unites us together. It cannot divide us. Rather, it will help us to understand each other more. This implies that we see ourselves as one body.'

Interviewer: 'What are you looking forward to in your current situation?'

Participant: 'Forgiveness and reconciliation of our uncle with my husband who is suspected to be responsible for our childless condition. I still believe that God will answer our prayers. I want peace in our compound to avoid further suspicion and malice.'

Interviewer: 'What sort of help will enable you to cope with your childless condition?'

Participant: 'Childlessness is perceived with prejudice. People look at you as an "outcast" or "defiled" person. Each time I cry in our bedroom with anger and frustration "Why me?", I find it extremely draining to live with the overwhelming desire for a family and to experience the resolution of loss and failure when you cannot conceive. Sadly, I always have the feeling that I have let down my partner, loved ones, and my blood relations. Any possible treatment that will lift our childless condition is what we pray for. I have contacted friends and some families to join us in prayer. In this way, I learn how to discuss my fears, worries, and concerns. I always allow God to bear my sorrow.'

Transcript (C—V3)

Socio-Demographic Data

The participant comes from V3. She is childless. She is thirty-two years of age and is a petty trader. She has been married for nine years. She is an Anglican.

The interview centres around three key questions based on the following:

- Women with *Ariri*
- Women without *Ariri*
- Coping mechanism(s) available for women

The key guides to the first interview's questions are centred on 'women with *Ariri*'. This shall decide whether patriarchy can negatively affect or result to women's *Ariri*. These questions were asked as follows:

Interviewer: 'What would you call your present condition?'
Participant: 'A childless condition.'
Interviewer: 'What are the social circumstances that affect your condition as a childless woman?'
Participant: 'I grew up in a family of five. I'm thirty-two years old and the eldest in the family. I married very early as a result of poor living conditions in my family. Some of my peers were supported at school, but I sacrificed mine in order to help my brothers and sisters to be educated like other children.

'I married a man my parents arranged for me. Both parents were friends and local farmers in the village, and that's how our marriage was planned. When we first met, we agreed to marry each other. We had a traditional marriage, which was later solemnised in the church. After our marriage, there are certain things I couldn't handle because of my age. The first complaint I received from my husband was my inability to cook properly. I was humiliated by such a complaint as a woman. I felt bad, which made me think. My mother-in-law was there to support me, which I considered a big help.

'After long expectation of a child, my mother-in-law stepped in to help the situation. She was worried and anxious about our condition. I see myself in the middle of the road. I find it difficult to find my feet. Some of the married women of my age were concerned and kept advising me to divorce my husband as soon as possible and look for another man since I am still young. The moment I heard about people's advice, the more confused I became. My husband didn't even care about our condition. He flirts with other women and drinks a lot. This is how I see myself at the moment.'

Interviewer: 'How would you describe your childless condition in the Igbo language?'

Participant: 'Traditionally, the Igbo society takes childless conditions very seriously. A childless situation is surrounded with mixed feelings and suspicion. It goes with the misconception and male bias or prejudice. In most cases, women are blamed for everything. If a woman has no child, there is no chance of inheritance. She is socially excluded from the property because her infertility is a great shame to the family and their ancestors. This supports the saying *Nwakego*, meaning childbearing is wealth. Parallel to this, if a woman gives birth to a first son, she is closer to the *obi* of her husband. A first son is entitled to inherit the *obi*. This implies that *obi* symbolises male authority. *Obi* is considered sacred because the elders (titled men) gather therein to make decisions and policies regarding *Omenala*—local custom and cultural practices including widowhood and infertility—childless condition. This is where *umunna* (the kin group) take decisions on family issues. '*Obi*' is significant, since it is where the ancestors are consulted through rituals, which is connected to dowry and marriage. As a matter of fact *obi* in the Igbo society signifies male lineage, acquisition of power, and supremacy. This is where men exercise there power over women. This social structure affects women in general.'

Interviewer: 'What occasion do you think usually provokes this condition?'

Participant: 'Family issues contribute to the provocation . . . experiencing successful children and parental support. As a woman, I prepared my marriage to have children. I never dreamt that I would stay too long now without a child. I still believe that what makes a woman is fertility. Dreaming of staying without a child is mental distress. Whenever I see women with new babies, it intensifies my worries. Different occasions trigger fear and anxiety, for instance, staying with my sister's children over the weekend. They call me Auntie, while I'm supposed to answer my children's name. Each time I hear the word "Auntie", I feel unhappy . . . it makes me to feel low and changes my mood.

'Other social factors, such as hearing children crying remind me of my childless condition. I feel jealous of their parents. I feel like those parents cannot take proper care of their children and if God gives me mine, I will take care of them better. Sometimes, when I go to market, I feel like buying babies' clothes and keeping them for the future, believing that, I will still have my own child. Part of me keeps telling me that I will have a child, but another part reminds me of my childless condition as a loss.

Another factor is the uncertainty that creates the fear in me, which I retain anger about people who I believe that they are gossiping or talking about me. In this way, I sometimes feel unloved and end up either crying or feel like killing myself.'

Interviewer: 'How does this condition affect the level of interaction with members of the family?'

Participant: 'Our interaction is never a smooth one. The rest of the family members despise me. Such an attitude creates tension, fear, and uncertainty, which emotionally distanced our relationship. Sometimes, it is difficult for us to eat together, especially when he is not in a good mood. In this way, I begin to doubt about my future in the family.

'Besides, I have serious problem with my mother-in-law, who doesn't accept my greetings. She makes up stories against me, which sometimes other women in the family are not happy about. On one occasion, we visited a friend who celebrated his wedding anniversary. We were all entertained with drinks and a nice meal. Unfortunately, we could not stay any longer because my husband got offended with his friend's joke, indicating that he cannot produce a baby. I felt embarrassed with this joke. My husband with anger left me at the party and went off home.'

Interviewer: 'What do you worry or fear most about your social condition?'

Participant: 'I'm afraid of the way the family will treat me. I'm always blamed, and I blame myself for the marriage. I regret marrying for the first instance. This feeling makes me stay alone. I'm afraid of public and social activities because of humiliation, and I've tried to avoid any circumstance that will push me to social gatherings or events where men and women will confront my childlessness. I am talking from experiences where some women have treated the childless women without respect and dignity.

'The worst situation is that I cannot make decisions regarding our marriage because of family prejudice. I'm afraid of my sisters-in-law because of their pressure to get rid of me. They're always calling me all sorts of names, instigating their brother to look for a second wife. Every time, I see them in our compound, I become suspicious about their evil plot.'

Interviewer: 'What have you done about this condition?'

Participant: 'We have tried several treatments like herbal and medical treatment but nothing has brought about any change. Some people told us that the hands of enemies have blocked our future and contributed to our fertility problem. We have consulted native doctors who used rituals—candles, white cloths, and black soap for our bath to ward-off diabolic attack on our marriage. My husband and I have tried all kinds of consultations to no avail.'

Interviewer: 'Are you still part of the family?'

Participant: 'At the moment, my husband and I still live together. We consider our childless problem as a major concern and anxiety in our life . . . it is very depressing.

'Another side of my condition is that my husband feels that I am responsible for our childless problem. Each time he picks quarrels, he calls me all sorts of names. What worries me the most is constant arguments, which sometimes lead to quarrelling and fighting. Whenever he is in the house, I feel insecure.

'My people have warned me several times to leave the marriage and come back home, but I still think that my husband could change at any time. Twice I have left our matrimonial house and went to my sister's place to stay because of his hostile behaviour. I prefer to save our marriage and live like any other normal and stable family.'

Interviewer: 'What are you looking forward to with your current situation?'

Participant: 'I'm looking forward for a better solution that can improve our childless condition. We are concerned about having our own child. People have gossiped so much about us, and I believe that no condition is permanent. My brothers and sisters have supported financially for our treatment . . . at the moment, we have spent a lot, but things are getting worst. I am looking forward to my family's financial support, which will enable us to continue with our treatment. We need to eat well and consider maintenance and such a concern bothers me.'

Interviewer: 'What sort of help will enable you to cope with your condition?'

Participant: 'I believe prayer has helped me to feel the presence of God in my life. Nevertheless, the childless condition still finds me in great pains and loneliness. It makes my entire life complicated and difficult. But with courage and strength, I come to hope for the best in the difficult circumstances that surround me. Each moment I see myself in suffering, it worries me a lot. Sometimes, I take each suffering as part of my cross and with prayers move on with life.'

APPENDIX 4

Exhibit III (1998). Report on Nanka Mayhem: 'Afu Afughi Ozu' *between husband and wife—complaint against ritual practice towards widow*

Ugochukwu Joe Okezie

According to Ugochukwu (1998), an informant from the town reported that the widowhood practice started in the community when one prominent citizen died in the village. The widow secretly removed valuable property of the husband and sent them to her maternal home before she informed the husband's relations (kin) of the death.

The widowhood practice is as old as the community. It's described as a way of life for the community. In most cases, the origin is very difficult to trace because the originators may no longer be living. In recent past, relations besieged the deceased's apartment and stole every valuable thing belonging to the dead, such as landed property, bank accounts, and so on, leaving the bereaved widow and children impoverished. Unfortunately, the decision of local custom and tradition where when the particular death occurred, they mapped out cultural restrictions and strict measures on women. For instance, the death of the husband in many localities draws up stories of accusation on widows to justify the practice of widowhood rites and seizure of husband's property.

To consolidate the practice, there is a cultural taboo, isolation, exclusion, humiliation, and stigmatisation of a widow within the community. The social stereotype is associated with how widows are labelled and looked at as 'outcast', 'profane', and 'bringing bad luck' to the members of the family. However, the ritual practice goes with suspicion and all kinds of accusation attributed to a widow as responsible for the death of her husband. Nwankwor (2003) indicates that the subordination of women in almost every traditional society has its myths and folklore. A widow becomes sub-human, a murderer, a suspect, and persona non grata. The retrogressive cultural attitude against adult survivors ensures the persistence of the most of the harmful practice where sex inequality is a strong belief and the majority of women are placed under depersonalising social pressures and severe sociopolitical discrimination.

Ritual practices involved the local custom and traditional practices on widows as a mark of the bereavement process *ino n'ekpe* or *ime ajadu*. On a general note, there is a common belief that death is the lot of any widow who objects to any of the demands of the local custom and traditional practice. She has to be subjected to all kinds of dehumanising ceremonies. Ritual is a process through which local custom imposes and inflicts emotional pains on adult female survivors. In addition to the study of Nwankwor (2007) with the traditional religious custom of 'Ichu Iyi Iri' in the light of widowhood in Amaokpala, death is always a common belief when a widow objects to any of the demands of the custom. From all indications the implication for the custom and practice amounts the feeling of inferiority complex that is dehumanizing to the human psyche and sanity of the widow—person in grief for the dead husband. Other manifestations in stages of widowhood that are common to survivors include: Prolonged grief, lamentation, frustration, sadness, unhappiness, insecurity, oppressive denials, and confinement.

Most localities in the Igbo land are still neck deep in tradition and culture that force women, most unjustifiably under incapacitating inhibitions. In another part of local community, a widow is flanked on both sides by *umuada* with suspicion. She is forced to drink the water used in washing the corpse of her husband to declare her innocence of his death. In this respect, it is a cultural taboo for a widow to see the corpse of her late husband, and no man is allowed to see her except her own sons if she has any. Cannon (*mkponala*) is shot to mark the beginning of widowhood. A widow is given a short knife (*mma-ekwu*) as a symbol of the widowhood rite. This is an indication that she is now 'unclean' and 'defiled' and must be isolated. Evidence from the local custom show that no man goes near the widow's house at night, and no widow is allowed to go next or near her husband's grave during burial. According to Ifebunandu (1978), a widow assumes the state of temporary dumbness. She dares not talk aloud or call out to the hearing of people outside. She must not go to the farm or be entertained by visitors or shake hands with any one, and any condolence gifts meant for her must be dropped on the floor or given to someone sitting beside her.

Aja Ani ceremony is a last phase of widowhood, which is a requirement or sometimes a precondition for the widow to be in a position to fraternise with members of her husband's family. It's usually done by midnight. This ritual takes different shapes according to the community. In some areas, the widow is first introduced to a ritual cleanser known as *nwa nri* (the traditional chief priest who will have sexual intercourse with her) to lift the taboo placed over her. There is a cultural belief that if she resists doing so, any man who attempts carnal knowledge of her invites death on himself. Hitherto, *Aja ani* practice requires a widow to be taken to the stream by the daughters of the clan; she is shaved everywhere, and the hair is thrown into the stream or buried, and she is bathed (Nwankwor, 2007). In every ceremony of *Aja ani*, there is an attempt that a widow will have an affair with anyone chosen by the kin, either the in-law or someone else. This man goes to the traditional priest of the local shrine and reports that the widow has had an affair with him. The traditional priest (eze *muo*) makes a demand of what has to be used for cleansing and performs the rites before she goes off home. On getting home, she does not enter her compound but stands outside the compound while the senior person or head of the family goes in to get an outfit for her to put on before she enters her compound. The next day, she sets off to the market to make a public appearance and later comes back home unescorted.

I would like to observe from the fieldwork that women's stories represent diverse experiences in rural communities where there is a common belief that death is the lot of any widow who objects to any of the demands of the custom. This is virtually the same for all women in West Africa, especially in South-Eastern Nigeria, where the situation of women is oppressive. For example, *Aja ani* ritual exposes women's into traumatic condition. The threat, oppression, exploitation, and pressure on widows and sexual abuse increase the related risks of potential HIV/AIDS victims, which is a major concern for women's rights and health. Culturally, the ritual practice renders women more frustrated and emotionally disturbed. However, much less is known that extramarital sexual relationship with men could expose women to the risk of HIV, since both the time from infection to AIDS and the time from AIDS to death are believed to be unpredictable. In this regard, the international law such as CEDAW and Africa Charter on Women's Rights reflects and reinforces women's protection against all forms of harmful traditional practices. The law prioritised that women should be able to exercise their freedom without constraint. WHO Report (1997), in similar way, considers women's vulnerability as a health priority. Public health awareness in rural communities should help to educate citizens on the social consequences of the obnoxious practices that endanger women's lives. Harmful traditional practice suggests the emotional abuse, which causes women to suffer multiple difficulties as their bereavement deepens. Even after these rituals, women continue to feel demeaned (guilty, shocked, and embarrassed). The International Covenant on Economic, Social and Cultural Rights (1976) highlights the prevalence of risk factors on women's rights and health and other social policies that are important steps in women's welfare.

Action Woman (Quarterly, 24 June 2004)
'Domestic Violence on Women's Inheritance Rights'
Barrister Joy Ezeilo (WACOL)

The reporters linked poverty to denial of inheritance rights to women. Through this report, economic dispossession of women stands as a complex problem, inhibiting the actualisation of women and their children's rights in South-Eastern Nigeria. Worthy of note are the live narratives of various myriads of injustices and discriminatory practices against women, some of which are manifestly harmful. Amidst tears, a twenty-four-year-old widow with two children testified how her brother-in-law, after the death of her husband, seized all the documents relating to the late husband's possessions. She is at the risk of being thrown out of the family. Due to financial hardship, she withdrew her children from school. She was told not to farm in her late husband's land.

Daily Independent (6 March 2007)
'Societal Abuses and Discrimination Against Women'
Rotimi Durojaiye

The paper reported societal attitude and behaviour towards widows after the death of their husbands. Among most traditional cultures, widows suffer from cultural taboos and dehumanising treatments, which have been their lot over the centuries. The situation in southeast geopolitical region becomes worse when they are denied their fundamental human rights. However, it does need to say that those responsible for customary law provide little or no support for widows, especially when they are deprived of their husbands' property rights. If we turn the pages of history, widows have suffered all forms of violence and abuse and have almost been excluded from public life. For example, in some localities, widows are perceived as murderers and are forced to drink water with which their husband's dead bodies are washed to declare one's innocence.

The women's rights group implored the National Assembly to pass the United Nations's CEDAW. The Ministry of Women's Affairs and the National Assembly, in furtherance of its campaigns against persecution of women, condemned traditional practices and forced and arranged childhood marriages towards women. *Punch* recommend that an investigative study on harmful widowhood practices and discriminatory inheritance laws and practices be carried out, adding that such a study would aid social and legislative advocacy towards the elimination of these practices. The *Punch* commended the House of Assembly for being the first parliament in Nigeria to pass bills prohibiting harsh widowhood rites and female genital mutilation.

APPENDIX 5

Punch (Thursday, 29 November 2001)
'Benin Chief Condemns Assembly over Widows' Bill'
Teslim Oyakanmi

The Edo State House of Assembly has been commended for its gender sensitive style. The commendation was given on Tuesday, in Benin, by the Roots and Fruits Women Farmers Society of Nigeria (RUFARM). The group, in a statement by its Project Coordinator, Mrs Nogi Imoukhuede, a copy of which was made available to the *Punch*, commended the House of Assembly for being the first parliament in Nigeria to pass bills prohibiting harsh widowhood rites and female genital mutilation. The women's rights group implored the National Assembly to pass the United Nations's CEDAW (1979) 'to achieve gender equality'. The group said it sent a petition signed by people from thirty-two countries, to the Presidency, Human Rights Commission, Abuja, the Ministry of Women Affairs, and the National Assembly in furtherance of its campaigns against persecution of women. It listed such persecution as violence in the home, sexual harassment at school and work, rape and defilement, sexual exploitation, punitive widowhood rite, harmful traditional practices, forced childhood marriages, sexual violence in conflict situations, and discrimination against girl child. It condemned the death sentence, by stoning, passed by the Upper Sharia Court, Gwadabawa, Sokoto State, on Safiya Hussein Tungar-Tudu over allegation of adultery. The group stated that that aspect of Sharia law is discriminatory and against the natural course of justice. It thus condemned the decision of the court to set free the man who allegedly impregnated Safiya. 'It takes two to tango,' it said. The group promised to contact other women's rights bodies and NGOs to ensure that Safiya and others do not suffer from discriminatory laws in Nigeria.

Punch (29 November 2001)
'The Plight of Widows in Edo Sate'
Teslim Oyakanmi, Benin

The plight of the widows in Edo State is very pathetic. A widow in Edo State is condemned to a life of rejection, trauma, deprivation, and poverty. The practices vary from area to area; however, there are two broad patterns of practice in Edo South and Edo North. Mainly the Binis and Ishans inhabit Edo South. When a man dies in Edo South, the wife is usually suspected to have a hand in his death, no matter how old the man may have been. The practice is usually for the women to be confined to her room and the man's family will be invited and informed. Upon arrival of the family, there is severe mourning and then accusations and counter accusations. The interrogation and inquisition then begins. This generally has put the women as an accused before her accusers. In order to prove her innocence, the woman is desperate to do anything demanded of her in the name of tradition. Her husband's spirit is usually invoked, and she is made to swear before him. In the purely traditional families, the corpse is washed, and she is made to drink from it. When the burial properly begins, she is made to sit on tree branches, her hair is shaven, and she does not bathe during the seven days of the burial ceremonies. She is served food on a broken clay pot, which remains unwashed throughout the period; she is also made to eat with her left hand. The rites are fraught with so much danger and hostility that the widow usually has her family members guarding her throughout. On the last day of mourning, after some rituals, she is made to bathe in the dead of night. This is usually the most dangerous as there have been occasions when the widow has been physically attacked by the husband's family members. She is usually protected by men from her own family. If the husband's family is Christian, the widow may be spared the ordeal, but usually there will be non-Christians among them who will insist that some aspect of the tradition be carried out. By the end of the ordeal, the widow is so traumatised that the cordial relationship, which previously existed between families, is terminated. After the rites, if the man was polygamous or if the widow was the only wife, but did not bear him a son, she is asked to leave her matrimonial home. There are known instances of women who have been driven out of their matrimonial home after forty-five years of marriage. The widow has no right of inheritance. If the widow is lucky to have older children, the children begin to look after their mother. Where the widow is young, she is pushed into penury because the family begin to divest her of all her husband's property. If the widow was a full-time housewife, the sudden loss of status and the traumatic experience has been known to drive some into depression. The children are also not catered for, and she is left to fend for them.

In Edo North, the widowhood rites are similar but also the women become inherited by the deceased's brother. It is very common in Edo North for a woman to bear children for two brothers. There is need for sustained advocacy and mass enlightenment in Edo State. We should uphold the aspects of our culture that enhance our dignity and abolish laws that are repugnant to natural justice, equity, and good conscience. It has been well established that culture is dynamic. The 1999 Constitution enshrines the fundamental Human Rights of the Nigerian city and Section 34 of the 1999 Constitution of the Federal Republic of Nigeria upholds the right to human dignity. We are saying that female genital mutilation and harsh widowhood rites derogates from the Nigerian Constitution, such customs are therefore illegal and unconstitutional. Women's Rights Watch commends the Enugu State House of Assembly for being the first State to prohibit punitive widowhood rites.

APPENDIX 6

Complaint Management: Ensuring legal system of 'Will' making if a man dies intestate' under customary law of inheritance

What is a 'will'?

The term 'will' signifies an instrument used by an owner of property to transfer his interest or estate in the property upon his death to any person of his choice (Udemezue, Okonkwo, and Ohia, 2002). A will is usually a document by which a person makes a disposition of his property to take effect after his death. The person who makes a 'will' is called the 'testator' while any person who benefits under a will is called a 'beneficiary'. A person normally makes a 'will' during his lifetime, distributing his/her property to spouse, offspring, relatives, friends, and so on, but these beneficiaries do not get to acquire these properties until after the death of the testator. For a document to pass for a 'will', it must inter alia dispose of a property; where a document does not dispose of any property at all, it cannot be said to be a 'will' (Barrister Ezeilo, 2002).

In the precolonial era, writing was unknown to the various local communities and households in Nigeria, and as a result of this, 'will making' was done orally, usually in expectation of death, and in the presence of witnesses who must not be beneficiaries under the disposition. Where a person dies leaving a valid will, he is said to have died 'testate', but where a person dies without making a will, he is said to have died 'intestate', and the property shall devolve according to customary law of inheritance. A will is usually prepared by a legal practitioner because of the technicalities involved in the making of a will; however, any other person, even the testator himself, may prepare the will.

Laws governing 'Will' in Nigeria

The laws governing the operation and administration of wills in Nigeria are as follows:

- The Wills Act of 1837 and The Wills (Amendment) Act of 1852: These are statutes of general application still applicable in the eastern part of Nigeria.
- The 'Wills' law of various states of the federation. Some of the states in Nigeria have re-enacted the received Wills Act 1837 with modifications and alterations, for example, Wills Law of Western Nigeria 1958 and Wills Law of Lagos state 1994.
- High Court (civil procedure) Rules of the various states of the federation governs procedure to be followed in probate actions.
- Case Law: These include laws made by the courts on wills.

Essentials of a valid 'Will'

For a will to be said to be valid, certain conditions must be fulfilled. Some of the formalities of making a valid will are provided in Section 9, Wills Act of 1837, which reads as follows: 'No [w]ill shall be valid unless it shall be in writing and executed in the matter hereinafter mentioned, that is to say, it shall be signed at the foot or end thereof by the testator or by some other person in his presence and by his direction and such signature shall be made or acknowledged by the testator in the presence of two or more witnesses present at the same time and such witnesses shall attest and shall subscribe the will in the presence of the testator but no form of attestation shall be necessary.'

The following essential requirements appear from the above provision:

1. A 'will' must be in writing or typed and not oral. Oral wills may be valid but are not covered by the Wills Act.
2. It must be signed at the foot or end of the document by the testator himself or by another person (appointed by him) in his presence and by his direction. The testator must sign or acknowledge before the witnesses subscribe; otherwise, the 'will' will be void for bad execution. Signature here will include any mark intended to represent the name of the testator, for example, thumb print, a cross, an initial, a rubber stamp, an so on.
3. The signature must be affixed in the presence of two or more witnesses present at the same time.

4. The witnesses must attest and subscribe the 'will' in the presence of the testator. To attest is to see the testator signing while to subscribe is to sign the will as proof of attestation. Note that a blind man can make a will, but he cannot, in law, witness a will because of his disability, which prevents him from attesting to the making of the will by the testator.

Apart from these conditions, there are other conditions, which must be satisfied for a 'will' to be valid, which include the following:

5. The 'will' must be voluntarily made and executed by the testator. This means that the will must have been freely made without any form of influence whatsoever by any person on the testator such as to affect the testator's mind in the making of the will. Persuasion is allowed in law but should not amount to pressure; pressure, of whatever character, if so exerted as to overpower the volition of the testator, without convincing his judgement, will amount to undue influence, which will invalidate the 'will'.

6. The 'will' must be made by a testator with testamentary capacity for it to be valid. Testamentary capacity means the capacity and ability to make a valid will. Testamentary capacity involves two elements:

    (a) *Age:* Section 7 of the Wills Act provides that the minimum age at which a person can make a will is twenty-one years; therefore, a person below the age cannot make a valid will. Certain persons are, however, exempted from this age requirement, that is, soldiers in actual military service, miners, or seaman at sea.

    (b) *Sound Disposing Mind* (Mens sana in corporis sana): A person must posses the mental capacity or sound disposing mind to make a will. This simply means that the testator must not be suffering from any disease of the mind or of the body capable of affecting the mind of the testator in the making of the will. Where it is established that the testator was not of sound mind while making the will, the 'will' will be invalid. There are three criteria for ascertaining whether a testator had the requisite testamentary capacity for making a will, namely:

        (i) The testator must understand that he is giving his property to one or more objects or persons of his regard.
        (ii) The testator must understand and recollect the exact extent of his property.

(iii) The testator must also understand the extent of those he intends to include or exclude from his 'will'.

In order to make a valid will, the testator must have the intention to make a will and must intend that his wishes should take effect on his death. The testator must know of and approve of the contents of his will so that where the contents of the will are not the wishes of the testator but the record of another person, then the 'will' will be invalid.

According to Section 15 of the Wills Act 1837, a will must not be witnessed by a beneficiary to the will or his spouse, except the gift to the beneficiary is a charge or direction for payment of debt. Therefore, where a person or his spouse is a beneficiary under a will, such a person or the spouse must not witness the will. If that person or spouse witnesses the will, the gift to him fails. Nonetheless, the will remains valid.

Importance of making a 'Will'

- Where a person of testamentary capacity dies without making a will, his property will devolve according to the traditional rules of inheritance operating in his place of origin, but where there is a valid will, the property will devolve according to the provisions of the will.
- A will prevents the emergence of family problems upon the death of a property owner of testamentary capacity.
- It will also ensure that the family, that is, wife and children do not suffer unduly as a result of scramble for property with family relations.
- A testator can, in his 'will', appoint trusted people whom he believes will carry out his wishes as his executors or trustees or both.
- A testator may, in his 'will', appoint guardians for his infant children.
- Where a person dies intestate, his property cannot be shared by his family unless his personal representatives first apply to court and obtain letters of administration, but where there is a valid 'will', the executors appointed under the 'will' will only apply to the court for letters of probate.
- It is the best way to safeguard your assets and to make sure they go where you intend them to go.

Who can make a 'Will'?

According the Wills Act 1837, any person above twenty-one years (both male and female) under his own hand, so long as the requirements for due execution of a will are met. Such a will when made will for all intents and purposes be enforced by the courts; it is however much better and advisable for a qualified legal practitioner to prepare a 'will'. This is mainly because of the intricacies and technicalities involved in the making of a will. Also a blind or disabled person can make a will either personally or through a representative of his choice, so long as the contents of the will are read over to him, and he appears perfectly to understand the contents and accepts it as a true reflection of his desires.

Revocation and amendment of a' Will'

A will may be revoked or amended anytime before the testator's death. He may either revoke the entire will or revoke or amend a part of the will. A will may be revoked in four ways:

- *Marriage:* Revocation by marriage is provided for under Section 18 of the Wills Act 1837, and it automatically, by operation of law, revokes a will. For example, if a will was made in March 2008 and the testator marries in September 2008, the subsequent marriage of September 2008 revokes the will of March 2008.
- *Later Will or Codicil:* This is provided for under Section 20, Wills Act 1837. The 'will' being ambulatory, that is, revocable, can be amended with a codicil or making a new will outright (A codicil is a miniature will used to alter, amend, or otherwise vary the contents of a will or of another codicil or any clauses of a will or of another codicil. All the rules and laws applicable to a will are applicable in equal force to a codicil).
- *By Writing, Declaring an Intention to Revoke a Will:* This is equally provided for under Section 20 of the Wills Act 1837. The document intended to be revoked being a testamentary document, you must comply with Section 9, that is, sign the letter in the presence of two witnesses present at the same time, and they in turn will attest to the signature.
- *Revocation by Destruction:* Destruction here may be by burning or tearing of the 'will' by the testator or by some other person in his presence and by his direction. Cancellation of a 'will' does not amount to revocation. For a 'will' to be said to have been validly revoked, there must be a physical destruction of the 'will' together with an intention to destroy (animus revicandi) one without the other will not constitute revocation by destruction. Therefore where a 'will' is torn during a fight between husband and wife, gumming together can revive the

will. But where the will is burnt, it cannot be revived, since it is no longer in existence.

Revival of a Will

Revival of a Will is provided for under Section 22 of the Wills Act 1837. This is the procedure whereby a revoked will or codicil, which is rendered non-operational, is resuscitated and thereby made operational. A revoked will that is in existence can be revived; the one that is no longer in existence cannot be revived. A revoked will can be revived in two major ways:

- *Re-execution:* This entails a re-observance of the provisions of Section 9 of the Wills Act of 1837 and a re-execution of the revoked will.
- *Codicil:* A codicil can be drafted to revoke or amend an existing will or to revive a revoked will. A clear intention to revive must be stated in the codicil for revival to be effective.

The effect of the revival of a will is that the will is restored and becomes operational, and the revived will takes effect from the date of revival and not from the date when the original will was made.

Some General Rules to Note in Making a Will

- Start early.
- Define your goals early. The further ahead people plan, the more options they have to treat people unequally.
- Be aware of the limitations of wills, for example, under Section 3 of he various wills laws of states, testamentary freedom or freedom to make a will is subject to customary laws of inheritance. The section provides that a person can only dispose of land if it is not subject to customary law, that is, if the land is not communally owned or the customary laws of inheritance expressly provide for who is entitled to the land. For example, under the traditional Igbo customary laws of inheritance, the eldest surviving son of a man is entitled to his principal place of residence; upon his death, the father cannot by his will divest the son of this entitlement.
- Wills become public documents after a person's death.
- Give away as much money as you can while you're still alive, but be sure you keep enough to support yourself while you are still alive.

- Look at your 'will' at least every five years to make sure the law has not changed.
- When buying a property, make it joint ownership so that it automatically passes on to the surviving spouse.
- Ensure that the executors you appoint to administer your will are younger and trusted persons who will survive the testator and carry out his last wishes.

GLOSSARY

National and International Organisations

NGO—Non-governmental organisation
CIRDDOC—Civic Resource Development and Documentation Centre
WACOL—Women's Aid Collective
WON—Women of the Federation of Nigerian Lawyers
CENGOS—The Coalition of Eastern NGOs
NANGOH—Network of Non-Governmental Organisations for Health
FORWARD—The Foundation for Women's Health, Research and Development
DOVENET—Daughters of Virtue and Empowerment Initiatives
NCWS—National Council of Women's Societies
AWID—Association of Women in Development
WILDAF—Women in Law and Development Africa
IWLD—Institute for Women, Law and Development
JDPC—Justice Development and Peace Commission
PASDEV—Partnership for Sustainable Development
ACHPR—African Commission on Human and Peoples' Rights
OAU—African Magna Charter on the Rights of women in Africa adopted by the Organisation of African Unity
UNHRC—United Nations Declaration on Human Rights
CEDAW—Convention on the Elimination of All Forms of Discrimination Against Women
UNDHR—Universal Declaration of Human Rights
ICESCR—The International Covenant on Economic, Social and Cultural Rights
ICCPR—The International Covenant on Civil and Political Rights
UNIFEM—United Nations Development Fund for Women
PFA—Platform for Action World Conference on Women Beijing

Codes for identification of participants' ethnicity and informants in the study

Participants

W: widowed with children
C: childless wives (e.g. married women without children)

Villages

V1
V2
V3

Others

EM: eminent men (clan heads or paramount chiefs)
EW: eminent women (chairs of the womenfolk)
M—NGO: men from the NGO
W—NGO: women from the NGO
DS—NGO: documentary source from the NGO and agencies

Igbo terms for indicators of 'Ariri' (a cultural—specific mental health problem)

Exclusion	igupu mmadu
Self-isolation	mmadu inoro onye ya
Discrimination	nkewa
Marginalisation	ikpa oke
Oppression	imegbu mmadu
Neglect	ileghara mmadu anya
Humiliation	ileda mmadu
Intimidation	iyii egwu
Blame	ita uta
Stigma	oru ejiri mara mmadu
Stereotype	isi otu akuku ele mmadu
Ostracism	isupu mmadu n'obodo

Clinical characteristics of 'Ariri' (mental health problem)

Low self-esteem	mmadu ileda onwe ya anya
Insecurity	enweghi obi sirike
Excessive worries	oke echiche
Anger	iwe
Fear	egwu m'obu itu ujoo
Agitation/frustration	ahu mgbakasi
Irritability	mgbakasi ahu
Lamentation	ikwa ariri
Despair	inwe obi nkoropu
Sadness	obi ojoo
Unhappiness	obi igba njo
Shock	obi mmapu
Panic attack	iku ajija
Persecution	mkpagbu
Suspicion	nyocha m'obu inyocha mmadu
Paranoia	isi adighi mma
Self-esteem	ugwu m'obu mmadu inwe ugwu
Confidence	inwe ntukwasi obi
Empowerment	inye ikike

Index

Lightning Source UK Ltd.
Milton Keynes UK
UKOW040623270213

206876UK00003B/104/P